DIARY

OF A

BROKEN MIND

DIARY
OF A
BROKEN MIND

A MOTHER'S STORY, A SON'S SUICIDE,
AND THE HAUNTING LYRICS HE LEFT BEHIND

Anne Moss Rogers
with Charles Rogers

BEACH GLASS
BOOKS

Published by Beach Glass Books, 2019
Manufactured in the United States of America
First Printing September 2019

Front and back cover photographs courtesy of the author
Interior family photographs courtesy of the author
Book and jacket design by Ray McAllister

Anne Moss Rogers, 1962-
Charles Aubrey Rogers, 1995-2015
    Diary of a Broken Mind: A Mother's Story, A Son's Suicide, and the
    Haunting Lyrics He Left Behind / by Anne Moss Rogers with Charles Rogers
ISBN 978-0-9987881-6-6

Over time,
Tears of agony become tears of remembrance.
Agony becomes ache.
A hole in the heart becomes a wound with scar tissue.
Denial turns into acceptance.
Despair and isolation turn into purpose and clarity.
Deep depression turns into moments of melancholy.
Helplessness turns into humility.
Love with nowhere to land evolves into a need to give back.
And instead of carrying your child in your arms,
You learn to carry him in your heart.

—Anne Moss Rogers

**In memory of my youngest son,
Charles Aubrey Rogers
April 26, 1995–June 5, 2015**

CONTENTS

CONTENTS

PUBLISHER'S NOTE

This book is a departure.
It is a departure, certainly, for Beach Glass Books. Our catalogue is replete with coastal books and historical books. We have published children's books and books of true crime and essays, with novels on the way.

But never have we published a book like this.

Few have. This book is a departure even from others that one might think are in the genre. Books about the suicides of young people are available. But books that take a reader deep into the life of a family whose child dies by suicide, with telling recollection and heartbreaking detail, yet with an overriding sense of hope, are far fewer. Anne Moss Rogers, now a nationally recognized speaker and writer on suicide prevention, has written an extraordinary memoir, with insight both personal and expert, aided by the words left by her deceased son.

It is an important book. *Diary of a Broken Mind* is a timely work for those families who have faced these difficulties and tragedies—and so very necessary for those who may face them ahead. It is a book important for the rest of us, too, who want and need to understand.

This is a book you won't forget.

Ray McAllister
Beach Glass Books

AUTHOR'S NOTE

TRIGGER WARNING: This is a memoir that tackles tough topics and contains a lot of emotional content. Most chapters including such content contain a "trigger warning" at the outset. If you are struggling with mental illness, addiction, and/or thoughts of suicide and if this is triggering in any way, please stop or take breaks. There are a few instances where method is mentioned briefly, although there are no details.

Your life is important to me. If you've ever experienced thoughts of suicide, reach out to the hotline, a parent, trusted adult, friend, a counselor, or find a support group. The moment you start talking about it, the easier it gets.

There is only one you. If you left us, we'd be robbed of your potential and all your gifts. We don't know what you could be. Stay with us so we can find out.

SUICIDE HOTLINES
If you are experiencing thoughts of suicide, please reach out.
United States: 1-800-273-8255
United States Text hotline: Text "help" to 741-741
For other countries: Search "suicide crisis lines."

INTRODUCTION

So play this when your day is gray,
when hope is dim
When happiness is growing slim
Listen to me rap then reverse the grim
Burn the hurt,
let my words do the work
—Silver Lining, by Charles Aubrey Rogers

When the police delivered the news that my youngest son, Charles, had died by suicide, my heart seized and, in the split second before my lungs could find air and the wails of my soul in agony could erupt, I had the urge to yell, "You have it all wrong. That's not how this story ends."

Rewriting that ending is not possible. There are no bargains to strike or do-overs. And the months and years following my twenty-year-old son's death on June 5, 2015, have been all about learning to live without the child I raised and what to do with all that love that has nowhere to land.

Losing a child to suicide does not "hurt more" than any other cause of death. It can't hurt more. However, suicide is a special brand of grief that comes with the baggage of additional guilt. I was

1

sure my son's suicide was glaring evidence of my failure as a mother. *Why did my child choose to leave me? Why wasn't my love enough? What did I do wrong? Why didn't I see the signs?*

I yearn to make that last five years of our family life rosier and more romantic, and the horrific ending less sharp and jagged. I wish I could smooth out the roughness of the phrase, "He killed himself." There'd be a different visceral response to "He died of cancer." I imagine it would be softer, like a vignette around a picture. Suicide is heavier because it carries with it complex emotions, with confusion leading the way. Others struggle to understand it, there is often blame, and everyone has an opinion, whether it's an educated one or not. It is the cause of death that gets whispered. I refuse to do that because it doesn't honor my son's suffering.

Charles was the younger of my two sons and appeared to relish every moment of life. Always in motion, he was one of the most popular kids in school. He was hypersocial, made everyone laugh, brought people together, reached out to others, listened to their fears, and shared their sadness. No one thought Charles was the kind of person who would kill himself.

Remarkably self-aware for his age, there were times when he recognized his life was spiraling out of control but fell into the trap of self-medication with drugs and alcohol, which led to a heroin addiction and his death by suicide. He had other issues, too: Attention Deficit Hyperactivity Disorder (ADHD), depression, anxiety, and a sleep disorder he had since he was a toddler that played into the severity of all his issues.

His suicide wasn't personal. Charles wanted to end unimaginable emotional agony, and the physical pain of heroin withdrawal. In that irrational moment of intense pain, he was incapable of realizing how much his death would hurt those who loved him. His brain lied and convinced him he was worthless and there were no other options.

The purpose of this book is to share a gift: something few other family members and friends have following a suicide or a drug-related death. I have the words my son left behind, written as sophisticated, hip-hop rhyme schemes that offer a window inside the mind of someone who lived with and died from depression and addiction. It

Introduction

is a lyrical journal of my son's emotional experience; music that is beautiful, sobering, and most of all revealing. True to the nature of depression and substance use disorder, Charles' self-loathing was a recurring theme in his writing and he let his soul bleed on paper to find relief from depression and suicidal thoughts.

There are sparks of beauty and revelation in his lyrics that sit on the soul while the angry raps spit from the page. The songs about love and family cradled me; the raps about drugs and alcohol dragged my soul into the ugly hole of addiction.

I call Charles' journals his Rap Diaries. They have curse words; many are self-deprecating and dark, and not always politically correct. He was a religious antagonist and in constant struggle with his own faith. I didn't edit his work, take out religious references that may offend readers, or change his dark songs to happy tunes. Lyrics that showed an uglier side of myself, his dad, or Charles himself are printed here as they were written. And words that best expressed his point of view are woven into my story.

Concerned that rap was a bad influence, we made attempts in middle school to steer his interest away from this style of music. The commercialized rap marketed to tweens and young teens catered to their emerging rebellious nature and fed our fears as parents. The homogenized, pop-culture rap is what Charles called "crap rap." This, he argued, was not the same as artistic rap, stories from the soul. He wanted me to know the difference and, engaged as his pupil, he presented a convincing argument for artistic rap.

He recorded his poetic thoughts in spiral notebooks as well as black-and-white granite composition books that he bought from the drug store. Over the years, he filled up thirty or more of these journals. At the time of his death, we were left with a mere six of them. Kids at the therapeutic boarding school he attended took many of those journals and I asked his counselor why. To me, that was the worst possible violation. She said Charles shared his words with others and connected in a way that made them feel they had to take a piece of him with them. It was a part of their survival.

The songs were handwritten in stream-of-consciousness style. Those lyrics poured onto the page in perfect rhyme with minimal punctuation or editing, no line breaks, and he crammed the words on the page, using every available space including the margins. Most of the spelling and grammar is correct except where he took creative license.

He was quick on his feet with stand-up comedy and on stage, always adjusting his humor to the audience and holding them captive. The spotlight loved Charles; that's where he came alive. When he would freestyle—raps created and performed in the moment—his friends and fans were in awe of how easily and fast the words would flow, and they craved those words like a drug.

About a year before he died, Charles and I were sitting on the deck outside of our Midlothian, Virginia, home where he and his older brother, Richard, grew up. A few of his videos had been posted online and he had shown none of his writing to me, although he did share some song titles. I would have been alarmed by the lyrics and my instinct would have been to insist on professional help. He didn't want help, at least not the traditional kind. A tortured creative soul, he was never able to follow a path he didn't carve himself.

On the deck that day, I asked Charles, "Why are all your raps so depressing? Can't you write something more lighthearted?"—as if I could wash away his darkness and push him into the light. That question demonstrated a complete lack of understanding of the genre of rap and what it meant to him. I had essentially told him the darkness in his soul was too ugly to put on display. No wonder teens and young adults are such masters at hiding their depression.

I hope the words written by my son help readers understand the complex brain attack known as suicidal thinking, the gifts that often come with it, and the mental illness that often triggers it. I hope my story and his help people recognize what it's like to live with someone who suffers from diseases that are not often recognized as such: the agony and heartache of both the sufferer and the family. Just maybe, it will help others learn how to love someone who is lost inside addiction or mental illness.

Charles wanted to be famous. My husband and I had doubts he could have handled fame, but he meant for his raps to be shared.

Introduction

After years of holding onto them, I'm ready to love and let go because those words helped me understand depression and the "why" behind addiction and suicide.

Left to right: Charles, Randy, Anne Moss, Richard. Taken at my mother's house in Fayetteville, North Carolina.

CHAPTER 1

THE CALL

If there's a God, where is he?
I tried to pray but the line was busy.
—*Letter to God*, by Charles Aubrey Rogers, song on YouTube

Charles calls me for the first time in two weeks since he walked out of detox after relapsing on heroin.

Four days prior we had sold our home. Maybe now we would free up some cash to help our son. We are woefully short of that right now, having spent hundreds of thousands of dollars to help him. The mental health system is broken and exhausting, and the desire to throw up my hands and say, "I give up," is tempting. But this is my child and I can't do that.

The despair in Charles' voice nags my tired brain and radiates through my heart. "Mom, I have nothing," he said after pawning his last possessions: his computer and his bike. He especially loved that bike.

The previous week, he had texted me about a visit to the doctor for his twisted ankle and gotten defensive when asked about the pain medicine prescription.

> "This is the first time we've talked in two weeks, Mom. And the first thing you do is accuse me? You didn't even ask about my ankle."
>
> "So how is your ankle now?"
>
> "You don't care."
>
> "You tell me you are not using and I can see you did fill the pain medication prescription on our insurance. Are you willing to go back to detox?"
>
> "I didn't use it, Mom. But see, you don't care. I'm not addicted anymore and I've been applying for jobs."

He had insisted earlier he had an addiction to OxyContin but not heroin. "Heroin addict" is a phrase drenched with shame and ugliness, and who wants to be associated with that? The street drugs are more dangerous because they can have any mix of deadly substances. Charles won't admit it, which makes me angry but I resist yelling, take a deep breath, and press on. Manipulation is part of the disease, but an admission would help anchor the conversation and guide what happens next.

Emotionally spent and gripped with fear of losing my child, everything is running together like a mess of melted crayons. He's been out there, "living with friends," for the two weeks since his relapse. My beautiful child, sucked up in the ugly world of addiction. Is he going hungry? It was hard for me to imagine a child of mine wondering from where his next meal would come.

Several times during a two-hour conversation I tell him I love him and hang up to catch my breath because he is yelling and his verbal assault is coming at me like machine-gun fire. But this is the first time we have spoken on the phone and I desperately want to connect with him. He calls back right away and we continue to talk.

In our final conversation, he asks about treatment options. This is it; this is when he is going to ask for help. But there are no additional funds right now to send him to the rehab where he had just been. Insurance is unlikely to approve it and the last bill has not yet been paid. The last few years of boarding school, funded by a home equity loan, has left our bank account hovering at subsistence level. I tell him about a local treatment option that won't cost us until we can get our hands on more funds and then decide where he goes from there.

Charles asks, "So if I went to that detox, how would I get there?"

That's when a mother in a normal state of mind would have said without hesitation, "I'll come get you right now and take you there." Instead I respond with, "Ask one of your friends to drive you," thinking he's within walking distance of that detox location and surrounded by his buddies. This inexplicable, bizarre response would repeat in my head for months, even years.

For the first time since we've been on the phone, there is an abnormal silence from his end that inflates my fears. I am unaware he is going through withdrawal and alone in a rundown apartment he has been sharing with a lot of other active drug users. He despises being alone.

Oftentimes as parents, we try to share ownership of recovery when we need to step back, and I thought he needed to own this one. But something was off.

Is he is committed to the idea of recovery or just desperately wanting to be out of the situation he is in? Is that rock bottom? Am I being manipulated again? Is this enabling? The line between addiction and recovery is razor thin and shifts at any given time. If only my husband, Randy, were here with me and not out of town. But Randy had said we'd get Charles this weekend. *Was he ready? Do you ever know that?*

Trying to sort between truth and fiction—what to do, what not to do, with so much noise in my head—is siphoning all that's left of me. The despair in his voice that was nagging me before is now a flashing neon sign with sirens. Another argument erupts. It is my fault for diving into the emotional tsunami instead of maintaining a level head. I had learned a more productive type of conversation from my four years at Families Anonymous, but right now, it has skipped town without a forwarding address.

Good God, Anne Moss, what does it matter what specific substance he is abusing? He is asking for help, isn't he? One more deep breath to calm my nerves but my head feels swollen and useless.

We never return to the conversation about going back to detox despite my trying to steer it in that direction. He insists the failed drug test at the recovery house that prompted his return to detox was wrong and he was cheated. *This again? Haven't we gone over this?* More yelling and then he's barely audible, almost whimpering, and it's a strain to even hear if he is still there. Struggling for calm, I try to interject again but he is still on a rant about the failed drug test at the recovery house. "But Charles…," My end of the conversation is drowned out. *We need a cooling-off period.* I tell him I love him and hang up.

Emotionally wrung out and with a pounding headache, I hear the phone ring again. First my mobile phone, and then the landline. The sound in my ears matches the incessant ringing. A strange thought torments me: Is this a moment I will regret? My mind is struggling to analyze the conversation and grasp at the corners of his despair to figure out what's underneath, but it's outside my reach. The indecision—*Should I? Should I not?*—torments me anew. When he would get overly anxious or mad, he'd hypertext or call relentlessly. In the past, I would cut my phone off for a few hours to let him gather his sanity.

He then sends a text.

"Mom, I'll go to fucking rehab, just listen to me."
"Mom, I'm trying to tell you something and ask for help but you won't fucking answer."
"Mom, PLEASE ANSWER ME."

Tired and spent, I text back.

"I am. I have a job and there are things I have to do. I want you to get help when you are ready. Are you ready? Really?"
"We sold the house and there are calls we have to take."

My mind plays ping-pong between call and not call. Two hours of unproductive conversation has not given me a single clue as to what my next move should be. This is when a magic fairy should waltz in and give me the secret code to this. *Where is my damn fairy godmother when I need her?* I waffle between yearning to hear what it is he has to say, and being exhausted, and just wanting all of this to stop. Then

The Call

all phones go quiet. A split second of relief is followed by terror so intense my body shivers involuntarily. I struggle to grab hold of any part of that conversation but there is a giant roadblock between his despair and my understanding.

There is a phone call that must be made about the house sale before 5 p.m., and my presence is required at a work-related road race in less than an hour. *How does anyone run a normal life in this chaos? How many times have we dropped everything we were doing due to a Charles crisis?* Spent and confused, my emotions explode into a waterfall of tears and racking sobs.

Staring at the phone is not making it ring again. Maybe that last text message about the house was too dismissive. He might not even know we sold the house. There is both fear of talking to him again, and a mother's instinct to get to the underlying reason behind the despair in his voice. Now that there has been a cooling-off period, I make the decision that if he answers that last text or calls again, I will call back.

He still has not answered. Panic squeezes my heart. Damn it, what am I missing? Surely there is someone who is willing to talk to me to give me some perspective. There is no hotline to any of the mental health professionals he'd been to regularly since most of them were back at the boarding schools. His lack of compliance for the therapy appointments set up locally once he returned home ended as expensive no-shows, so there are no contacts there either.

Randy, my husband, answers his phone on the third ring and our conversation is short. He thinks our addicted son is just trying to get money, but my conversation with Charles seemed more like a cry for help, not cash. Randy assures me he'll be home the next day and that we'll go to get him Saturday. "I'll be back tomorrow, around 5 p.m.," he says. I am relieved not to have to face this alone. Randy has been required to go on a company trip and is expected to listen to presentations and share with his group. Somehow my phone call with Charles begs for immediate reaction, but what kind?

I decide to call Becky, a member of my Families Anonymous support group. She is very reassuring as I share anguish, helplessness, and plenty of tears. Per support group rules, she doesn't give advice. None of us is qualified to do that. Becky knows how this feels, having endured her own son's cycle of drug addiction. That shared experience does help me find a much-needed moment of peace.

I'm a co-owner of a digital marketing firm, and there is an expectation for me to be with my employees for a road race. The day is damp and ugly, like my current mood, and it's the last place I want to be. But getting out will make me feel better. On the way there, my mind bounces between wanting to call Charles and going to get him, wherever he is in Richmond—and waiting this out. *Where would I take him? And where is he living? Did I ask?* I made a promise to call him back if he texted a reply to my last one, and there is no answer.

At the turn signal to the road race, I contemplate calling him back one more time. *No, it's better for me to just go run this race and clear my head. Running always does.* Maybe it would help me find the missing piece of the puzzle that is bothering me. My gut is screaming but my thinking brain is not cooperating, having taken flight sometime at the beginning of that phone call.

I turn left to go and meet my employees at the road race.

THE NEWS

Life can crush your perfect world in under a second.
—*Hell on Earth*, by Charles Aubrey Rogers

It's June 5, 2015, and I'm at a board retreat for the Richmond Chapter of the American Marketing Association, which had appointed me vice president of sponsorship. After that last text, there had been no communication between me and Charles, although my husband and I briefly discussed options. The desire to dash from the room to call Charles is overwhelming, and then, just as quickly, it passes. My thoughts and energy have been siphoned by dread and fear. My limbs are heavy while my mind feels watery and unhinged. Just standing takes herculean effort.

Everyone is buzzing with conversation and laughing. For the board photographs, I mask my despair with an artificial smile that would taunt me throughout my year's tenure in this position. No one in this room knows our ugly secret, that my child suffers from depression and is now addicted to heroin. My husband and I ourselves have only known for about thirty days.

The last five years of our lives have been consumed with putting out fires, searching for the source, and applying solutions that exploded in our faces. Charles' sleep disorder as a toddler was the first sign of a problem, followed by the ADHD discovery in first grade, and signs of drug abuse starting with marijuana and alcohol in high school, which then graduated to harder drugs. The diagnosis of depression and anxiety at age seventeen finally gave us some answers but there was a frustrating lack of resources. My greatest fear was that heroin would find my child, and when it did he was seduced into thinking he couldn't live without it. Heroin told him that he was the greatest human being in the world, and then the most worthless. *How do I fight that invisible enemy?*

My head hurts and the tension has my shoulders bunched up around my ears all day. I finally manage to get my mind back into the room and engage in the conversation, and for a while I feel blissfully distracted. But it doesn't last.

There is a group go-carting activity after our all-day meeting. I take a halfhearted spin twice around the track, make polite excuses, and go to my car to head home. This is where I've wanted to be all day, and now it's uncomfortable, too. My husband's out-of-town trip has left me feeling more untethered than usual. *How does anyone do this as a single parent?*

I call Charles. No answer. My mouth goes dry and my heartbeat sprints from my chest and into my throat. He often did not answer. But something is wrong and it has punched the air out of my lungs. A few deep breaths push the worry back down long enough for me to focus on the task of driving home.

Once at the house, I stand and stare out my back window looking across my deck into the woods, momentarily entertained by the vision of both my children playing out various scenes in that pitiful excuse for a forest in their many YouTube productions. Sudden, soft pressure on my left shoulder and a shudder through my body interrupts my reverie. *What was that?* After spinning around expecting to see my boy, no one is there. The dog is turning around in circles in obvious distress. He never does this.

Convinced Charles has been in the house today, I check every closet, under every bed, and even go into the attic. No one is there.

The News

Fear settles in my shoulders, which are hovering around my ears again, straining my upper back, now knotty and sore. After I tried to settle into a seat at our kitchen counter, my husband walks through the door. Relief takes temporary residence and we decide to go out for dinner. *Why can't I get comfortable anywhere?*

Not long after we arrive at the restaurant and order, Randy gets a call on his mobile phone. My mind and body freeze, every muscle on high alert. It has to be something about Charles. And it is. When my husband hangs up, he tells me the Richmond police are at our home in Chesterfield County and for a moment the tension that's been holding me captive releases its grip. *He's been arrested. That means he's alive and safe.*

But they didn't say that. Seized by dread, my skin prickles, leaving me cold. I am completely immobile. *Why would Richmond police go to our home in the county? He's twenty. There's no way they are making a courtesy call to tell us our child has been arrested. They are coming to tell us he is dead. Please don't let him be dead. Maybe he is in the hospital? No. I don't think they come to tell you that. Or do they?* I want to hang on to that hospital thought and believe it, but logic is weaving its way through my mind, calculating a desperate inventory of rational reasons as to why they are driving to a parking lot to meet us.

I touch Randy's elbow and say, "Do you think…?" He says, "I think so." My body goes cold, my breathing ragged, and my head feels adrift, as if it's lost its mooring. *Don't faint. Don't jump to conclusions. It could be anything.* Meanwhile my husband is talking up other scenarios. *Why not let him? They are coming to tell me my child is dead. This can't be real.* My mind and my movements slow to a crawl.

The bartender comes up and asks us if we want our check and I nod and pay the bill as if we are normal people who have just had dinner. I no longer feel like "normal people." *Did we eat the food?*

It takes the Richmond police twenty minutes to get there and with each minute, hope crumbles a little more. My mind volleys between wanting them there to find out and not wanting them there. Not knowing means there is a pilot light of hope still burning.

My husband stands up and tells me they are here. He is out there so fast. *How did he do that?* I, however, am moving through quicksand because the answer has arrived. The police are parked in a nearby space in one of those nondescript, gray, standard-issue undercover cop cars. An African-American police officer is standing formally at the back door, his hands clasped together in front of him. My husband has already gotten into the front passenger seat. There is someone in the driver's seat, probably another officer. They are dressed in dark gray suits with ties. This can't be good.

Still standing across the street, I irrationally yell, "You're coming to tell me my son is dead!" Stunned with fear, my feet carry me across that street because now the officer who'd been standing by the back door opens it for me and closes it behind me. It's a warm June day. *Why am I shivering?* The police officer in the driver's seat is turned sideways so he can see me in the back and my husband in the passenger seat. *Please, please, please let things be OK.*

"I have some sad news to share with you. Your son Charles was found dead this morning in an apartment on Monument Avenue," said the police officer.

There's no air in my lungs and when I rebound from the shock, I wail, "Noooooooooo!" My husband and I scream agonizing wails of agony: the worst possible human sounds, the excruciating cries of grief and loss. Anyone within earshot would have suffered the crushing heartbreak in those cries. My heart drops out of my chest. Rocking and wailing, the sounds of the ocean crash in my ears and there is unrelenting pressure on all sides of my head. *This can't be me hearing this. It's not true. This is a dream.*

The other officer who was standing outside is not there anymore. *Where did he go?*

"Can we see the body?" I ache to see my son again one more time. My husband asks if they are sure it's him. The answer is yes, they are sure, and no, we can't go to the morgue to see his body. Confused, we question the officer. They do it all the time on TV. How can they deny us this?

The officer tells us there are many deaths at this apartment, mostly drug-related. It's a place where those who suffer from addiction come and go. The despair at that place wrapped my son like a blanket. I heard it leaking from his voice and it resonated in my heart when we talked yesterday. My mind takes a brief detour to Monument Avenue, the most coveted street in Richmond with its historic million-dollar row houses and manicured yards on cobblestone streets. The seedy residence described doesn't fit the picture.

The officer goes on to say addiction is an awful disease and he's never seen an epidemic so widespread. This man has seen the scourges firsthand and it's etched on his young face.

Then my husband quietly asks, "How did he die?" For some reason, this question stuns me. *How do you think he died? He was addicted to heroin, for God's sake.* I am prepared to hear "overdose." But the officer says, "He hanged himself," and my husband begins to bang his fists on his lap and the glove compartment. He is wailing in inexplicable emotional pain and I stare at my husband's explosion, unable to move.

What did he say? The statement hangs in the air, outside of my consciousness, trying to get into my head, but confusion and denial are obstructing its path. *Did he say a hanging? Like a suicide?* With this cruel twist of a knife, my heart burns. Rocking back and forth and wailing guttural, inhuman sounds, I have a primal urge to grab the edges of yesterday and bring it back so we can do the day over with a better outcome. *We love him. How could he kill himself?* When my wail of agony finally escapes, it sounds like a wounded animal being tortured. This moment of horror will repeat itself multiple times in the coming weeks, months, and even years.

My brain can't form questions. *Where is the escape route?* My raft was moored to a pier and then suddenly someone cut the line and it went drifting out to sea. Brushing at my arms, I try desperately to get out of my skin and into a life somewhere else where this isn't happening. And then a vision of me floating above and looking down at myself sitting in the police car appears in my mind. *Oh, this is just a movie of me hearing this awful news.* Another wave of reality hits and the fantasy flies away, too fast to snatch back. For a split second, it was warm and comfortable.

The officer in the vehicle is trying to maintain his composure. This has to be hard for him, too. He's gentle, empathetic, and soft-spoken. He tells us he has a twenty-year-old son, too, and can't imagine hearing this news, and hands us a piece of paper with his name and phone number.

Charles had such beautiful curly hair. That curl in the back near his ear and neck, that was my curl and it fit perfectly around my finger. Playing with it annoyed him. "Mom, stop. I'm not a four-year-old," he'd say. I cherished that sweet boyish grin, those funny jokes, that amazing talent. He was working on his second iTunes album and he loved his music. *What happened? Didn't he love us?* My broken mind fades in and out like radio with a sorry signal. I don't understand.

Then it hits me. We'll never see him again and there's a strange urge to call him to ask if it's true. *That phone call the previous day was a cry for help. Wasn't there a text message, too?* My face feels hot. It needles me like an epic missed opportunity but my head is too full of noise to remember it.

The first feelings of "coulda, woulda, shoulda" hit. In that last call, his despair and mine made me ache but I couldn't figure out what to say or what to do next. *And this cost me the life of my child? How is it that I'm such a shitty mom my son would kill himself?*

We want to drive home and have to convince the officers to let us leave because our pain is too naked right now. It's a twenty-minute drive home. Longest. Drive. Ever. Whimpering but not wailing, I have got to hold it together for my husband's sake since he's behind the wheel. *What do we do next? There is a list. Really?* Just a one, two, three list that has next steps in case Charles died.

In May of 2015, right before the house went on the market, I made a list to quiet the nagging premonition he was going to die. It was like carrying an umbrella. If you have an umbrella, it won't rain. But it did rain. He did die. The list no one ever wants to use will tell us what to do next.

As soon as we are home, we collapse on the kitchen floor and release the agony that was put on hold so we could make it here. Sensing we are in unspeakable despair, the dog panics and jumps in the middle of our collapsed pile of pain. As bad as this is, and it's brutal, hearing the news was the worst, at least that part is over. It's what gets me to the next minute, and the next.

Charles' girlfriend calls, and it's a struggle to keep myself together. I ask her to pull her car over and she yells, "Tell me." Sharing the news is like reliving it again. Her wails and pain pierce my soul. The poor girl is blaming herself. "Please call your dad," was all I could say before erupting in tears again.

Who found him? When did they find him? What was that text? That text was significant but my mind is a skipping rock on a pond and can't land. The memory of that last call yesterday nags at the back of my brain. *Oh my God, he was suicidal.* Suicide was not on my radar at all. That was the missing piece. Nobody ever talks about suicide. There was never a mention in all those years after his diagnosis of anxiety and depression. The addiction had come much later, although he had years of self-medicating with drugs and alcohol. I can grab only one piece of that text right now.

"I have to tell you something. Pick up the fucking phone."

That last conversation had lasted for more than two hours. The despair in his voice was urging me to do something. I told him I loved him. He had to have known that. One more declaration of my love. But it wasn't enough to save him. *This was my fault.*

We call our family that night to deliver the news. In our state of ugly naked grief, my husband and I make the decision that the last chapter of our son's life would have to be the beginning of a new one for us. While I feel worthless, his death can't be the end of my own life. Who would carry his legacy forward?

How will we ever survive this? How can we go on without our youngest child?

We just will. We just will.

How striking that the shoes Charles was wearing when he died were his favorite pair of Converse "Chuck Taylors," featuring his favorite super-hero.

CHAPTER 3

LETTER FROM HEAVEN
AS I KNOW CHARLES WOULD HAVE WRITTEN IT

My demons up against me and I'm facin' them now.
I wear the face of a clown.
I feel so unloved, because of the monster created from drugs
—*Just to Hurt*, by Charles Aubrey Rogers

Dear Mom,

The angels and me are rapping our asses off up here. They don't even care when I say the f-word.

I miss making you laugh, throwing the ball to Andy, hanging out at the river with my friends and family. I don't miss emptying the dishwasher, mowing the lawn, or having to clean the toilet. That's one thing about checking out. No chores. There is also a ton of candy here and I can eat a treasure chest full of it and get no cavities. It's heaven. (That's a little joke for you.)

About that last call. I know there was a lot I didn't tell you, so here goes. After relapsing at the recovery house, the manager took me to detox. My friend, Mac, from The Family School was there, too. Remember him? We decided to leave for just one more party. After that, I didn't find my way back.

21

DIARY OF A BROKEN MIND

My friend Jay put me in a hotel for two nights after I posted that message on Facebook, the one that said if I died, no one would notice for thirty days. No one else called. My friends had stopped calling and texting because I was always high, always too much, and they didn't know what to do. I know you and Dad didn't either. You didn't know this but you were finally unblocked from my Facebook page so my friend could print family pictures you had posted. Did you see all of them in my backpack? The letters you sent me when I was away were in there, too, every one you ever wrote me.

That apartment I was living in for two weeks was a hellhole where strangers came and went. There were no locks on the door, dirty mattresses on the floor, bullet holes in the wall, and people fighting all the time. Others lived there, too: people who had walked out of rehab or detox or were asked to leave their house. All were homeless and unloved like me, just junkie throwaways, too ugly for society.

I had been alone for days when we talked on the phone that last time. You know how I hated being alone. That's why I always wanted to have people over to spend the night. Because at night, those feelings of wanting to kill myself were the worst. It was like those thoughts were on repeat and why it was so much harder to sleep. Remember my roommate, Henry, at Wasatch Academy from Thailand? He would lie down and fall asleep, just like that. How the hell did he do that?

As my insomnia got worse so did my drug use and everything else. Who would have imagined me, the funny guy, had depression? When you feel ugly and depressed every day, it just wears you down. I insisted depression was a phony diagnosis because you would have worried and wanted me to take antidepressants. Would they make me a zombie? Would they suck away my personality?

None of the medicines the doctor prescribed ever worked. And we always had to wait so long for appointments. Nobody ever helped. Instead, they made me feel ashamed and they shamed you, too. After a while, I gave up on doctors and therapists. The other drugs made me feel so good at first. That was before they turned me into a monster.

When I was fifteen years old, I wanted to kill myself and smoked pot instead and that feeling went away. How could something that made me feel that good be wrong? Weren't taking drugs and drinking better than killing myself? And I slept, too. Marijuana seemed like the answer. But when one drug would stop working, I tried something new. It was always

22

Letter from Heaven

more. And then it was impossible to stop because it became an obsession. That first hit of heroin made me feel like a king and then I kept chasing that feeling. I didn't want you and Dad to know it was heroin, even in the end. I'm sorry I lied. A heroin addiction wasn't part of my plan. You know my dream was to be a rap star.

You should have seen me freestyle, Mom. My friends loved it and told me I had a gift. When rapping in front of a crowd and they were into it, everything felt good. After handing out CDs of my first album from iTunes, people would come back and tell me how much my music meant to them and my whole world lit up. But it never lasted. It needed to last.

Those words in perfect rhyme came so easily and the paper would absorb all my hurt. It was my only relief from the pain and sometimes even that was not enough. My art was my gift and it was hard for people to see it through all the other noise out there.

The reason I was by myself in that apartment was because Mac and the others who'd been staying there with me left to go to the West End to find drugs. They asked me to go but I had fucked up my life so much and didn't know how to get it back and was too ashamed of what it had become. I didn't call in that two weeks but had hoped you would call more. But you didn't and that's when the feelings of worthlessness got worse because my mind started to convince me you didn't call because you didn't care.

And when I called you, my head was so messed up from withdrawal, and the pain wouldn't stop. I thought you had given up on me. All that needed to happen for me to get better seemed like so much. It wasn't just the physical pain and the restless legs; it's that my head kept telling me no one would care if I just ended it. Did I want to die? Not really. I just wanted to stop the pain and I wanted to stop hurting you and Dad. Wouldn't your life be better without me in it?

I thought you would hear it. You did hear it, didn't you? But I could not get out what needed to be said. Dad thought it was a call for money but that wasn't it. I needed you to save me because I couldn't save myself right then.

Just so you know, that was me who hugged you the day I left the earth. You were right about that.

I love you,
Charles

Diary of A Broken Mind

Whatchu need? I CAN GET it, if I talk it, I live it, I make music
for Sick kids with Slit wrists, to Scare Mormons at picnics Sweet and Sensitive
mixed with twisted Sick SHiT, Dark shit and Bittersweet Symphonies that'll get
you lifted, Sin Hymns flows that can Be hard to sit with, my pen hits Spots
you thought you had forgot Existed, cause the Devil lives in the tongue I spit
with and Angel's Bleed in the ink that writ this, A split sense like
god lives In the 3rd G when you list it, 666, flip em all to 9's then fix it
as a kid I used to ask to get Crucified on Christmas, cause the
yellin of Redrum in my Cerebul-um was to to Difficult to live with, rip
the voices out my head and ask WHAT IS THIS? How come Im not
like the other kids? How come Im different, I sent God an Email, I guess
he missed it

this is just the Diary of A Broken mind
No hope inside

A page from Charles' rap diary. He often wrote edge to edge on the
paper and I had to figure out the line breaks.

CHAPTER 4

DIARY OF
A BROKEN MIND

Lyrics by Charles Aubrey Rogers, aka Reezin' the Revolutionary

W*hatchu need? I can get it,*
If I talk it, I live it.
I make music for sick kids with slit wrists
To scare Mormons at picnics
Sweet and sensitive
mixed with twisted sick shit
Dark shit and bittersweet symphonies
That'll get you lifted

Sin hymns flows that can be hard to sit with
my pen hits spots you had forgot existed
'cause the devil lives in the tongue I spit with
and Angels bleed in the ink that writ this
A split sense like God lives in the third six when you list it
666 Flip 'em all to 9's and fix it

25

DIARY OF A BROKEN MIND

As a kid I used to ask to get crucified on Christmas,
'cause the yellin' of red redrum in my cerebellum
was difficult to live with,
rip the voices out my head and ask what is this?
How come I'm not like the other kids?
How come I'm different?
I send God an email
and I guess he just missed it

(Refrain)
This is just the diary of a broken mind
no hope inside,
Feed my soul to mics¹
and walk through life
with closed eyes,
This is just a diary of a broken, of a mind,
of a broken mind, of a broken mind

As a young'un, I asked my mother if she was all right
She didn't look okay
She started cryin' and said the fault was all mine
She started screaming, "CHARLES STOP!"
and crying like nothing was fine

I was perplexed like, "STOP WHAT?
Why are you crying HUH?
Tell me MA!"
But she kept wailing and wouldn't respond,
Sayin' it was all my fault and something was wrong,
that's why you feel the pain in every word in this song
cuz at that time I knew I had a broken mind

In the back of my head
I can still hear her cry
blame myself for every sin and every lie

---

1   *Feed my soul to mics*: an abbreviation for microphones.

Diary of a Broken Mind

I know God could hear her whine
but didn't care
My dad had to carry her up the stairs
I knew I was nothin' but damaged goods right there,
that's why sit up at night and I pull out my hair

(Refrain)
This is just the diary of a broken mind
no hope inside,
Feed my soul to mics
and walk through life
with closed eyes,
This is just a diary of a broken, of a mind,
of a broken mind, of a broken mind

Mickey Mouse, I grew up without
I listened to 50 cent, Eminem talk about pulling gats out [2]
and blasted it throughout my house
Let the words leak through my brain
till it claimed my mouth

Hip hop raised me.
that was my route
till it became the only way to get the pain out
Little fuck with my listenin' bad
locked in my room with a pen and a pad
ready to show the whole world what I'm pissed at

Never liked school
didn't wanna to be just like my dad,
no interest in finishing class
my only wish was to have my bliss exist through my rap,
for people to bump my shit and give me daps [3]

---

2   *Eminem talked about pulling gats out*: 'gat' is slang for a pistol
3   *give me daps*: to give someone daps is to give them a handshake or 'fist pound' as a greeting or form of respect.

DIARY OF A BROKEN MIND

to tell me the only thing that helps
when they're feelin' like crap
I heard the word of God and I write that
but the devil talks, too
He gave me a walkthru,
told me my pen's a spiked bat.
I like that
So I listened to 'em both and let my pen host
Angels and demons close when I write rap

(Refrain)
This is just the diary of a broken mind
no hope inside,
Feed my soul to mics
and walk through life
with closed eyes,
This is just a diary of a broken, of a mind,
of a broken mind, of a broken mind

I started smoking weed at 15,
Before that, I was just a sick teen
that never lit green,
And I graduated to pills 'n lean alcohol
and other shit on the scene
The world treated me like I was just a fiend
and my teacher said successful
was something I'd never be
like money was something
I would never see

He said to me, "Charles, rap is dumb.
It'll never make you any sufficient funds.
Quit while you're young."
But I played the devil's song and angels sung
I took a deep breath out of my grateful lungs
And mixed my hate with love,
passion in my brain that had developed a taste for drugs

Diary of a Broken Mind

I became numb and out of touch
I needed to reach the top
and started to crave with lust
I was never regular
and wouldn't behave for much

Rap became enough
It was my soul
It traced in my blood
Locked myself in my room with the door banged shut
Felt it in my veins
The rush, the beat became my drugs

Obsessed with blowing up
and seeing my enemies eat slugs
It fixed in my broken mind and Charles died
REEZIN' ROSE,
A revolutionary, visionary
painting beautiful pictures real and scary
That make you feel reality too much
That makes you feel chewed up
Lifts or get you crushed,
spittin' new stuff
Turn the speakers up
and listen to the sick pup
that used to piss in cups,
And I won't quit till I'm RICH AS FUCK,
Made an album for the haters
every trax a dick to suck

(Refrain)
This is just the diary of a broken mind
no hope inside,
Feed my soul to mics
and walk through life
with closed eyes,

DIARY OF A BROKEN MIND

This is just a diary of a broken, of a mind,
of a broken mind, of a broken mind

Charles recorded "Diary of a Broken Mind" with his friend Max when he was at Wasatch Academy, a boarding school in Utah. When I asked Max to look over this rap song to help me get it right, he said, "I remember recording this with him! This was always one of my favorites of the music he wrote." This boarding school had a studio with an instrument microphone and this song is on SoundCloud under his name, Charles Rogers. The school ultimately pulled the plug on their recording because some of what they were rapping was too graphic in nature and not always politically correct, even for a school that allowed greater allowances for creativity. Charles was always pushing boundaries to the edges of uncomfortable.

He references me in this one, as he did in many of his songs, refers to a night when I just had had enough. I had no idea he took my breakdown so personally. My husband, although a strong man, did not carry me upstairs but I sank to the floor that night in despair and he helped me upstairs.

This was when I knew our lives were headed in the direction that it was and it crushed me. It was hard to watch my child self-destruct with substance abuse, and I was powerless to prevent it. Nothing in the normal parenting books worked.

He says I said other things but that's not the case because the words wouldn't come. He had been yelling questions at me, and all I could say was, "Charles, stop."

It is humiliating to lose it like that. But sometimes a person has to fall apart before regrouping again to fight another day. And that's what I did.

CHAPTER 5

THE SPARK THAT LIT
THE FLAME OF FUN

As dark as my life's like,
I can still smile at the bright side
and see the silver lining
even when it's nighttime.
—*Silver Lining,* by Charles Aubrey Rogers, YouTube

My second child, Charles Aubrey Rogers, was born April 26, 1995, in Raleigh, North Carolina. When he was nine months old, my husband, Randy, got a promotion and we moved from Cary, North Carolina, to Midlothian, Virginia. My oldest, Richard, was three.

It was the middle of January 1995 and a case of walking pneumonia had zapped my energy throughout the moving process, although the diagnosis was not made until we were settled in our new home in Midlothian. It had taken years to build a thriving freelance copywriting business in the Raleigh area and my life had been humming along nicely. News of the promotion and the new location that went with it blew apart a carefully constructed support system of friends, family, and caregivers, leaving me feeling unmoored, without identity. With two young children, saying goodbye to family and friends had not been part of my plan.

My career had started in Richmond, Virginia, as an advertising copywriter in the eighties writing print, television, and radio ads right after graduating from UNC-Chapel Hill, so it was not an unfamiliar place. It had taken years to develop business connections in Raleigh where I had worked hard to become established as a freelancer, and working part-time allowed me to stay at home with my children. In 1995, I had been out of the Richmond market for close to a decade.

I had suffered from depression while pregnant with Charles but didn't realize it until the clouds of doom parted and the sun shined through the moment they said, "Push," and he was in my arms. Depression had not been an issue at all when pregnant with Richard. The postpartum blues that followed a couple of weeks later after either pregnancy were nothing compared to the darkness that took over my personality while pregnant with Charles.

However, when we moved from North Carolina to Virginia, my lightweight postpartum blues were amplified. Moving within the first year after giving birth is a vulnerable time for a woman as it can trigger episodes of postpartum depression and even thoughts of suicide, although I never experienced the latter. Added to that recipe were feelings of loneliness, the pneumonia, and lack of sleep that comes with moving with two small children in the dead of winter during a brutal cold snap. There were no friends or babysitters to call on for a break. This was pre-Internet, so finding outlets for us as a family was slow and difficult. Day after day of routine with no friends or family left me quick-tempered and out of sorts, which leaked into my parenting. I was miserable and cried myself to sleep every night, and took my resentment out on my husband.

When summer came I was excited to get out and meet new people at the pool, but my children hated it. Richard hid under a lounge chair and refused to come out despite being red-faced and drenched in sweat. Because of his older brother, Charles was not going to go near the water either and cried inconsolably. There was no making them get into that pool for my sake. No coaxing, cool floats, promises of ice cream, or pool toys did the trick. After several tries and many episodes of crying behind dark glasses, the pool idea had to be abandoned as a way to meet new friends.

Neighbors and their children came out of hibernation to play in the tot lots in June and July. It was a new neighborhood, still sparsely populated with a lot of construction. And the grief of leaving the people and the place I loved took a long time to overcome.

Charles was always a charming child with his shock of white hair and engaging personality, a natural extrovert. Richard, older by a little over two years, was an introvert and not a child who liked or embraced change. Richard was the problem solver, more about precision and order and it was Charles who established himself as the icebreaker. He was all fire and brimstone, passion and emotion. When he cried, he invested everything into it. When he laughed, it showed from his eyes to his toes.

They were each other's best friend and worst enemy.

I remember going to the mall one day and Charles wanted to climb on all the coin-operated animals and spaceships near the food court. There was no keeping him in a chair or stroller, and I envied parents who had more complacent children who nodded off in infant carriers.

As soon as he climbed out of his seat, his brother followed. They just wanted to scramble on top of the rides. All of a sudden, there was a crowd of kids around Charles and he was leading an expedition on top of spaceships, horses, and donkeys. Most of the parents were just staring at him and still others were glaring at me as an irresponsible parent who didn't set limits. With Charles, my sensation seeker, choosing the battles to fight and the ones to let go was a constant struggle.

The truth is, Charles never used things the way they were intended, which either excited people or incensed them. He never had to be pushed outside his comfort zone because that's where he

33

lived. Trying to establish boundaries with him was difficult and he challenged me to the equivalent of a duel every time. He, a natural devil's advocate, pushed limits, found and exposed loopholes, and more than once left me wondering why some rule was there in the first place.

My effervescent little boy was the spark that lit the flame of fun. Others were drawn to him, and this trait would follow him throughout his short life. Whenever Charles walked into a room, he'd be the highlight of the party. But he was never satiated by a fun event; he always left wanting more, feeling melancholy when it was all over. As a toddler, he was constantly asking for friends, play dates, trips to the park, and more. Like fun could last forever?

He always hated being alone. When he was put in time-out, he would badger us to death. I would say, "Ask one more time and you've earned another fifteen minutes," having learned that if I said "one more hour," there would be an expectation to stick with that and he'd make it intolerable by knocking a ball nonstop against the wall, humming something ad nauseam, or some other annoying habit that would make me sorry time-out was ever invented as a parenting strategy.

There were no guides for raising a kid like him. His brain lit up at night and he didn't sleep well, which troubled me because it could never be fixed. It was odd to have a child that age go nonstop every minute of the day and not pass out exhausted at night. His diagnosis of Delayed Sleep Phase Syndrome (DSPS) was not made until he was a teenager, and is typically a sleep disorder that has its onset in adolescence and lasts a year, maybe two. But with Charles, it started at about age two. DSPS is a disorder that makes it hard to fall asleep until after a certain hour, which can advance as the child ages. In first grade, my husband or I would read him a story, put him to bed, and two hours later he would be calling our names and begging us to read him another book. He was lonely at night but at the time I saw it as stubbornness to give up on the day when in fact, it was more than that.

As a young child, Charles was the one who would scramble into my lap or his dad's to cuddle. No one gave love so freely and openly. He adored family and his friends and was loyal to a fault. Later, it was this undying love that made him feel such shame for his thoughts of suicide and drug use.

When rescued from time-out, after a nasty spill or emotional episode, he'd pat my back to soothe himself as he was held. I loved that. While it started as a baby, he even did this as a teenager. Just a light pat with his right hand, both arms scissored across my back. It was an embrace of love that took my heart hostage. It grounded him. And it grounded me, too. That special human contact he delivered with unconditional love was the one thing my crushed soul craved the most after he died.

As a lot of children do, Charles pursued his independence with a passion. If Daddy or Richard did it, why couldn't he? He was four years old when he decided he was a big boy and didn't need baths anymore because those were for babies. Daddy took showers. Richard took showers. It was time for Charles to do the same.

For his inaugural shower, he tried taking the remainder of his packet of candy with him under the running water and I had to tell him to leave it on the counter until he was done. So he handed it over warily, issuing a warning that he knew exactly how many Gummi Bears were left in his snack pack. He knew I had a taste for Gummis, especially the red ones. When he finished his shower and got out, before he could be toweled off, he was scanning the counter for his remaining candy and grabbed the bag. He looked up at me and said one was missing and to prove it I had not eaten it, he demanded, "Stick out your tongue." A red tongue would be evidence of a guilty party. Knowing how possessive Charles was about his candy, I complied and he said, "Mom, stick it out all the way."

Rolling my eyes I said, "Charles, what are you talking about? It is stuck out all the way." He then complained, "It's crooked." Exasperated, I looked in the mirror and stuck out my tongue only to discover it was crooked. Meanwhile, he went about finishing up his candy and brushing his teeth.

Some troubleshooting on my part revealed that the left side of my tongue was crooked because it was paralyzed. How does a tongue become paralyzed? All of a sudden, I was slammed by a freight train: Something was really wrong. After a doctor's visit and an MRI, a brain tumor was discovered on one of my cranial nerves, specifically the hypoglossal nerve, the one that controls the tongue. The right side was normal, the left side had little sensory feeling and no motor function at all. It was a benign tumor but it was wrapped around the left internal carotid artery next to the brain stem and it would later be discovered it had grown into a bone in my skull. It was not malignant but it was a major ordeal having a rare skull-based tumor and I underwent two brain surgeries, one in 1999 and another in 2000, to have it removed. That was followed by a cranial reconstruction in 2003 to correct a physical deformity of my skull that followed the surgeries.

To my young children, then four and six, the ghastly stapled scar and shaved head were a shock despite our trying to set their expectations prior to my surgery. Charles worried that blood would be gushing from the wound at all times and wondered how all of us would be able to stop it. He imagined the point of entry would always be open, exposing my brain, and he was relieved the Frankenstein-ish scar with staples kept the brain and blood inside my head. While he ended up loving the scar and couldn't get enough close-up looks at the crusted blood that clung to the staples, this was a major event in our family and Charles was traumatized more than Richard. He had real anxiety that Mommy would die, despite conversations to alleviate that worry.

After total removal in 2000, the tumor sneaked its way back. From his music, we discovered later that he suffered considerable anxiety over its return, something he didn't show outwardly. In 2018, three years after his death, I underwent Gamma Knife radiosurgery to finally fry it. Left on its own, it would have done permanent damage and eventually killed me. Charles was always proud that he saved my life and his worry over the tumor was something that was referenced several times in his music.

The Spark That Lit the Flame of Fun

Mom is still sick
Tumor in her brain and shit
She's acting like it's nothing
So I'm acting like it's nothing,
but I still got pain for it.
Buried deep: next to my guilty conscious
under rocks and leafs...

The early brain tumor drama happened when Charles was in preschool and Richard in kindergarten. Two years later, Charles could not wait to start school. His remarkably developed vocabulary and progress in reading, as well as his ability to make friends, made the transition smooth and peaceful. But the honeymoon period ended after kindergarten, and from first grade on, calls from teachers regarding lack of organization, inability to pay attention, and failure to do homework became the norm.

By third grade, Charles was diagnosed with ADHD. We didn't try medication until fourth grade, and it was on and off. Deciding to medicate was controversial. Studies had shown high-risk behavior for unmedicated kids; still others argued that giving a child stimulants was like giving them methamphetamine and would trigger drug addiction later. All of this stirred up considerable internal conflict for years. It was never a comfortable subject for me, and I wanted to do the right thing. Figuring that out was difficult given that opinions were definitely in one corner or another. No one dared discuss the topic openly for fear of reprisal or worse, parental judgment. In the end, his father and I tried to make a decision that suited our child, given the situation at hand.

While there were a lot of issues related to school and homework over the years, he embraced any and all extracurricular activities, especially ones that allowed for creative expression and anything related to Halloween, his favorite holiday. For an upcoming costume party at the elementary school, he decided he was going to go as a bloody bunny. A costume from first grade was dragged out of the dress-up box and, to my horror, Charles wedged his extraordinarily thin body into that white, velvety bunny costume. Now that he was a fifth grader, the legs were way too short so it looked like a pair of capri pants, and some of the flocking from the costume had worn thin. He added the bunny ears, splattered fake blood on the front and borrowed a toy machine gun to complete the cringe-worthy ensemble. Given that every day with Charles presented multiple issues that required negotiation, I ended up letting him go to the event dressed exactly as he wished. Besides that, he was delighted with his creation and had been working on the idea in secret all week. It was not likely to go over well with parents and teachers. At the time, I didn't consider the sensitivity of the Columbine tragedy, which had occurred in 1999, about six years prior.

A child dressed up as an elaborate TV set greeted us when we arrived. It looked like a parent had spent a long time crafting every digital detail. That kid might as well have taken his victory lap because his costume was the clear winner over the plastic-mask superhero costumes from the drug store and assorted student-made creations. Charles came up to me about fifteen minutes after arriving and told me all his friends thought he'd win. They found his costume hilarious. It was certainly original. That skin-tight costume was as egregious as Charles, and as usual there were daggers in the stares directed at me by parents who disapproved. Surely, I was out of my mind for letting him dress in that audacious costume.

His friends were sure he was going to win and crushed when the TV costume took top prize. Charles didn't even take honorable mention. The teachers were judges and not about to choose something as inappropriate as a bloody bunny. He would have been more likely to win dressed as a pimp or prostitute. But, good God, my husband and I laughed like crazy. The way he ran around and entertained was classic Charles.

For fifth grade graduation in the spring, Charles wanted to wear a white tuxedo. White must have been his color of choice that year and he obsessed about that tux every day for two months. No way were we going to rent a seventy-five-dollar miniature white tuxedo that might not even exist. But Charles was relentless. He wanted that white tux so I ordered a cheap one off eBay. It was not an ideal fit but it was priced at twenty-five dollars and he could not have been happier had I taken him to an all-night theme park. His rail thin physique and long legs always presented challenges when it came to buying pants but some creative sewing made the fit presentable enough. Over the years, Charles got his twenty-five dollars out of that tux. He loved it and wore it in videos, for Halloween, and even to dances. A picture of him with his friends in their standard-issue blue blazers at fifth-grade graduation, him holding proudly the lapels of his white tuxedo, is one of my favorite photos. No one embraced "different" like Charles. At middle school graduation he begged to wear it again but this time there was no way. He had grown a foot so the pants were Bermuda shorts and looked ridiculous.

There were early signals that alarmed me during this time but not five-alarm style warnings of what was to come. The ADHD and his anxiety related to being prepared for class were two of them. When I did notice traits that seemed out of the ordinary, whomever I told usually dismissed my concerns as behavior he'd grow out of. Teachers told me what the problem was but never offered solutions because they didn't have any. And when his fifth-grade teacher and I tried to get Charles an IEP (Individualized Education Program), we were told, "He's too smart," as if that has anything to do with not being able to concentrate.

In middle school, we tried months of biofeedback for his ADHD in lieu of medication, none of which was covered by insurance. Unfortunately, it was not effective for him long-term, maybe because he had other undiagnosed issues. One of the side effects of biofeedback sessions was supposed to be sleepiness. But it never happened, which was a huge letdown given his sleep issues that were by this time worsening. He was enrolled in a smaller private school called Millwood by sixth grade, which turned out to be a good move for him, although initially he missed his buddies. There were a lot of strategies used to try to get him engaged. But the truth was, Charles saw no point in school and struggled to invest himself despite being highly intelligent. The cumulative effect of all those phone calls from teachers about one assignment or another probably contributed to his low opinion of himself. He always excelled in English and drama, however, because he liked those subjects and the teachers who taught them. He was a gifted writer with a vivid imagination and a lively class participator. No one wanted to present the same day as Charles because his book report performances were always original, engaging, and entertaining.

Charles was often asked to come to the library and read to the younger kids. They loved it when he came because he was animated and funny and made stories come alive: a natural-born entertainer. He did take ADHD medication for a while in middle school and then we'd try without. His grades were always better on the medication but that was hardly inspiration for me to keep him on it. It was in high school when he said it amplified his anxiety so we let him make the choice and he never took it after ninth grade. The fact that medication left him with no appetite and that it might be contributing to his sleeplessness were problems for a child so thin who didn't sleep well to begin with. So the risk didn't necessarily outweigh the benefit for him.

Charles was always on the phone and knocking on doors around the neighborhood, talking kids away from their video games and into the cul-de-sac. It always took him a while to coax people out of their houses but many times he managed to get a large enough group of kids to orchestrate a game with Charles rules: rules that always seem to favor him. He loved all games and on into teen years, he was a social coordinator for bringing together groups of people for wall ball, dodgeball, basketball, ping-pong, badminton, golf, baseball, a board game, a bonfire, making a video, or taking trips to the river or the park.

There were many times when Charles would knock on doors and no one would come out. He'd come home dejected that no one wanted to play, which always made me ache as I internalized his hurt. My child craved human connection. Put simply, Charles wanted my life growing up in the seventies. Back then we were outside all day, every day, playing dodgeball, chase, and riding bikes. In the seventies, no one asked where we were going and the only rule was to be home

The Spark That Lit the Flame of Fun

when the streetlights came on. My mom got us to the dinner table by going outside and ringing a large, handheld cowbell, to which we responded on first ring about fifty percent of the time. We slept like zombies because we were so tired at the end of the day. My cousins, a grandmother, an aunt, and uncle were all in the same town where we lived.

Today, families are not often in the same town, leaving people feeling more isolated and alone. That was the environment Charles had growing up in early 2000, technology having seduced our children into more time with video games and virtual role-playing. Those digital screens were far sexier than beautiful sunny days outside, and I wondered at the time what this effect would have on our children in the future. My kids were the last ones in the neighborhood to get video-game consoles. Somehow I thought my mutiny toward a screen-obsessed culture would prevent the technology revolution from robbing our children of the outside playground as the staple of cherished childhood. But my husband and I caved because our kids were bargaining and bribing their way into friends' homes to play. While I embraced technology and change myself, I saw through Charles' eyes how it affected children, and resisted.

We were a normal family, living a normal life. My husband and I dreamed of what our children would be one day, admired how smart and adorable they were as we laughed at ourselves for thinking we had the smartest and the cutest kids in the universe. Randy was a great dad, coaching recreational league baseball during their school years, which they loved. And I coached or co-coached basketball, was secretary of the PTA, volunteered in the classroom, and stayed at home and freelanced so there could be more quality time with my children. We played in parks and cul-de-sacs, went to science museums, theme parks, and took trips with family to the beach.

I protected my children from cars in the street, worried when they got sick and ran a high fever, feared they might die in a car accident, get childhood cancer, or be abducted.

When Charles was a teenager, my worries graduated to drug overdose, a drowning, or even a shooting. It never occurred to me that my child's worst enemy was in his own head, that his brain would betray him like it did, tell him he was worthless, and convince him he'd be better off dead.

I just couldn't imagine it, or wrap my head around it. Until I had to.

CHAPTER 6

BROKEN PUZZLE

Lyrics by Charles Aubrey Rogers, aka Reezin' the Revolutionary

*D*ear God, give me my friend back
Dear God, where you live at?
Are you giving love? Cause I didn't get that.
Sent you a prayer, guess you missed that
But I spit at the devil and he spit back
I hit tracks fast and cause whiplash
pain from memories remain and drift back
I was always the kid that never fit
and wished that I could focus and get class

Maybe be less awkward
and have a pretty girl kiss down my six-pack
In 5th grade, my teacher never let me play at recess,
a mess,

couldn't relieve stress
depressed and ADHD
As a child I used to think my teacher hated me
cause she made me feel so fuckin' stupid
I don't know what my use is
I guess I'm useless,
a loser writin' putrid music

(Refrain)
I'm the last piece in a broken puzzle
To a broken puzzle
Never fittin'
I'm just sittin' near the trouble
It's difficult findin' air to breathe
concealed within bubble
Can't sleep,
death is the only way to keep peace from the struggle

I got sent off
Rumors and others spread
But I still write raps
as sick as the tumor in my mother's head
I lived in an institution
where they were constantly spewin' lies
like the truth is DEAD
They used to take my music,
treat me like a nuisance,
they said my dreams a fluke

I watch these kids slit they writs
and hear bulimics puke
When am I comin' home?
I'm getting pissed and God doesn't hear shit
Even when I'm scream to the roof,
I spit that real till your ears bleed from the truth

(Refrain)
I'm the last piece in a broken puzzle
To a broken puzzle
Never fittin'

Broken Puzzle

I'm just sittin' near the trouble
It's difficult findin' air to breathe
concealed within bubble
Can't sleep,
death is the only way to keep peace from the struggle

I could never sit still
Doctor prescribed pills, "This kid's ill"
I already wrote my will,
I don't know how long I'll be here till
Dope kills,
but I let the opiates fill my brain,
but the effects don't remain

I'm stranded strange stuck
in the same mundane thing
in this lame game
Fake rappers tryna claim fame
just like puppets on string
auto tuned so they pretend they can sing,
wake up
and see you're a slave to the mainstream

Charles proudly poses in his beloved white tuxedo for 5th grade graduation with twin friends, Casey and Dustin Hux.

CHAPTER 7

THE YOUTUBE YEARS

She held me in her tummy for 9 months
And I repaid her with lies and lighting blunts
And I spit on her gift of life by trying to die once
Like, 'Goodbye Mum'
Things are different now
My life, I appreciate mine.
—*Out of Reach*, by Charles Aubrey Rogers

It was in 2006, when Charles was in sixth grade and Richard in eighth that both of my children started YouTube channels as the video craze hit their generation. By 2007, my children were absolutely gripped by it and I bought them an iMac and put it in the hallway of our home so we could monitor their activity. They started out with just the computer webcam and then Richard graduated to a video camera, that being his favorite possession ever.

For years, my home would be the stage for making crazy

videos. Sam, Jacob, Daniel, Alex, Scott, Johnny, Robert, and other supporting characters were always at my house playing a part. These were Charles' peeps and they would all hang out together throughout their school years.

Richard had his crew, too. Charles would do the occasional cameo in Richard's movies and vice versa.

Richard and Charles developed YouTube followings, Richard as Cyberkiwi27 and Charles as Timeboy1408, and my home would be seen by millions in the coming years. This video-production obsession made the dress-up box the most popular plaything in our house for more than a decade. Stocked with shark and dinosaur heads from costumes past, props like toy guns, fire hats, plastic axes, severed limbs, capes, dreadlocks, crazy hats, hand mitts with claws, and so on. It was a plastic footlocker so full of costumes, the lid would never close.

To my generation, these videos were stupid and pointless. To the emerging one, they were hilarious antics and stunts. Neither child was allowed to use his real name on YouTube and I had rules that had to be followed or the video would be taken down. Of course, these boundaries were challenged multiples times.

Concerned about increasing time spent on YouTube, I decided to have a conversation about the dangers of the Web with my children. As they sat down for the lesson, they rolled their eyes and I began by giving them my standard speech that they could balk, squirm, and talk back, which would mean the conversation would take twice as long. That always gave them pause and inspired them to cut the complaints and settle down.

So I launched into various scenarios that predators use to get young kids to give up information or lure them into a meeting them in person or even a chat room. Unlike most parents my age, I was well versed in the Internet and computers. As a digital marketer, these tools were not foreign to me; neither were tactics used by online predators.

About a day after that lesson on Internet safety, Charles popped into the kitchen during dinner preparation. Richard was sitting at the kitchen counter doing homework, a departure from his favorite spot, the kitchen table. Charles was standing there stock-still and we were both staring at him. He launched into a story that took a moment to understand.

He told us he had met someone very nice on the Internet, and his name was Jim. He then said "Jim" had asked for nude photos of him but since the man said he was a doctor and I had told him that a medical professional was the only person who could ask to see him naked, he had immediately complied and sent the requested photos. Richard and I laughed until our sides hurt. He was acting out the scenarios I had told him about in my Internet safety lesson, and had made up a fictional predator named Jim. He was making fun of my lessons and he had an engaging way of acting this out. At least I knew he understood, and of course "Jim" was a fictional predator Charles had invented.

For several nights following, Charles would waltz into the kitchen wide-eyed with some other outlandish story about his friend, Jim. Jim wanted to meet at the mall because he had lost his dog and wanted Charles' help finding him. He told us that Jim would be by to pick him up and, because he was in a hurry—the lost dog and all—he'd meet Charles at the corner of our street. Was it OK if he left for the mall with this new friend he had met on the Internet? And by the way, was it OK if he also went into a van to test video games while at the mall?

Richard and I would wait nightly for the performances as he played out every single scenario I had described. These vignettes would have been great educational videos. They certainly had enough of a YouTube following at the time.

With the videos the kids were making, they got friends together, organized shoots, wrote scenes, planned wardrobes, and were constantly outside with friends. They objected to my having guidelines but they knew this was part of the deal of being allowed to do them in the first place.

Over the years, there were some videos that had to come down, and still others slipped through the cracks. Other parents were not always happy with me, a reoccurring theme. It was their opinion I was giving my kids too much creative license. They wondered why I didn't just put my foot down and put a stop to this. They wanted me to "control" my children. To me, parenting is about fostering gifts and talents, guiding my kids in a direction, and allowing them to learn from mistakes. Charles was not controllable, but he was not a behavior problem either. He simply pushed boundaries and questioned rules, which made people uncomfortable. I could choose to fight that, or accept him as he was.

We had established rules and limits on the videos but it was a challenge to stay in front of it. It would have been fine if all the other kids in the neighborhood and two schools hadn't wanted to be in one of the famed productions. That's when other parents would object. This was all new territory, and pioneering a strategy that didn't quash their imagination and steered clear of outright parental controversy was always a hard call.

There were worse things they could be doing and because they made so many videos at my house, I was able to keep them in my sights.

In watching them, many mysteries were solved including why pine straw might be on the back of my winter coat, why there were dents in the mailbox, breaks in our siding, scratches on car doors, mystery spills on the deck, and so on. Kids do a lot of things behind our backs. My kids videotaped what they did and published the evidence on YouTube.

I had a flash of video fame on Richard's channel. The audience could see me in the background fixing sandwiches during a passionate fight-to-the-death scene happening in my family room. It was business as usual as far as I was concerned. But to viewers of the channel, this attitude was dismissive of a brutal murder taking place in my den, which, to a bunch of teenagers, was utterly hilarious. Strangers and even parents approached me in the grocery store line or while selecting produce or cereal to tell me how funny their kids thought it was and how the whole family had howled with laughter. You could say I was the first reality series star.

The YouTube Years

During this time, it was nothing to walk downstairs and see a rubber arm sticking out of the ground in the back yard, a cape over a bush, or see them performing some wild stunt: murdering someone, or witness one of them drinking an unidentifiable liquid from a carton (always something normal disguised as something disgusting). Or perhaps it was a gross substance Mom didn't need to know about.

Richard was a natural with video, Charles less polished. And it was Richard who had the greater following and would go on to make it his career.

One day Richard made a video and uploaded it to the upstairs hallway iMac. It was seen and shared by a famous YouTuber with millions of followers who commented on how funny it was. By that evening, Richard had had about seven hundred thousand views on the video, and the number was climbing fast.

It was Christmas Eve and we were all riveted to this new trend, called "going viral." It had been only a few hours and we surmised that by the next morning it could possibly be a million. We woke up the next day, and instead of running downstairs to open presents, we were all intrigued to find where the number was now.

But the video was mysteriously gone.

Richard was very upset and an investigation revealed it was Charles who had deleted it. We were confused as to why he would do this. In trying to defend himself, Charles told us that Richard had logged onto his YouTube channel and added background that read "I am gay" all over it. In a move of revenge, he logged onto Richard's account and deleted the video. We were crestfallen because we had been cheated out of the results of our exciting new adventure. And I wasn't overjoyed at the negative reference between my boys to homosexuals, either. The conversation of language, inclusion, and acceptance would happen at a later date.

From that moment forward, Charles would become very private about passwords and refused to share any of them with me, no longer allowing the computer to store them. One of my rules was that I had to have the passwords and it became harder to keep up with what he was doing. This was an abrupt change in his personality and I had to find other strategies of securing them or limiting his use until he gave them up.

Overall, middle school for Charles was innocent enough. I know now that this was when his struggles began, but he was consistently engaged with all of his activities: baseball, after-school clubs, and making movies. I believed he loved life because he made so much of every day but now know he was trying to fill himself up, and was often left wanting more. Sugar was part of his attempt to fill himself up, to feel better, as were most of the things he did.

CHAPTER 8

SNACK TIME[*]

Lyrics by Charles Aubrey Rogers, aka Reezin' the Revolutionary

O h, pass me a Laffy Taffy
and some Sour Patch Kids,
I'm about to have a snack bitch.

Cheetos, Fritos, Cool Ranch Doritos, Taco Bell burritos
Pass me dem Skittles
'cause you know I bout to eat those.
I'm suckin' down a Frosty
like blood fo' mosquitoes,

Krispy Kreme donuts
make me go nuts.
I'm robbin' pepsi towtrucks
just so I can get some sodas.

---

*   This is one of the few lighthearted songs in his collection. I so wish he had a video on this. I would love to have seen his performance.

DIARY OF A BROKEN MIND

(Refrain)
I be all about the snax,
I be all about the snax,
I be all about the snax,
I be all about the snacks
I be snack snackin' on some chips,
snack snackin' on some shit
cuz it's snack time bitch,
it is snack time bitch!

Purple Slurpees and Hershey's,
RedBull cuz I'm thirsty.
Churros and cheese curlies.
It's 2 o'clock in the morning,
I SNACK EARLY!

The snack is back
snack attack, I'll snack on that
I go to the gas station
and buy out
the whole snack spot.
I snack a lot,
this snack is hot,
just ate all the snacks I bought.

Cereal packs of pop,
crackin' rocks and tater tots,
Can't take the Mott's
cuz I am not about the applesauce.

I'd rather have some apple jacks,
ice cream bunny tracks,
sackfullofnax
Utex mix 'n match,
a Twix and a half,
Kit-kat fudge—
some bricks of that,
RACKS ON RACKS
of big fat snacks.

Snack Time

(Refrain)
I be all about the snax,
I be all about the snax,
I be all about the snax,
I be all about the snacks
I be snack snackin' on some chips,
snack snackin' on some shit
cuz it's snack time bitch,
it is snack time bitch!

Maybe onion chips,
French onion dip
and Starburst bricks
Snacks,
I'm all about that shit.
Cream soda sips,
shreddin' beef jerky.
In my lips with bags of rips,
frosted flakes, pancakes, milkshakes,
bits of steak on my plate.

Snacks to the face,
snacking race,
no snacks to waste.
Cookie dough unbaked,
cinnamon bun cake
Sitting back eating snacks on a Sunday—yeeuh.

Funyuns mothafucka, yea,
FUNYUNS MOTHAFUCKA,
Got some Funyuns mothafucka,
I like Funyuns mothafucka.
Chips be flavored like some onions mothafucka (CRUNCH sfx)

I be snack snackin' on some chips,
snack snackin' on some shit
cuz it's snack time bitch,
it is snack time bitch!

Cheezits and chocolate,

55

you don't snack bitch you just talk a lot
So putcha your snax up if you snacking,
Eatin' all the snacks,
motherfucka need a napkin.
Licorice snack dish,
snack on the average.
You don't even snack bitch.

Pop tarts, toaster strudel,
gushers taste like magic.
Snacks I got to have it,
I got stacks of all the snacks
and bags of pepper jack.

Bananas and some yum yums,
Gummies with Capri Sun.
Snackin' whatchu dreamed of
chewing on sum tum-tums.

Honey buns, Oreos double stuff
and some gum.
Lookin' handsome while I'm snacking
grams of breadcrumbs.
Yeah son, whatchu know about snacks?
Whatchu whatchu know 'bout snacks?
I BE ALL ABOUT DA SNAX

CHAPTER 9

SIGNS OF WHAT WAS TO COME

… I bet when I'm deceased,
at peace when my final season ends,
they'll listen then and say ain't another rapper dope as reezin' is,
or was, 'cause I'll be done with the dust unable to feel the love.
—*Hollow Man,* by Charles Aubrey Rogers

Charles was an enormously popular in high school, not just funny but thoughtful. If someone new came to school, he was the first to introduce himself and ask that kid to sit with him and his friends at lunch. He was the first to knock on the door of a new neighbor even while the moving van was still outside. I loved those things about him.

However, one of the traits that really bothered me was his addiction to candy. He loved snacks and convenience stores and would stand in that aisle and ponder his final decision as if it were a major case on which he needed to render a Supreme Court verdict.

This candy debate was a bone of contention between me and Randy from early on, and the buying of one piece was our parental compromise. Teaching good eating habits is nearly impossible in a culture of processed and fast food saturated with sugar and caffeine, and it was my attempt to get a handle on it before it blew up. It didn't matter because if it was terrible for you, Charles loved it, craved it, begged for it, and found a way around it. If I said, "one bag," he'd find the deluxe, bargain size and insist that it was within the boundary that had been set. If he had been told at the grocery store, two choices only, he would debate each new item he picked up and try to wedge it into the category of nutritious or claim another family member had asked for it so it wouldn't qualify as one of his two. It was rare that either of us would take Charles to a grocery store because too many needed items were left behind for meal preparation because he'd used up our available brainpower in intense product deliberation.

My early days of painstakingly cooking and freezing our own baby food from organic sources, a real challenge in the nineties, was pointless because it didn't stick. So much for creating a good foundation of nutrition, and I do know how important it is when it comes to being both physically and mentally healthy.

Sweets were not introduced early in our home and it was rare to find candy in the house other than small snack bags like Gummi Bears that they'd get once a day or in their lunches. My husband, on the other hand, was not so strict, but how can you be in a culture like ours? I fought hard against sugared cereals but didn't always win. For some kids, that good feeling sugar delivers is addictive. I'm not blaming my husband because they introduce sugar as rewards as early as preschool, so it wasn't as if I was going to win unless I packed him away in a bubble.

One day while switching out winter for summer clothing, I found a stockpile of candy wrappers under his bed, and I sat on his bed and cried. He was about ten years old at the time. Substance use disorder ran on both sides of the family, and I knew that his stash of sweets confirmed what I had long suspected: a sugar addiction.

Charles' friends said he would walk in, go to their kitchen, grab a soda and candy, making jokes and entertaining them the whole time he raided their supply. By the time he was eighteen, he had serious tooth decay in his molars and had to have two root canals. That child had more cavities than genuine tooth structure.

I don't think this habit alone pointed to future addiction, but there was a mounting body of evidence that he had the personality traits for substance use disorder. Hoarding candy, together with other troubling signs, made me worry that he would one day become addicted to something much worse.

The problem was there were no strategies or studies for preventing future addiction. Or at least they weren't readily available. Not buying candy and trying to steer him toward more nutritious choices was not working and I knew that making wartime at the dinner table would make things worse. He picked at his food and then wanted to get snacks instead. At a certain point, a parent can't force someone to eat what he or she wants him to eat.

It's no wonder Charles loved Halloween the most, especially the trick-or-treating. At six foot two inches tall, one hundred thirty pounds, and nineteen years old, Charles still went door to door in costume with a pillowcase that would come home filled to the top. Halloween had two things he loved most: dressing up and free candy.

Another personality trait that alarmed me was his relentless pursuit of fun. I never knew what to call it, and once the Internet came into our lives, I looked up multiple phrases to get more information but could never define or attach this behavior to potential future problems.

The memory that comes to mind to illustrate this was a trip we took to a theme park when Charles was around eleven, his older brother, Richard, about thirteen. Each got to invite one friend. It was not crowded that day and my youngest tore through that theme park like a boy attached to a rocket launcher, dragging his friend on every hair-raising ride or roller coaster. With no lines to slow him down, he could get off a roller coaster and back on the same one in less than a minute, his little friend panting to keep up and barely able to find his feet beneath him before Charles raced up the gangplank for a redo. This was an eleven-year-old thrill seeker's version of pure ecstasy, and while I thought it would tire him out, it did just the opposite by refueling his tireless temperament.

Once we got home from this all-day outing, Charles wanted to know if we could go to Busch Gardens, about an hour away from our home in Chesterfield County, Virginia, right outside of Richmond. This was at 5:30 p.m., immediately after an entire day of riding rides at a hot theme park. I was exhausted from just trying to keep up with him all day and responded, "Sure. Let's plan that for a couple of weeks from now." But he meant right then and challenged me on my reasons for not getting up and going immediately. What could possibly be stopping me?

I laughed and said we'd have to plan for another day. So he shifted tactics and begged to have four friends come over for dinner and a sleepover. Once this was denied, he asked if we could have just two friends over for dinner, which would always turn into him pleading for them to stay overnight. If they stayed overnight, he'd keep those kids up all night playing games, which meant I'd be up several times telling them to keep it down. Because he kept friends awake when they were supposed to be sleeping, our list of people to choose from was getting shorter. Parents didn't like grumpy, tired kids the next day, and I cannot blame them.

After his death, I learned that his relentless pursuit of fun was the result of a broken reward system[1], a concept that was introduced to me in a lecture at a conference hosted by the College Behavioral and Emotional Health Institute (COBE) at Virginia Commonwealth University. Further research revealed that some people, about ten percent of the population, are born with a pleasure center that's deficient in dopamine, so when they take an addictive drug that releases dopamine, they are absolutely euphoric.[2] A year after that revelation, I would discover this behavior could be labeled "sensation seeking," one of four personality traits identified by the Preventure study for showing a predisposition to addiction, lead by Patricia Conrod, Ph.D., from the University of Montreal.[3] The

1   Broken Reward System" Study—Action of drugs of abuse on brain reward systems, 1982. www.ncbi.nlm.nih.gov/pubmed/6127721
2   Attention-deficit-hyperactivity disorder and reward deficiency syndrome. www.ncbi.nlm.nih.gov/pmc/articles/PMC2626918/
3   Clinically Combating Reward Deficiency Syndrome (RDS) with Dopamine Agonist Therapy as a Paradigm Shift: Dopamine for Dinner? www. ncbi.nlm.nih.gov/pmc/articles/PMC4586005/

other three personality traits are: hopelessness, anxiety sensitivity, and impulsiveness.

Charles had all of the above traits but it was the sensation seeking that drove his constant requests for play dates. Had he taken the test to determine which trait was most prevalent, it would have been that one, with negative thinking taking close second. All during his childhood we had a revolving door of friends and activities at our house. If he was awake, he was a nonstop social coordinator and event planner.

Those traits that show predisposition for addiction—most of them characteristic of mental illness, too—are also behaviors one finds in the most successful and innovative entrepreneurs, the most gifted actors and musicians, our most decorated Olympians and athletes. Creative geniuses often have one or more of them.

In a culture where prescriptions for pain have become so normalized and available, at a point in development when children lack coping skills, and in a society that is increasingly disconnected, a lot of kids who suffer these traits self-medicate to numb the pain, as Charles did. Early introduction to substances increases the risk of addiction, ending up in prison, or early death.[4] This is why Jasmin Vassileva, Ph.D., of VCU Institute of Drug and Alcohol Studies and I have partnered to make an evidence-based, personality-targeted coping skills program, or something like it, available in Virginia and U.S. school curriculums. The idea is to promote positive coping strategies and prevent negative ones like cutting or substance misuse.

In 2006, I wanted to change Charles' trajectory and get him focused on his future. But Charles was a "here and now" kid, and no amount of lecturing was ever going to change that. I went so far as going to the school to discuss adding coping strategies and commonsense education to the curriculum, but got nowhere with that.

Charles was always sick, too: stomach pains for which we could never get a diagnosis, and pains in his back, arms, and legs. The nurse at every school he attended knew him by his first name. He caught

---

4   Clinically Combating Reward Deficiency Syndrome (RDS) with Dopamine Agonist Therapy as a Paradigm Shift: Dopamine for Dinner? www.ncbi.nlm.nih.gov/pmc/articles/PMC4586005/

everything that went around, the flu, a cold, stomach virus, and ear infections.

Getting sick often is an early sign of possible mental illness. Physical health is affected by mental health and it would not be until 2014, that it would be proven in a ground-breaking landmark study called ACEs.

The Adverse Childhood Experiences Study (ACE Study)[5] was a research study conducted by Kaiser Permanente and the Centers for Disease Control and Prevention. The study demonstrated an association of ACEs, such as neglect and abuse, with physical health and social problems as an adult. Our culture may separate physical and mental health, but our bodies and brains do not. The brain has no idea what society is doing and it develops per the environment it grows up in.

From teachers and administrators, Charles was consistently hearing, "You are not performing up to the standards for which you are capable," which had a profound effect on his opinion of himself. He was also "disciplined" for his coping strategies such as listening to music in the wrong areas of school, and was once suspended for a panic attack because administrators didn't understand what they were seeing. My son also took to heart the austere treatment I received when trying to stand up for him or get him help, which contributed to his own feelings of despair and hopelessness. All of this contributed to his taking matters in to his own hands, and translated to relying on drugs and alcohol to cope.

Experiences I might not have considered traumatizing at home may very well have been so to my sensitive and vulnerable younger child. Early in the process of his drug abuse, we relied on punitive discipline to alter behavior; frustrated by lack of results, I resorted to yelling my way to a solution that was lazy and unproductive. There were abrupt changes that alarmed me, too, including his sudden lack of motivation and loss of interest in outside activities. Our education system as a whole had evolved into a nonstop series of standardized testing that summarily sucked the creativity and innovation from the curriculum and homogenized the school experience. Education

5   Adverse Childhood Experiences (ACEs). www.cdc.gov/violencepre-vention/acestudy/index.html

became all about memorization and test scores.

Charles showed me a video to illustrate this point: "Do Schools Kill Creativity? TED Talk by Sir Ken Robinson." It was exactly how I saw the education system, but to realize that he did, too, was a shock. My son was a gifted and highly talented child, yet our current system had no idea what to do with an innovator like him. There were teachers along the way who fostered and appreciated his talent but the larger system would crush his creative spirit.

The sign that worried me most, that we could never get our minds around, was his sleep problems. Lack of sleep contributes to mental health problems. As a grieving mother, my worst days are always following a night when sleep is hard to find. When he was alive, just thinking about how miserable he was not to be able to sleep kept me up at night. Sometimes I stayed up with him, which meant there were two sleep-deprived people in the house. His issues went beyond the diagnosis of Delayed Sleep Phase Syndrome (DSPS). Anxiety and ADHD played a part. And something we have not yet identified. But more than anything, lack of sleep exacerbated his feelings of loneliness, which was a contributing factor to his frequent thoughts of suicide.

Before we made the no-phones-allowed-in-the-room-at-night rule, his friends from middle school later told stories about Charles texting them messages of misery late at night. We were the first generation of cell phone-owning children so there were no studies, no protocols yet to follow, but I was uneasy about this technology and its effects.

Early intervention would have been effective for Charles, and it is why I believe every pediatric, family, or primary-care practice should screen young people for suicide risk. Together with Lisa Horowitz, Ph.D., of The National Institute of Mental Health (NIMH), I have advocated for the four/five-question Ask Suicide-Screening Questions (ASQ) tool because it's quick and has saved young lives. The majority of those who die by suicide have had contact with a medical professional within months of killing themselves. Charles had seen a clinical professional at two facilities within a week of his suicide, neither of whom did a screening.

When it came to finding resources and answers, I certainly gave it a gallant effort: advocating, begging, calling, asking questions, and researching. But I could not make something exist that did not exist, and resources that may have been available were unknown to me despite turning myself inside out to find them. Charles' problems were coming at me like an angry, swollen river after days of heavy rainfall. I was helpless to stop it and didn't know where to turn or where to start.

CHAPTER 10

RUN FREE

Lyrics by Charles Aubrey Rogers, aka Reezin' the Revolutionary

*P*roblems just pilin' all around me
  Wish I could just wilin' in Hawaiian Islands
Taking shots of crown
Let the alcohol drown
Take a look around
All this bullshit surround got me down
Wish I could just run free, run free,
to the fuckin' sound

Turn the music loud
Now I'm sprintin' through the clouds.
Clear your mind free
Your doubts we gon scream,
we gon shout till we blow them speakers out.

DIARY OF A BROKEN MIND

Time for peace is now,
I just wanna run away like a race,
Painkilla music, get numb to the bass
runaway
Feel the sun in my face

(Refrain)
I just wanna run free, run free,
I just wanna run free, run free,
I just wanna run free, run free,
just wanna run free, run FREE

Floatin' high above the ground,
never touch down,
never ever comin down
High off all the sound.

Sick of all the pain,
I am sick of all the hurt and the burn
Ima runaway runaway
and never return.
Never COMIN' back
Leanin' on clouds up in heaven
with my rap feelin' free at last
Floatin' through the present
I ain't focused on the past,
Mind on the money
I am focused on the cash
Just broken beyond repair
Feels like no one's even there
God ain't even care
It ain't even fair.

Runaway, runaway
I can't be brave
Sit and stare till I gotta go,

Run Free

up, up, by bye, Geronimo!
I'm comin' home, comin' home,
just a scared little boy all alone,
Momma don't pick up the phone when I'm callin' home
And it's gettin' hard so you know I gotta go.

(Refrain)
I just wanna run free, run free,
I just wanna run free, run free,
I just wanna run free, run free,
just wanna run free, run FREE

Close my eyes till I don't exist
Floatin' through the black,
peace and bliss
Peacefulness, escape the place where evil is,
Escape it all cuz I can't face it all.

I just run, run cuz I ain't gotta place at all,
Melt into the music while I face the wall.
Up in outer space and I chase it off,
I'm in a place that's lost,
Palm trees, white sand bright,
tan with a can in my right hand,
Like this is the life man,
This is the mothafuckin' life man,

Pfft
Yea right man,
Ima float and fly away up above it all like fuckitall,
High enough to touch God
before I just fuckin' fall.....
Before I fall on the floor with ya'll
But I gotta go, gotta go, gotta go, gotta go
Can't stop me,
no, gotta go, gottugoupup,
Bye Bye Geronimo

DIARY OF A BROKEN MIND

(Refrain)
I just wanna run free, run free,
I just wanna run free, run free,
I just wanna run free, run free,
just wanna run free, run FREE

CHAPTER 11

FAMILY LIFE STARTS TO UNRAVEL

I still feel like a lost child holding a crayon
Trying to paint a picture to explain myself as a man
But I'm still left wondering if I even can.
—*Out of Reach*, by Charles Aubrey Rogers

It was high school when our family life started to show signs of trouble. From the time Charles turned fifteen until he died at age twenty, our lives were chaos as we struggled to navigate one crisis after another in a complex mental health system. Charles was sixteen and in tenth grade when I finally installed spyware. His safety trumped his right to privacy. I was seeing many alarming changes in him. He was not being honest about passwords, and monitoring his activity had become too difficult. Something more was going on and I programed the spy software to cut off the Internet at 9 p.m. or 10 p.m. in our home on any given night. I didn't want my night owl up trolling in the wee hours.

No laptops or Internet-ready devices were allowed in their rooms at all, which was easy considering he didn't have a laptop, and mobile phones at this time were not all smartphones although it was becoming more commonplace. He had an iPod but it was a large one that stored songs only and had no Internet access. We also had an alarm system installed because his nighttime prowling was something we could not monitor when we slept.

The spyware revealed a lot I was not prepared for. The onslaught of what he was doing and all he was involved with was shocking but I got an inside view of other kids who were suffering and saw an alarming trend of drug abuse far before a lot of people were talking about it. He was often high late at night when we were asleep. Who was doing drugs, what drugs they were doing, and who was dealing were all revealed in those spyware conversations. One substance lowered inhibitions, and then it was open season on alcohol, popping whatever pills or drugs were lying around no matter what they were.

It was in these conversations I first discovered teens would find out who had just had wisdom teeth removed and target that kid to give up his prescribed pain medication. The teen who sold the medication would get his cash and the person who bought it would then sell it to other teens and, in some cases, keep some or all of it for himself. Selling the pills was an attractive way to make money and feel important. Oxycodone, an opiate with Tylenol, is legal heroin in a prescription bottle and an easy way to get high. It's often a gateway to the street drug heroin and full-blown addiction. Oxycodone was routinely prescribed and handed out in 2012 by oral surgeons following wisdom-teeth removal, who had been told by pharmaceutical reps that these drugs were safe.

Charles' close friends didn't quite know how to react to his increasing interest in drugs. It was beyond what they were doing and often conversations went as this one, revealed by the spyware, did.

Charles	you wanna do me a favourrr?
Friend	what is it brother?
Charles	GO TO UR MEDICINE CABINET BRING ME UR DRUGS
Charles	jelly beans*

Family Life Starts to Unravel

Friend	*drugs
Friend	no problem <u3
Charles	WORD
Friend	hehehe
Charles	kidding
Charles	unless you have hydros or some yummy yummy wisdom teeth stuff
Charles	hahahahahaha
Friend	;) you know me
Charles	did u have u ur wisdom teeth removed?
Friend	not yet
Friend	i don't know when i will
Charles	oh. youll have fun
Friend	fuck no
Friend	it sucks ass
Friend	i know from you sam and caleb
Charles	i didnt get painkillers... and mine were extracted
Charles	youll get vicodin
Friend	<u3
Friend	no painkillers? whyyyy?
Charles	CUZ IM A MAN
Friend	FUCK YEAH
Charles	dont worry. im pretty sure i made up for it
Friend	how?
Friend	;)

Other kids, not just Charles, were abusing medications like Robitussin. The kids had a method of getting high off this cough medicine and it was called robo-tripping. Symptomatic of this abuse were robotic, stiff movements along with the usual drunk-like behavior. Armed with a list, I went and cleaned out all medication with abuse potential. Most would be surprised at how many substances this involves.

The Tramadol (the dog's medicine) was one of the ones that missed my purging session, and later I found the supply seriously depleted. My dog didn't climb up into that cabinet and take it. And it wasn't just Charles scouring my cabinets, it was friends who had

71

come by once and not the familiar faces who had been at my home for the past ten years making YouTube videos and playing basketball in the driveway. There had been leftover Concerta at the back of the cabinet, and that was all gone.

It's tempting to blame all the drug-seeking behavior on friends. But those who are struggling tend to find one another. I wanted to believe that Charles was influenced by "the wrong crowd," and probably most parents do, but spyware indicated that he also swiped medications from friends' medicine cabinets as they raided ours.

Reddi-wip had to be banished from my household because it was always flat, and my counselor tipped me off that it was because teens would suck the fumes for a quick high. Any and all alcohol was locked up; my husband and I stopped drinking anything at all. Not that either of us at the time were big drinkers. Once we stopped completely, it was eye opening to see how dependent the adults in our culture had become on substances to help manage life. These kids with whom Charles was collaborating online, school friends mostly, were abusing anything they could find, anything to escape whatever issue with which they were dealing. An overall feeling of inadequacy had met up with an environment of availability.

The nineties had brought on a period of normalization as it pertained to using substances to treat both physical and mental pain. During that decade, prescribing for pain became more commonplace, and as that happened the quantity prescribed increased, which made leftovers in medicine cabinets more common. When my child tried something and it was no longer there, he found alternatives in everyday medications that could be bought over the counter or in a grocery store. He had gotten those ideas from online collaboration.

It's where I found out he was smoking pot and how often. We discovered he'd tried LSD and some dangerous party drugs from China with names like 2-CE. Our most vulnerable population was getting sucked into this culture early. Kids who'd suffered depression or a trauma such as losing a parent were also susceptible. The only problems they were learning to solve were math and science and no one seemed to be asking these kids about their home life. They were left to figure out how to cope with monumental family issues on their own, so they often defaulted to using a substance to make it go away because they knew of no other option.

My husband suspected Charles knew about the spyware and he was pretending. It's my belief he had no clue. The spyware was undetectable and I could login from my computer anywhere and see the screenshots and get the data. It's not hard to understand why Randy's brain could not believe our child was really this out of hand. It was unbelievable, and overwhelming. Knowing it was true didn't put me at any advantage.

The question was, what could we do about it? To figure that out, we saw a counselor to help, to get the two of us singing in the same choir. We needed to be a united front and we were, quite frankly, at a loss for what to do. Taking away car keys doesn't stop a depressive suicidal from abusing drugs and neither does drug testing. Being able to monitor activity required me to go undercover in my own home, which was uncomfortable, and if he found out, it would unleash a wrath of anger. I had to be careful what I said.

My child needed help and a diagnosis. We saw mental health professionals, made phone calls and researched but no one ever said the magic words, "psychological evaluation." Even when we had testing done, they'd give me a vague assessment that he was high risk but never defined the term. Since Charles was often in the room with me when the results were presented, I was never comfortable asking them to explain that further and expected a written report to follow to elaborate. But it never did. Despite having the signs, no one ever mentioned he was at risk for suicide or substance use disorder, though those early tests had to have shown that he was. The mental health professionals we saw in 2012 didn't want to be the ones to say the correct phrases or have the tough conversations. One medical professional prescribed what I would consider to be inappropriate medication for a teenager who was abusing drugs.

During his sophomore year, Charles and Richard were both chosen to be on the homecoming court. It was a proud-momma moment. I escorted my eldest, who won that year as a senior, and Charles, a sophomore, was escorted to homecoming court by his favorite teacher, Mrs. Fretwell. That night stands out because there was so little joy in our household during those years. Soon after, Charles' drug use escalated. From his music, it was obvious he suffered from

73

depression and had been tortured with thoughts of suicide, which is what drove his substance abuse. His behavior from age fifteen on was risky, and he had a cavalier attitude about life, a trait I would learn later is indicative of depression.

One day in Charles' junior year, there was a call from the high school that he had listened to his iPod during lunch, past the designated area where students were permitted to do so at lunchtime. I remember thinking, "Are you serious?" This apparently required my immediate attention. They showed a video still of Charles standing just a foot beyond the line.

In all seriousness, the administrator carefully pointed to the line and where Charles was standing beyond to further corroborate his heinous crime.

I was at a loss to understand the severity of the infraction. When Charles told me his side of the story, he said, "Mom, my anxiety was eating me alive and you know that's how I cope. I was working up to a panic attack, and listening to music is what keeps me sane." He was accustomed to listening to music to calm himself, and in so doing broke some cardinal rule at school. While I was trying to explain this to the administrator, she was discussing a zero-tolerance policy, a term people use when they are too lazy to make rational, informed decisions.

At the time, the school was run like an old-fashioned juvenile detention center; the only thing it lacked were bars on the windows and doors. Time and again, I'd get called for the most bizarre infractions, for either of my boys. Even Richard was called in for a psych consult for creating a picture in art class where he had drawn a tattoo of El Salvador on the arm of his subject. If this was indication of a school shooter, I'd missed it. Richard was a fabulous student and time manager, and we would have found these meaningless infractions comical had they not been so annoying.

Charles thought he was ugly and broken: typical traits for those who suffer depression. As a child, he had had so much self-confidence, which had completely eroded by the onset of his mental illness in early adolescence and middle school. Disciplinary treatment in high school perpetuated his feelings of worthlessness.

Calls from teachers and administrators about homework or falling asleep in class were becoming more frequent, which prompted a visit back to Special Ed to meet with the counselor to look into this. We needed answers as to why he was more withdrawn and unmotivated. While some of it might have been drug use, that wasn't the whole story. There was an underlying problem driving that abuse, and we needed the testing that could be done at school to find out what was going on. The Special Ed counselor, who was very accommodating, said there should definitely be some testing given the number of absences and complaints from some of his teachers. I thought, "Finally, we'll get a diagnosis so I'll know what the issue is." By then, it had been years of trying hard to get him the right resources, and there still were no answers.

In one of our meetings prior to implementing the testing that would take two to three weeks, another counselor—not Special Ed—leaned over to ask if we had found a medication yet. Feeling uncomfortable about sharing this information but also desperate to get feedback since there was no one to ask or compare notes with, I told her. She leaned back with a look of horror while Charles stared straight at her. Then she said in the world's loudest whisper, "Have you seen the side effects of that medication?" My heart sank. Charles saw the look and heard every word she said. It had been hard enough to get him to try medication, and this one had been showing good results thus far.

The side effects she was expressing doubt about were present only at doses four times what Charles had been prescribed. And besides, we were only trying a class of mood stabilizers. The stigma for taking anything for mental illness in 2012 was still strong, but I was not expecting this counselor to "pill shame" us in open court like that.

My face was red hot and the visceral feelings of anger took days to subside. As soon as we left the session, Charles turned to me and said, "I'm never trying another antidepressant as long as I live." Despite the fact that it was not actually an antidepressant, I knew when Charles got this stubborn, he meant it. My heart sank. There had been significant difference in my child that week. There had been a spark of hope, and it was again crushed by the very person who was supposedly there to help us. This behavior was unprofessional, and it is one of my regrets that I didn't address this with her directly because right after this meeting was when the kids were dismissed for summer break. My self-appointed job acting as advocate and navigator in a mental health system that was a labyrinth of confusion had been stressful and time-consuming. Chasing down loose ends would often be interrupted by some other new development or event that required immediate attention.

The results of the testing gave us no diagnosis; there were some answers for us but not so much from the testing itself. Part of the exercise was to have the teachers write a letter. The one who didn't like him at all wrote a scathing report, which was expected, and I couldn't help but laugh under my breath. Charles was not a bad kid. He could be frustrating and he was suffering, but it wasn't like he was swinging from the rafters or throwing jars of mustard at kids' heads. There was a cause for his behavior, as it is with all children and it was odd to me that a teacher couldn't see that. Teachers either loved him or hated him. So I'd read one letter that gushed about how wonderful he was and listed minor issues. Another painted him as a possible future criminal as a result of assignments not done on time and falling asleep in class. It was hard for a kid with a sleep disorder to embrace boredom at 7:30 a.m.

One teacher's letter stopped me cold. It said, "I suspect Charles may be suffering from depression." That was the first time anyone, including all the mental health professionals we'd paid dearly for, had ever mentioned depression as a possibility. It was hard for me to wrap my head around it since he'd always been so funny and lively most of his life.

Clearly, something about Charles had changed. Later, I would ask one of his counselors if he might be depressed. Instead of saying, "Let's do a psychological evaluation," he said there was no way Charles had depression. He said depressed kids always ask for help when they are in a depressive episode, and Charles had not. Case closed.

The revelatory letter had been from Charles' favorite teacher, Mrs. Fretwell, from his favorite class, theater. She had a special bond with him, and I trusted her.

Was it depression? It would be another year before I would get that diagnosis and it was not in Virginia.

Family Life Starts to Unravel

Early on, we hit roadblocks when there was clear opportunity for early intervention and education that could have changed the trajectory of my child's life. But the timing was not right, since our culture was still in the mode of sweeping under the rug any indications of mental health issues. No school wanted to be branded as having "drug problems," so the subject was summarily dismissed. No one talked about it. No one acknowledged a growing problem that I was starting to see had the potential to snowball. And just a few years after 2010, it did.

A proud momma moment: Charles on Homecoming Court in 2010 at Cosby High School in Midlothian, Virginia, escorted by Kerry Fretwell, his theater teacher.

CHAPTER 12

JUST BE

Lyrics by Charles Aubrey Rogers, aka Reezin' the Revolutionary

G rab my notebook and flip inside,
I hypnotize different minds
with the shit I write.
When I spit in the mic
and you hear shit you don't like
it means you didn't listen right.

My brain doesn't connect correct,
the lost mind of a genius.
I write with the tears of a phoenix,
let my soul sink into my ink
You couldn't even dream this.
If you can't comprehend it
then lean in,
open your thoughts
and let me slide in between them.

DIARY OF A BROKEN MIND

I think this world was an accident,
God never meant for it to be,
it makes no sense to me
that our sorrows should be his scenery.

(Refrain)
Relax.
just breathe,
it's just life,
I'm just Me,
and you're just You,
so Just Be

This is for the kids that never fit in much,
and the ones that do,
this one's for you,
for when you're down and blue.

I found the sun and hold it,
this world is dark with cracks of golden,
I'm burning hot like scolden' molten lava,
hold my pen and it'll singe
like you forgot the sleeve on your Java

Choose your team,
cops or robbers?
But shit ain't black and white,
like I wish it all was,
havin' trouble to fill this wallet,
alcoholic, or whatever you call it,
I got problems and I solve it with this solvent.

Bury me with a Bottle in my coffin,
"I like your words Charles,"
She listens while I'm talkin',
I pulled your chair
so you could sit with me,
But every time I look
your chair is empty

Just Be

(Refrain)
Relax.
just breathe,
it's just life,
I'm just Me,
and you're just You,
so Just Be

Being yourself,
because you're like no one else,
I stand in fire on snow as it melts.
Broke with wealth
whispering you a story to tell,
but I'm not sure you can fathom my rappin',
so, I'm just asking the world questions
directed at our maker
and the only response is vapor.
I've been shit on, spit on, told to quit.
But I still put the pen to this paper,
music of symphonies for sick friends.

I'll be your nicotine,
just breathe,
I won't let you forget me,
try to kill me and I'll take you with me,
I talked to God and said, "Let's be friends,"
Outside of Heaven's Gate
but he wouldn't let me in

Charles in the middle, holding a skim board, his brother to the right, with all their cousins at the Outer Banks in North Carolina.

CHAPTER 13

WHAT SHOULD I CALL IT?

TRIGGER WARNING:
Suicide method mentioned briefly.

I'd re-attempt suicide
I already tried
I'm not dead
I only died inside.
—*Forgive me, I had to release my pain*, by Charles Aubrey Rogers

Charles was sitting still on the sofa. This was unusual for a kid who was always in motion. I had passed him going up and down the back staircase twice and knew something was wrong.

"Charles, are you OK?"

He started to cry, and I sat myself down at the other end of the sofa and hugged him. He seemed so small all of a sudden even though he was fifteen going on sixteen.

"Mom, there's something I need to tell you."

"Go ahead."

"Remember a couple of weeks ago when I didn't want to go to school?"

He never wanted to go to school so I wondered which morning this may have been. A 7:30 a.m. start time was hardly ideal for a teenager with a sleep disorder and previous attempts at finding a high school with a later start time had been unsuccessful.

Then the memory became clear. There was one morning in particular when he looked bewildered and out of it. I had been a drill sergeant that day trying to get him moving, which inspired a jolt of guilt.

Finally, I say, "Yeah. I think I do."

An empathetic pause in the conversation allowed him the time to work up the nerve to tell me whatever he needed to say. He started to cry again and I reached out and put my hand on his knee.

"I, um …. the night before, I took a handful of pills. That night, I didn't want to wake up again. At least I think I didn't. But in the morning, I opened my eyes and couldn't believe I was alive. I was happy to be alive."

Stay calm, Anne Moss. We were both crying but I needed to be careful here and not make him feel punished or ashamed. The next question came out calmly but inside, my fight-or-flight response was on high alert.

"Do you think you were trying to kill yourself?"

"No. I mean I don't know. I'm not sure. The last two weeks … I have felt terrible. I thought about you and Dad, Richard, and Andy. How sad you'd be if I died. I feel careless. I'm so sorry…. I'm not sure what that was or why I did that. It scared me. I won't ever do it again."

Saliva in my mouth was thick as paste from panic. Inhaling slowly without his seeing to calm my nerves, I replied, "I'd be devastated if you died, Charles. I love you. Your dad loves you. I sure hope you don't do that again. Is there a reason you were feeling so low? How can we help?"

"I don't know. I don't remember. It's like I just felt awful and wanted everything to end. I don't really even remember much."

Neither of us could define the moment.

What should I do? What should we call what had happened? There was no emergency right then so taking him to the hospital was not a logical option. So I just listened to Charles; we cried together and held each other.

"Thank you so much for telling me about this. I know that took a lot of courage," was my response. Fighting still to maintain a calm, cool exterior didn't reveal the tsunami of emotions and fear that was twisting my insides. If only I had known to follow up and consider it a suicide attempt.

A common, yet highly inaccurate belief, is that people who survive a suicide attempt are unlikely to try again. That's what I thought because that's what I wanted to think. Surely my son would not check out on us and leave us with all that hurt. Didn't he love us too much for that? But the truth is, if someone has an attempt, his or her chances of completing a suicide are that much higher because a history of previous suicide attempt is the strongest predictor for future suicidal ideation, suicide attempts, and completed suicide. Almost two-thirds of those who die by suicide had a history of a previous attempt, and it is a serious risk factor. All of these facts were unknown to me.

I thought we'd dodged a bullet, as if he'd "learned his lesson" and would never do that again. Despite all the counselors and psychiatrists we'd seen up to this point, we had no education on suicide. This is most likely what they had meant by "high risk" on the testing we had done but no one interpreted this phrase for us.

As a parent I simply couldn't imagine things would be so bad for my child that he'd resort to taking his life. Didn't he have a pretty good life? Hadn't I done a reasonably good job of raising my child? Besides that, statistics of teens dying by suicide from 2010-2012 indicated it was still a rare event. It doesn't have anything to do with how famous, rich, or great one's life is. It's a moment of excruciating pain that drives a person to want to end the pain.

So on our next visit to a doctor—not our usual family doctor— Charles was with me, and I told the doctor about it and asked if what happened could be defined as a suicide attempt. Both of us wanted to know, and Charles and I were literally poised on the edge of our seats for an answer. The doctor just motored right past it and gave me no answer. I brought it up again at the pediatric psychiatrist's office and would ask again in the coming years, and always got the same glazed look.

The word "suicide" would hang in the air awkwardly to the point I wanted to snatch it back and tuck it into my pocket. The only thing that drove me to keep asking is that no one had answered my question. I should have pushed it but wasn't sure if that was the right thing to do and I was probably more than willing to accept that everything would be OK. But it grated on my conscience.

There were so many references to suicide in his writing; they did take his notebooks at the therapeutic boarding school and read them. I simply can't believe no one thought to say anything to us about it. We went up there for family work, and he was under eighteen at the time. He also shared those notebooks with others who had those thoughts, as well as his friends. I could understand his peers not really taking those references in his music seriously or thinking they needed to tell us. They were just teenagers.

About three years after he died, while listening to a psychiatry show on *Doctor Radio*, a caller nervously described a similar scenario to the one we experienced and she asked the psychiatrist on the show if that was considered a suicide attempt. I yelled at the radio, "Yes! Yes! It's a suicide attempt. It is. Consider yourself warned."

Fortunately, the doctor on the air gently but clearly educated the caller that it was a strong predictor of future ideation—attempts and completed suicide—and carefully outlined her next steps.

I am unaware if Charles had another attempt, although there are vague references to it in his writing. He talks about the "shame on his wrist," and he wore about ten friendship bracelets on one of his wrists. There are also a few references in his music to psychosis, which is characterized as disruptions to a person's thoughts and perceptions that make it difficult for them to recognize what is real and what isn't. I wonder if he suffered periods of psychosis or perhaps the drugs triggered these episodes or he took drugs to make them go away. But several times he told a story in his music that didn't happen, and those give me pause. His brother revealed, after Charles died, that he did tell him he was hearing voices.

CHAPTER 14

FAMILY MATTERS

Lyrics by Charles Aubrey Rogers, aka Reezin' the Revolutionary

G randbobby used to make my card disappear,
    and pull a quarter out of my ear,
Momma how'd I end up here?
Life was so different,
I was so innocent,
Who knew I'd ever act like a criminal,
My love for you is far from minimal,
Daddy was my hero,
He's who I wanted to be like,
Taught me how to ride a bike,
Taught me how to live my life,
But you know me,
I never listen to advice.

I write this for family,

DIARY OF A BROKEN MIND

The ones I see on holidays annually,
I'm grateful for everything you handed me,
For my cousins n' my grandmas,
For my aunts, uncles and my grandpas.

Dad bought me my first Eminem CD in elementary,
Throwin' presidents at Marshall Mathers,
My favorite rapper till my wallet was empty.
Me and Richard used to bicker,
No one told me life would be this quick
only getting' quicker,

Who knew my little cousin would have a little sister,
Hey Owen, hey Amy,
I hope you feel my love when you play me,
I hope you treat your sister like a lady,
I remember you both when you were just babies.
Now you can say there goes my cousin
rappin' like he's Shady,
rappin' like he's Jay-Z,
Who knew my brain would decay from drugs?
I thought I'd go astray,
but my family stayed with love
Nights of stress, stayin' up,
I've seen enough,
what connection runs deep as blood?

(Refrain)
This is Family Matters,
Cause even when you're a famous rapper
FAMILY MATTERS

I'm still just a kid,
And Owen's gettin' just as big,
And Aubrey joined the guard,
Yeah, he really did,

Family Matters

Who knew you'd ever hear the Beat Bumpin'
and be able to say,
Yeah, that's my cousin stuntin',
Who knew I'd make a song that'd make you feel something.
Momma used to say I'm just like her brother,
I still remember summers at Meemaw's house,
Swimmin' in the pool and sleepin' on the couch,
How old is Aurora now?

Where did the time go,
The good, the bad,
remember the good?
Put the bad behind, yo,
This is for the ones who ain't here,
Who went too soon,
The ones we think about when we bow our heads,
This life's so fast,
Feels like I only got hours left.

Family as priceless as life is,
This time is moving too fast
I wish I could grab it, hold and have it,
Keep it there and show you all how much I really care,
I thank you every day that I'm here and breathin' air.

(Refrain)
This is Family Matters,
Cause even when you're a famous rapper
FAMILY MATTERS

Reese and Chris, went off to college and did good
like everybody knew they would,
And Chris is in other countries teachin' kids,
And my homies ain't my homes,
they my family,

Jacob Wakins, dog!

DIARY OF A BROKEN MIND

How long have you known me?
Packin' our little lunchbox,
Mommas takin' pictures of us
at the bus stop,
Plus Tucker Holt and Ty,
yea we all grew up.
I told you I's gonna blow up,
And Daddy I'm sorry I was such a screw up,
Wasn't born for school and loved to do drugs,
I clasp my hands and look for God,
I ask for forgiveness
And I'm something I'm now able to live with.
So play this track,
look back and say,
my nephew did this,
Yeah my grandson did it,
Yo that's my cousin spittin',
Yea that's Charles who write this.

I had to get some stuff off my chest,
I love my family,
I'm just a rapper,
So don't ask about our dirty laundry
That's family matters.
I remember the first time I rapped for my brother
and his words,
"You're gonna do it Charles,
you're the best I've ever heard."

The Moss's yeah that's my family, dog
The Morgantis, yeah that's my family dog
Sam and Will, you my brothers dog
Daniel you my brother dog,
And I ain't forgot about the others
You know I love my dogs

CHAPTER 15

A NO GOOD, VERY BAD DAY AT THE BEACH

Mom I'm sorry for my list of mistakes
I'm sorry for the pain
escape from hits I take
I'm sorry for the holes in the wall
All the alcohol
The broken dreams, stolen things and twisted schemes
I'm sorry for the bloody rage and fits of screams.
—*Out of Reach*, by Charles Aubrey Rogers

The summer Charles turned sixteen, we were planning to go on a family beach vacation with my husband's family. He didn't have his driver's license yet and our efforts to help our son and curb his drug use were not working. I had tried to talk to friends who had been through what we were experiencing; those conversations were stamped out like burning embers at a campfire, which magnified my isolation. As his depression and anxiety worsened, so had his sleep disorder and drug use. Richard was in his senior year of high school and I was hardly able to engage or to enjoy it. Guilt feelings over having ignored my older son in his best year ever weighed on my conscience.

While trying to find a treatment that worked for Charles' sleep issues, his risk-taking had escalated. Despite trying to get help locally and asking, we still had no clear diagnosis, one of my greatest frustrations. Was it drugs or mental illness? There were still so few answers, which left me feeling jaded and resentful. The panic, helplessness, and depression during this time led me to a doctor's office to try an antidepressant. This trip was about thirty days into giving that medication a try, and alarming premonitions continued to tackle me at night and scream in my ear. Fuzzy, black-and-white surveillance footage of Charles robbing a bank played in my head repeatedly, whether awake or asleep. Not able to take it anymore, I shared these fears with my husband who talked me out of irrational projections of my sixteen-year-old robbing a bank.

I prayed the trip with family to the beach would give us peace and a break. Despite perfect beach vacation weather, alarms in my head continued to ring all week; although there appeared to be no fire. More withdrawn than he usually was, it was difficult to coax Charles out of the basement, which was out of character since he loved being around family. Although sullen and withdrawn, he brightened up around my sister-in-law's extended family, which was large since she had come from a family of nine.

At a get-together that week with my sister-in-law's family, the Lynch clan, all the teens were begging the parents to let down their guard so they could have wine or beer, but the adults were not budging. There were way too many of them to set that precedent and I was grateful for the solidarity on that point. Charles was energetic and funny that night, which allowed me to relax the tension in my jaw and neck. Maybe that's why a headache had greeted me first thing every morning that week. He was especially engaged in a game they played that was a lot like charades and I can still see Aunt Margie hopping on one foot in a brown paper bag, Charles laughing, and his beautiful carefree brown curly hair a couple of weeks past due for a haircut.

Those memories were playing in my head on "go day" as we were

A No Good, Very Bad Day at the Beach

packing up to return home from our beach trip, when a young lady walked down the driveway. Meeting her at the halfway point, she showed me a piece of paper and asked if I recognized the young man in the photo. It was Charles. And it was a picture of him in a convenience store he had gone to multiple times that week.

He had told me about the couple who owned it, and really liked them. About four of the days we'd been on vacation, he'd gone there and ordered a grilled egg-over-easy sandwich, which he raved about. I looked at this young lady and asked why she wanted to know. She said it was a picture taken by their security camera at 3 o'clock that morning.

Fear gripped my muscles and strangled my throat. What was he doing in a convenience store at 3 a.m.? The store had not been open, and she explained that he broke in that night and had stolen a six-pack of Mike's Hard Lemonade, two cigars, and five dollars from off the counter.

What did she say? My brain wasn't allowing me to process the information. But my feet responded by carrying me upstairs at lightning speed to find Charles and get to the bottom of this misunderstanding. We nearly collided on the stairway.

"Where were you last night?"

He looked panicked and said he did not remember but followed me down, his eyes wide with fear.

Not something else. I can't take any more.

He walked outside with us in front of everyone packing up to go and stood shaking and looked down at the picture. It's like he didn't believe it until he saw it himself, which left me more confused.

How could he do this? For fifteen dollars worth of crap? Why? How? Had we not taught him right from wrong? How had I failed? Shock, fear, and confusion took turns tormenting me, shame and anger were burning in my face. My husband, feeling the same, was less outwardly emotional.

We all got in the car—me, Charles, and the young lady—while Randy drove the short distance to the store in our car where the police were waiting. I was yelling and crying, which was not helpful. Charles yelled back. My ears couldn't pick up any conversation because of all the noise roaring in my ears, and my ability to handle the news was compromised by my already fragile emotional state.

Like a lot of parents, I thought he was doing this to us when in fact it had nothing to do with us. It had to something to do with Charles. But what was it?

When we arrived, the front door was shattered and the shards of glass lay glittering on the pavement in the bright light of this tragic day at the Outer Banks. Black storm clouds were off in the distance punctuating the ominous moment of light and dark. How did he do that? And with what? Charles was not strong. He didn't even have a car but then this store was less than a mile from the cottage. Maybe he walked? Or rode his bike? How did he break that door? Did he break that door?

Ironically enough, at 5 p.m. the previous day, the store owners had installed their first security camera. At 3 a.m., Charles broke in. I was floored by this bizarre coincidence.

We were invited to come in and look at the footage of the crime as if we were coming for a hamburger and fries. Witnessing Charles in the video wearing exactly the same shirt he was wearing that day was surreal, and the room blurred and shifted as my stomach lurched. He was wearing the same clothes: the loudest and most conspicuous shirt he owned, which was black with a bright lime green and red splash on it. If he had been trying to get by with something, he did a lousy job of it. We couldn't see any expression on the video, but there was disbelief and shame on his face now. A quick flashback of my surveillance camera premonitions interrupted my thoughts. In the video, Charles tried a shovel first and then there was a time lapse before he came back with a sledgehammer and smashed the door, at which point there was an audible startled cry from the three of us who'd not yet seen it. It was like we were watching a scary movie together except that the unlikely perpetrator was standing next to us and there was no popcorn or candy.

The store owner, who was the boyfriend of the young lady who had walked down the driveway, looked at Charles in disbelief. He had taken a liking to him, as most people did, and said, "I cooked you sandwiches every day. How could you do this to us?"

There were no answers or logical explanations. I could see my husband crumble with shame. Then Charles' shoulders caved. He looked defeated and lost, which left me feeling hollowed out. Is he trying to trick us?

A No Good, Very Bad Day at the Beach

We somehow ambled outside in a state of disbelief, and the police asked to search his bag that we had just packed into the trunk of our vehicle not twenty minutes prior, when we had been just another family packing to go home from a family beach vacation. Not knowing there was a right of refusal, we handed it over. But then why would we not have allowed them to? The Mike's Hard Lemonade and the two cigars were in the compartment at the bottom. They handcuffed Charles and put him in their car. He looked so young, and I had the urge to scream, "He's just a baby!"

For some odd reason I thought this was the ideal moment for picture taking. Wouldn't we want a record of the momentous event later? Even odder, the store owner's girlfriend smiled in her photo while her boyfriend scoffed in disbelief at the both of us. Here we were, acting like old buddies taking a few photos of a beach vacation crime scene. Were we struggling for some level of normalcy? Maybe this would be some kind of lesson later? This was such bizarre action on both our parts.

In the meantime, Randy was doing practical, level-headed things like finding out where Charles was being taken and when we could see him. This nightmare had initially unfolded in front of my husband's family as well as my sister-in-law's and I was naked in my humiliation and failure as a mother; I ached for my child who was suffering. But didn't he bring this on himself? Does he not know breaking down a door and stealing is wrong?

Back at the cottage before we went to see Charles in jail, Randy's oldest brother, Rick, came up and talked to us. He tried to explain mental illness and addiction since he, too, had suffered from the humiliation of his own actions as a result of those illnesses. Still dumbstruck, there were no clear answers as to why Charles acted as he did despite multiple doctor's appointments and having spent thousands to find out. But I admired Rick for having the guts to come up to us and say something. Everyone was in shock and no one else was saying much because they didn't know what to say, including us.

It's a good thing I didn't know what was to come, but this was definitely a turning point. We tried to piece together what had happened as we waited to see him after he was arraigned by the magistrate, a story we heard more about later from Richard. We visited Charles after a few hours and in the meantime found out it was a low-security jail for adults. Was this a mistake? He was only sixteen.

We learned that in North Carolina, sixteen-year-olds are considered adults in the criminal justice system. At the voting polls, they are not adults until eighteen. And in a bar, they didn't reach the adult milestone until twenty-one. They couldn't even have a driver's license until sixteen and a half. I looked at Charles, who looked fourteen years old at the most. His eyes were puffy and rimmed in red, his nose was running, and his curly hair had not graduated from early morning bedhead.

We were allowed to see him, hug him, and talk to him. His dad held his hands as he sat across from him, his own eyes rimmed in red while tears spilled down all of our faces. Charles was overtaken by despair and told us he honestly didn't remember.

He said he woke up that morning thinking something was seriously wrong but he couldn't figure out what it was. I gently told him it was a struggle for me to believe what he was saying but did not accuse him. Something was not adding up, and he looked puzzled. Why? He'd not told us much and was always cryptic and stubborn with details. Richard didn't know a lot but said Charles was acting strange and annoying when he was driving a group of cousins from both sides of the family somewhere. Charles kept insisting that Richard stop and get cigars. He went on to tell us that Charles had stolen vodka from one of the nearby cottages, which gave me chills.

We had no choice but to leave him and make our way back from North Carolina to Virginia. We made the decision not to post bond yet and leave him where he was until we got a lawyer and figured out what to do. At least he was safe. Several people told us it was an "adult" jail but the Taj Mahal of jails. They insisted he'd be fine, and they weren't kidding. As jails go, it was pretty tame.

Two days after we got back we had a scheduled meeting with our counselor and I recounted the story. Our counselor was shocked. Charles didn't look the part. We shared the story that Charles said he didn't remember and I admitted my doubts about that story. The counselor looked at me and asked about his sleep medication.

We had been working on his sleep disorder for years and nothing was working so Lunesta had been prescribed by an adolescent-focused family doctor Charles had been seeing, a doctor about whom the counselor was wary. The sleep medication was not Plan A and not something of which we were proud. But after years of testing and effort, nothing was working. It was a temporary measure until our scheduled appointment with a sleep specialist, still a few months away. Appointments with this particular sleep doctor were difficult to get.

Charles had been warned not to drink alcohol while taking this sleep medicine but to boost its effectiveness, which had waned, he drank vodka and orange juice. He had been afraid to tell me it was no longer working. That's when the counselor leveled with us and said if he drank while taking that sleep medication there was no doubt Charles truly did not remember the incident or would have had a hard time discerning if it really happened. Several of his young male patients had had similar experiences and did things off their radar. Would we ever have a diagnosis now? By now his drug use was making it hard to get any definitive assessment and jail and court time wouldn't make the process any easier.

We were advised by our counselor to enroll him into an Intense Outpatient Program (IOP) to curb the drug use. Stories on heroin use and opiates were on the news often enough to kick up fear. When I talked to Charles about heroin, he laughed and said, "Mom, I'm not going to become a heroin addict." Does anyone ever get up in the morning and decide he's going to grow up to become a heroin addict?

A week later, we drove back to North Carolina, posted bail and enrolled him in the IOP in Richmond. The program was three hours, three times a week for eight weeks and parents were supposed to attend the Monday sessions from 4-7 p.m. On the other days, the teens met with their group and were assigned a counselor. Richard was a college freshman in the fall of 2011 so it was I, Charles, and my husband who attended.

At week seven, Charles had an appointment with his new sleep doctor. She was of Indian descent, very empathetic, and kind. More importantly, Charles really connected with her and she was one of the few who didn't shame him for his drug use, although she emphasized the importance of not mixing prescribed medication with illegal substances. We had tried to get him to do more of the light therapy recommended for his sleep disorder but when we discussed it with our counselor, he had said we were expecting far too much discipline for a child who was not emotionally mature enough to follow the rigid schedule it would take. He was right. We had asked Charles if he would try it but few sixteen-year-olds could follow the strict protocol needed for this particular therapy to work, and she was hesitant to prescribe more medication for this teenager particularly after what had just happened. It made me cringe, too.

While enrolled in IOP, he was not doing drugs, according to the pee tests. If he was, it was a form of substance that would fly under the drug test radar. He and the rest of us were all making an effort. A drug or mental health problem is not just the child's problem, it's a family problem and we all had to shift to understand and become more educated because it wasn't just his recovery, it was ours, too. If he was not sleeping, we had no chance to beat this drug issue. It was the worst possible catch-22.

The doctor wanted him to take trazadone but Charles knew immediately it was an antidepressant, albeit an old one and not a selective serotonin reuptake inhibitor (SSRI). SSRIs are a class of drugs that are typically used as antidepressants in the treatment of major depressive and anxiety disorders, and they have been known to have fewer side effects than older antipsychotic drugs.

Ever since the incident with the counselor at school, Charles had refused to try another antidepressant. The trazadone was the lesser of evils and had no abuse potential but he refused. In the end, she prescribed Restoril, generic name temazepam. She did so begrudgingly, and emphasized it was only temporary to get him through the IOP. I wasn't overjoyed about it either but we were at a loss at this point and it seemed the best time since he was clean. I wondered if this was a benzodiazepine. Xanax and Ativan, for example, are brand names of benzodiazepines. It sounded like one although I'd never heard of it. She told us this was not a typical drug of abuse and I neglected to ask whether it was a benzo. There was real fear he would repeat his beach behavior and mix it with other drugs. But that's why we were in this program and after the eight weeks there were several follow-up and urine tests.

Right after that appointment, I filled the sleep medication prescription at the pharmacy and we headed over to the Monday night IOP session. There had not been enough time to look anything up and the pharmacy had been too crowded to entertain a Q&A with the pharmacist and still make the meeting. At the session break that evening, I approached the facilitator to ask if it was an allowed substance for the program. Was it OK to take at his age? Did she know of alternatives or other therapies? Lack of education was making it difficult to make informed decisions.

I told her about the medication but as soon as it came out of my mouth, she looked at me as if I were dirt, turned on her heel, threw up her hands, and stalked away, saying, "Parents are so stupid!" Standing there shocked and humiliated, an emotion which I was becoming all too familiar, I tried unsuccessfully to choke back tears.

My son has just broken into a store and was facing charges in a state that considered sixteen-year-olds as adults, and I was desperate for information and empathy. It was the lowest possible point in my life thus far, as if someone had kicked sand in my face and rubbed it in my eyes. How were we going to survive this? Wasn't anyone on our side? My child and my life were falling apart, we were screaming, no one was listening, and no one seemed to care. My efforts to find a support group had turned up nothing still, and it was hard to believe that no one shared support group information as a regular practice.

We were at the end of the program at this point and she never answered the question. I never said he was taking the medication either. When it came time to do follow-up treatment, he signed up. But they never assigned him to an after-care counselor. I called for weeks after to find out why. Drug tests finally showed he was clean. Follow up was crucial to maintain that because most psychiatrists won't treat a patient who is using drugs. The follow-up was an integral piece of the program.

When someone finally did call back, he said, "We are not scheduling him because of the use of benzos," and he abruptly hung up with no further explanation or suggestion. I wanted to ask the caller about the medication but no one would take my call after that. So he didn't get the follow-up and reverted to self-medicating again.

I had carefully scheduled the psychiatrist a few weeks after follow-up started. But without a follow-up program, there was a lot of time in between with no support, creating an ideal environment for a sixteen-year-old to relapse. Due to a nationwide shortage of pediatric psychiatrists to meet the growing demand, there was no getting in sooner. Nine months later the group facilitator called to check in on Charles and left a message. In bright and chipper voice she said, "I hope you are doing well, and we just wanted to check and see how Charles is doing. Have a great weekend!" Obviously, they had so many young people churning through the program, they had forgotten I had been left standing there melting into the floor in my own humiliation. They didn't remember Charles or that he was not in the follow-up program at all.

My child was self-destructing in front of my eyes and I was powerless to stop it. Taking away the phone, the car, or any other traditional punishment was ineffective. Other parents not dealing with this would occasionally give advice about the effective punishments they doled out, saying things like, "I wouldn't tolerate drug use in my home. I have a tendency to put my foot down about things like that." The innuendo behind their bold statements implied we had not spanked him enough, hired enough tutors, taken away enough privileges, or showed him who was boss. Punishment seemed to make Charles more self-destructive. Later I would learn it simply made him feel like a loser. After eight weeks, my antidepressants were tapered and the remaining went into the trash since they didn't work.

At first, the IOP inspired us to work together. But lack of follow-up in the program left us dangling again and by spring it was clear he needed to go somewhere even if it was against his will.

Eight months after the breaking-and-entering was reduced to a misdemeanor, it was recommended that we hire an escort to take him to a wilderness program. We needed a diagnosis. We needed to try and save his life. It was the hardest decision ever, not to mention expensive.

CHAPTER 16

AN ALLEY
OFF MEMORY LAND

Lyrics by Charles Aubrey Rogers, aka Reezin' the Revolutionary

A beach cottage with the whole family
A little boy lies in bed depressed
Upset eyes, closed with no rest,
toss, turn, no sleep,
even after the Lunest…a sleeping pill

He can't sleep, chill, or event keep still
Weep soft like a willow
when tears hit the pillow

He forgot that he took the sleeping pill tho
So he starts to hope that if he takes a drink
It'll ease the pain, did he even think?

TAKE A FUCKING DRIVE

DIARY OF A BROKEN MIND

HE DIDN'T FUCKING THINK
That although an alleviating elixir
He didn't think of the mixture
Couldn't sleep, couldn't smile,
desperate for fixture
Desperate depression's the trigger

Who the heck could've ever figured
that the events of the evening would've left 'em traumatic and
grieving
Pain for the paint brush eternally bleeding
Vodka water bottle
down it all full throttle
Down it all
Rock Bottom
Stuck in a pothole

Vacation with every single family member
Bet he doesn't remember
Alcohol and sleeping pill
thought dismembered
Mind lost at a heavy fucking cost
Thoughts of trouble
reach for the shovel
Then down the street
to the convenience store
To smash the fucking door
Because he's a fucking idiot,
A FUCKING IDIOT,

Seriously kid what the fuck is wrong with you?
That you'd just blackout and do this
What the hell is going on with you,
Your little cousin Owen
You own him a real role model
Not a criminal who will down a whole bottle
and lose his moral compass
And lack a couscous act
An asshole pompous constant,
Breaking and entering without even remembering

An Alley Off Memory Lane

Barely able to stay stable,
cameras and alarm they got the kid on cable
Next morning he doesn't remember at all
But he remembers that call,
His dad yells
"Son they've got a picture of you inside this place.
They say you broke in and I can see your face."

No, no, he couldn't have done that
That couldn't be the case,
But it was,
His heart began to race
It's indisputable now
but he still wants to lie through his teeth
His dad says get in the car
We have to go to the store and talk to police

So mom and dad and boy
go on up the street
Mom sees the change and starts screaming
Ears buzzing and burning
This is a fucking nightmare
He must be dreaming
Wake up, he's gotta wake up,
Wake up from reality
God take me up and give watchu have to me,
You see that little boy was me,
A little boy scared
this kid don't fit
And you can't heal this shit
with a first aid kit
The pain and embarrassment
looking for where the life lessons from my parents went
Swallowed with anxiety and tears
Nothing hurt more than being the cause of his mother's sorrow
And having his father's voice get hollow
His face streaming with tears
Feel like I've failed when my own father says
"Son, you're going to jail,"

DIARY OF A BROKEN MIND

Looks me straight in the eyes
Feel like I've died,
Mom can barely hold it together,
Someone take me away from this
and make it forever

Cops see it as just another day
Family distraught,
guess we see it another way
I don't even know what to say
When the cops cuff me and take me away
Grandma crying, hugs me
I can't even hug back
Fuck that

The disappointment, the hurt,
doesn't come at therapy appointment
But I think of it often
distant pain never forgotten
Wish I could wipe the slate clean
and not know what the work pain means
I'm sorry I apologize
for the crimes and all my lies
And making mom go through hell a million times,
The drugs and the snortin' lines
I guess that's why I sit where I sit today
in this RTC¹ where the outside world can't see me.
It doesn't work and it hurts
Satan lives in my mind
He flirts dark thoughts for dessert
The shell of a man underneath the shirt
Mom begs me to stay but I turn 18 and had to walk away

---

1   residential treatment center

CHAPTER 17

KIDNAPPING HIM OUT OF HIS BED

TRIGGER WARNING:
Suicide method mentioned briefly

I was so angry when you sent me away,
in my own personal hell to stay.
I hated every day,
put me off on layaway
cause you were terrified by the way I lived my life.
—*Forgive me Momma*, by Charles Aubrey Rogers

Charles was a sweet soul but he fought demons we could not understand. We weren't qualified to fix this and not sure what the next step should be. All local resources available for his age had been exhausted.

Opening up my Facebook feed one day, I saw an update from a mom about her child's cancer treatment. She had hundreds of comments of love, support, fundraising offers, and meals, which inspired an instant flash of fury on my part followed by feelings of intense guilt and embarrassment. What's wrong with me? This was simply a mom who was hurting and posting an update on her son's status in the hospital.

While parents going through tough times with a child's illness got casseroles and cards, we got silence, gossip, and judgment. Few ever asked about Charles or about how I was doing. When the topic of our family's struggles came up, it would die like a flame with no oxygen, ushered out of the room like an uninvited guest. The message was for me to keep that ugliness under wraps where it belonged. Lack of emotional support was not something an antidepressant was going to solve for me.

In 2014, no one was bringing dinners to families who had a child in the psych hospital. No one had bake sales to help pay for astronomical mental health or addiction treatment.

Long gaps between appointments interrupted a continuity of care that all but guaranteed relapses, and spyware revealed Charles was into new party drugs with odd names. He didn't seem to care what he took or what risk any of it might pose. Once he was under the influence of a substance like alcohol, his inhibitions were lower and he'd take whatever anyone handed him or whatever a dealer was advertising that day.

One minute, he would be in the house and the next minute out the door without a word, then back inside, all in under ten minutes. Making a drug deal isn't a social encounter with lots of lingering and chitchat but a quick cash-and-carry exchange on suburban and urban street corners, in cul-de-sacs, parks, and tot lots. Anyone can have drugs delivered to a driveway or to the front door like a pizza. I call it text and deliver. As Charles' drug use ramped back up, so did my anxiety.

One day our counselor called me. He was a very busy guy, and this was unusual.

"Mrs. Rogers?"

"Yes?"

"I have some alarming news. I have information your son may be taking some risky substances and it's time we take that drastic step I mentioned."

"Oh no. I've been seeing that on his computer using the spyware I installed. Some new drugs called 2-CE?"

Kidnapping Him Out of His Bed

"New designer drug imports from China. You have an appointment tomorrow. Bring your husband. We have a lot to talk about."

I would rather have gotten a call to tell me my brain tumor was back. This next step was out of our reach financially. My kitchen renovation had not yet happened because a nagging voice encouraged me to wait because that money might be needed elsewhere. It was eight years of savings. There was also an extra 401(k) from a previous employment that might be needed. *Would this step actually make a difference?* We had to try.

He had cracked his skull while car surfing a few weeks prior. Car surfing is standing on the back of a truck or van while the driver does doughnuts in the street; Charles had fallen off the back of a vehicle, probably while high or intoxicated. No doubt the driver had been as well. His friends dropped him off at the emergency room and were not there by the time we arrived. At least they did that. Right away, I made the request that he not be given narcotics because I worried he'd become addicted to them. He was conscious and responsive when we arrived, which allowed me to exhale. His stay started with twenty-four hours in Pediatric ICU for observation, followed by a few days in the hospital. One of us was there most of the time except for the two hours I left to get a shower. In that two-hour time frame, he requested pain medication. Despite my request for Toradol, which had been sufficient to manage his pain up until then, they gave him a narcotic against my wishes. Similar medication had made me sick and triggered horrible dreams and vomiting. This was not the case for my youngest child and his state of counterfeit euphoria was obvious as soon as I stepped into the room.

Mad Momma immediately marched to the nurse's station to lodge a formal complaint, which was met with a laissez-faire attitude that up until now had not been associated with the formerly strict hospital policy we'd experienced. Their attitude told me they wrote me off as an autocratic, overprotective parent. No amount of screaming and yelling would have helped so I made a note to speak with the neurosurgeon about it when she came by on rounds.

He had been drug testing at that point, and it was after that hospital stay that we started to see occasional positive result for opiates. His drug use had graduated beyond marijuana but it was his abuse of the new party drugs imported from China—with a mixture of letters and numbers—that were causing alarm in the local area and the reason our counselor had called to warn us.

These synthetic hallucinogens were just the kind of escape he loved, and Charles couldn't get enough. Two teens in the area had dropped dead thirty minutes after just one hit. I was also suspicious he was selling something on the side to support his obsession. His music points to that theory. While it's not unusual for drug users to support a habit, I never thought this would happen in our family.

We met with our counselor and hammered out the plans to have him kidnapped out of his bed and taken to a wilderness program in Georgia. Defeated and overwhelmed with sadness and disbelief, we launched into plotting our son's legal and expensive abduction.

The recommended escort was a retired policeman who did this full-time and partnered with an off-duty cop to join him for the prearranged kidnapping. Charles would be cuffed and taken in their vehicle and they'd drive from Virginia to Georgia. We didn't think Charles would go willingly and we despised ourselves for having to take this step, but the uncertainty and desperation to save our child conquered any feelings of not following through. I thought of him as an airplane headed full speed into the side of a mountain. The kidnapping would put the brakes on his self-destruction.

Like a couple having an illicit affair, we sneaked out of the house to a hotel room to meet the escort and his partner. But instead of the thrill one might associate with that kind of encounter, this one oozed with deceit and sleaziness. My husband and I liked the older guy who was in charge. The younger man had that testosterone-charged attitude of tough guy, which bothered me. My child was ill, not evil, and the younger man seemed still of the mindset that you could scare drug abuse out of a child. Would he be too tough on Charles?

My son was not yet addicted at this point but headed in that direction and we wanted to prevent that. We also wanted to know what else was going on with him. Up to this point, there were no real answers or diagnoses despite all the testing, psychiatric, and therapy appointments. Locally, they'd used more of a spaghetti-noodle effect, throwing ideas against a wall to see if it would stick, not bothering to do any kind of real diagnostic assessment.

Once the decision was made to do a kidnapping, the time between planning it and making it happen was unbearable. It was prom time and about a week before his birthday. Charles was a junior in high school, sixteen turning seventeen.

He walked into our room one night to talk over his big prom plans. My husband was playing sudoku and I was reading a book in bed. He looked so young, skinny, and tall with that gorgeous loose, curly brown hair that the girls loved. Animated and beaming, he started to talk about prom and going with his neighborhood chums. My husband and I loved it when they were involved. There had been fewer visits from them in the past year, but when it came to friends, Charles had a ton. He was a people magnet although the recent crop of friends were definitely on the fringe, as others probably saw Charles as being.

He went on about what tie he was going to wear and how he was going to rent a top hat and tuxedo with tails. These plans delivered a sharp bite of regret.

My husband and I pasted smiles on our faces to hide the churning in our stomachs and the grief of losing the innocence of a normal high school experience. We knew it would probably be recommended he attend therapeutic boarding school following wilderness. It was unlikely he would be coming home for about eighteen months at least. No prom, no football games on Friday night, no more bonfires at the Rogers' house, no more plays featuring Charles and friends, and, the hardest of all for me, no more conversations in my home office after school. I loved those.

As he exited the room, my husband and I tried to keep from breaking down and crying. Once he was safely down the hall, we closed the door and cried, mourning the loss of "normal." We were thankful that Richard was already in college, away from this chaos, because I can't say we functioned well as parents that month. Most likely he would have been drawn into this drama as he had often been before he left. As close as my boys had been growing up, they had grown apart which was painful to watch. I would later find out Charles would call Richard and try to engage him in lengthy conversations about drugs. He'd become so obsessed with different psychedelics—LSD and other party drugs—and Richard found the conversations over the top and tried to talk his brother out of his drug use. Frustrated he couldn't fix it or get him to listen, Richard had to distance himself from Charles. College gave him the opportunity to stay out of it, which was a much-needed break for my older child.

There was much planning on the exit strategy for wilderness that included a slew of paperwork and mad dashes for large amounts of cash.

At 5 a.m. the day after the prom conversation, the escort pair arrived. Nervous as hell and feeling sick, we let them in to do what they needed to do. It was my job to wake Charles up, which made me feel awful because he'd probably just gotten to sleep. It appeared he was still high on something because once out of bed, he struggled to tie his shoes. His eyes were bloodshot and his gait was wobbly and suspect. It was more than lack of sleep, which did help me feel that we were doing the right thing. The retired cop and his partner took over and we went downstairs to our dining room per the plan while they got him ready to go. They were fast and explained to him what was going on and the behavior they expected. We had packed a tiny bag of toiletries and minimal clothing, as he'd be issued new clothing in wilderness for living outside eight to ten weeks. He hated spiders and that random thought gnawed at me while guilt consumed my insides.

Once the team headed toward door, we went to say goodbye in the foyer. Handcuffed in front, wearing his Superman high-top Converse tennis shoes, he looked ten years old and I had a bizarre wish we'd gotten him a haircut. It was unlikely he'd get one in the woods but it's not like he was headed to a family reunion. The escorts had a special way of guiding people by the elbow and shoulder should the person try to flee or fight. Charles had no fight in him. This was a betrayal, and his eyes shot us a look that said as much as he was escorted out the door.

We told him we loved him as he left. He said nothing.

It was April 2012. Once Charles got to wilderness, he tried to run away but didn't succeed. He was very angry as we suspected he would be. They assigned Charles to a group and for the first three weeks, he refused to change his clothing. No one ever told us this before or after but he was on suicide watch. His music revealed it.

Out of more than thirty groups and thirty years of the program, two kids from the same high school had never landed in the same peer group, but Charles ended up with a kid—Cal Reilly—from his high school.

Bullied at school for his many idiosyncrasies, Cal had had his tongue cut like a snake. Cal and Charles were the same age; they forged a strong bond and called each other "woods brothers." From what my son told me later, Cal drank a ton of coffee, to the point caffeine had become an addiction. In his music, Charles reveals that it was Cal who convinced him not to hang himself out there in the woods. (It was standard practice to initially take away shoelaces and drawstrings to prevent suicide.) I wouldn't find out about this until after Charles died.

To our relief, after about three weeks of fury, Charles began to soften and participate in the program. Given that it was some four hundred seventy-five dollars a day, we were relieved. Since they were in wilderness, we were allowed only letters back and forth. There would be no phone communication unless there was an emergency. His letters were eight-page rants: accusatory, angry, full of manipulation, with plenty of guilt tossed in. These letters were hard to read. But I made it my religion to write him twice a week, send pictures, update him on the news, and send him our love. Years later, every letter I ever sent to him was tucked away in his backpack that was returned to me after his death. I understood how much my son loved me and how much he hated himself for not being the kid he thought we expected.

By week four, he was actively participating and our ominous mood lifted. We binge-watched the educational parent webinars online while in a hotel room one night in Winston-Salem, North Carolina. We had gone to visit Richard at the University of North Carolina School of the Arts to tell him about Charles' trip—rather kidnapping—to wilderness and what was happening. He was surprised at first but then told us that we did the right thing and confessed that he had tried and failed to get through to Charles. He didn't know what it would take but maybe this would work.

As we were watching one of the parent videos, support groups were suggested. Our radar stood at attention. I had been looking and asking every counselor in our path and had not gotten a lead on one. I wrote down *Families Anonymous* and immediately looked it up to see if we had a local chapter. We did, and we put it on our calendar. It was there we found much-needed and much-craved support, and of all the things we did, this was the best move. When Charles died, it was this group of members who were at our house and at the memorial service supporting us with love: my family away from family.

It was in wilderness that Charles finally got a psychological evaluation. I had never heard those words: psychological evaluation. They were magic. In the chaos of everything going on, I'd try to investigate one thing and a crisis would crop up and require our attention, abandoning that search. There would be an appointment for me to get Charles to or some work thing I needed to do. I was a co-owner of a digital marketing company and keeping my professional life and personal chaos separate was difficult. I was always putting out fires and bracing for the next crisis.

The diagnosis was depression, Generalized Anxiety Disorder, ADHD Combined Type, and, oddly enough, something I'd never seen, cannabis dependence. The latter was a fancy clinical phrase for self-medication.

Charles did a lot of writing in the woods. We would get written updates about what was going on with the group, in addition to letters from Charles. They'd email pictures once a week and I would salivate waiting for Charles' sour-faced, angry photos. One of the boys would act as chief scribe and do the write-up.

One day I opened our group update email, started reading, and smiled. It had to be Charles doing the group write-up because it was so funny. I recognized that humor right away and on our next phone call with his counselor, Tony told us that it was indeed Charles doing the write-ups. I regret we didn't save those. His progress otherwise was not quick but we had hope even though his stubbornness had become legendary.

When they were teaching breathing techniques for anxiety, Charles would insist that this didn't work for him despite refusing to try it. To show the group, he finally performed the breathing technique and they all pointed out that it did work; they could see that it worked for him. Charles was not about to do that silly breathing and they were all wrong. That was one of the most frustrating things about him: his refusal to comply with any interventions that might have helped.

Altogether, Charles spent ten weeks in wilderness, about two to three weeks past the average stay. Ten years of savings had been used up in the first eight and it was recommended he go to a therapeutic boarding school after that, which had been expected. This would clean us out financially and we still had one in college. Since Richard was going to film school out of state, it exceeded our college savings for him. We knew we'd have to use Charles' college money to help Richard and he would have to take out a loan at some point. He wouldn't be the first child to have to contribute to his own education.

Charles didn't relish being kidnapped out of his bed and deposited into wilderness against his will. This is one of the angry photos we got.

CHAPTER 18

WILDERNESS SUICIDE LYRICS

Lyrics by Charles Aubrey Rogers, aka Reezin' the Revolutionary

*S*o they abandoned me
and stranded me
And look where the fuck it landed me
in a state of suicidal depression

Nobody loves me
I mean that as more than an expression,
Death has become my only obsession,
Stripped of my dignity
and every last possession,
I'm begging,
I'm pleading
But they left me here bleeding

Isolated with loneliness
as my only companion
only goal is to plummet to death

DIARY OF A BROKEN MIND

off the Grand Canyon
Can't sleep at night,
just wait for the bright
But I'm blinded by the light
and I'm blind with rage,
trying to start a new page
but I feel like an animal in a cage,
I miss my life,
I miss the stage,
But my future was sacrificed
so I hope for an afterlife.

I just can't stop,
I'm losing my mind,
my brain is on fast forward and rewind
at the exact same time
It's tearing me up,
It's just becoming too hard to give a fuck
I don't feel like a person any more,
I'm losing my touch with reality
and constantly living in a fallacy

My mind in goooone,
I sit alone all day looooong
I need help, I need your help
Somebody please reach out to me,
I need love, I need love
It's my only drug
It's the only thing that matters,
Oh I hope it matters....
Please let it matter

I feel isolated, constantly hated,
neglected and rejected,
Am I still human?
I can't tell,
I feel lost and can't be found,
I'm deaf in my eyes
and blind to sound
It's a curse,

Wilderness Suicide Lyrics

my brain's on reverse,
My morals have gone to shit
Black and faded,
my time is jaded
and my brain feels degraded

Welcome to the mind of an evil genius,
This is just a preview
Something you can review
I'm an artist
I'm a magician,
the pen is my wand
and rap my addiction

Crazy Brainiac
Speak fact, not fiction
the pad is my stage
and love is my prescription

Charles on the right with friends from a picnic at The Family School, a therapeutic boarding school in Hancock, New York.

CHAPTER 19

THERAPEUTIC BOARDING SCHOOL

TRIGGER WARNING:
Suicide method and suicide attempt mentioned.

So go ahead and tell me how its' gonna be
· *Tell me Ima 'wanna be'*
Tell me how I suck at everything in front of me
and make fun of me
That way when I'm there
You can act like you care
and act like it was fair
Even though you said I suck.
—*Scapegoat*, by Charles Aubrey Rogers, *Reezin' the Revolutionary*

B ecause therapeutic boarding school was such an expensive step, we looked for help in choosing one that would fit what Charles needed. I visited an educational consultant, Martha Kolbe, who had come highly recommended. She was in her late seventies at the time and everything about her manner and dress reminded me of old Richmond, Virginia, aristocracy.

Her office décor was reminiscent of both a stately library and a parlor of an old Southern mansion. It had several high-end dining room style chairs in a circle, mahogany bookshelves on two walls with detailed woodwork, giant windows overlooking the avenues on the first floor below, and a lovely but worn oriental rug to pull it all together. It was the kind of place where one would expect a butler to appear with a tray of tea and scones. I sat in one of the upholstered dining chairs and asked why there were so many. She said in many cases, whole families came to discuss this next step including grandparents who often funded the endeavor. The room grew larger and lonelier, and threatened to swallow me in my isolation. My husband would have come on that first visit and he came in later meetings but because of the chaos in our household over the last few years, he'd missed a deadline during one of our crises. Despite telling Human Resources what was going on in our family, his superior held it against him well past any normal statute of limitations. It was important he remain employed. He was so good at what he did but the lack of appreciation and lack of empathy regarding what our family was going through added stress to an emotionally difficult time. Fortunately, there were a few sympathetic friends where he worked, and I'm thankful he had that support.

The educational consultant ultimately recommended therapeutic boarding schools, one in upstate New York near Binghamton and another in Idaho. A therapeutic boarding school is a residential school offering therapy for students with emotional or behavioral issues. Troubled teens are enrolled to work on managing their mental health and learn healthier coping skills while getting high school credits for high school graduation. Classrooms are smaller, there is a higher staff-to-student ratio, and these schools are often out tucked into remote locations and restrictive about leaving campus.

Flights back and forth to Idaho would mean we would not get to see Charles as often. And he'd never see his dog, so we chose the other option: the school in upstate New York, The Family Foundation School (FFS). We could make the ten-hour drive there when funds to fly were not available since we would be traveling to the school for family counseling. My parents often helped by funding plane tickets when they could.

Therapeutic Boarding School

It was all we could do to afford this eighty-four-thousand-dollar-a-year step, which worked out to about seven thousand dollars per month after the ten-thousand-dollar down payment. Actually, we couldn't afford it but with a home equity loan could. We had gotten the loan prior to the 2008 mortgage crisis; up until then, it had gone unused. Martha Kolbe mentioned that the school had a scholarship foundation and I applied and was accepted, bringing the payment down to six thousand dollars a month. Even that was not wallet-friendly. We were grateful because it would be for the duration of his stay, which was a recommended eighteen months. While our household income would hardly have put us in the category of underprivileged, we were just working professionals with a son in college out of state.

Martha was kind and thoughtful, and that day when I told her our family's story, my composure crumbled. She remained quiet and empathetic, handed me a box of tissues to soak up tears that insisted on falling, and patiently listened as if she had hours of free time to act as my therapist. She calmly shared success stories of other children, which I needed to hear to rekindle my hope and not feel as if I were setting cash on fire by taking this step. There had been apprehension on what hiring her would cost but I didn't express that. Instead, I asked about making payment that day prior to leaving and she handed me a clipboard with a sheet of paper and had me fill it out.

As a woman who was independently wealthy and owned her own business, I suspect she had a soft spot for how financially stressed we were. When I did bring up payment, she always followed with the promise she'd send me a form to fill out for the purpose of later invoicing, which never happened. In the two years we used her services, I must have filled out that form four times. To this day, remembering that act of kindness makes my heart swell. When she said "Hello," in her even-tempered, measured voice, it would instantly make me feel relaxed and well cared for. We were emotionally dependent on her guidance and reassurance, and grateful to have had it.

The particular therapeutic boarding school she recommended focused a lot on drug use and curtailing that use. Some of the kids who arrived were in recovery from addiction. Still others, like Charles, had abused substances but had not yet become addicted. And then there were some kids just struggling with trauma or mental health concerns.

It had become commonplace for wilderness programs to recommend that teen patients go straight from wilderness to therapeutic boarding school with no home visit between. No matter what the teens said, history and studies had proven they would get back into bad habits or hook up with the wrong friends quickly; and that lapse, even a day, could undo weeks of work. We had witnessed this in action in that period between IOP and the psychiatrist visit earlier.

My first step was to tour the school while Charles was still in wilderness. I flew to Hancock, New York, and while there took pictures, and pasted them in a letter to Charles explaining how it worked and what it looked like, to set his expectations.

We then got an eight-page tirade arguing against therapeutic boarding school and why it was a bad idea. Mail from Charles at this time was always smoking with anger, making us feel enormously guilty. He knew how to trigger our feelings of self-doubt. If he'd had a phone, I'd have gotten a barrage of nonstop text messages. The following is an excerpt from his rant at wilderness. It's one of the few times he mentions depression.

"I miss my dog and my home so much it hurts. My paranoia is getting worse definitely. I think it's because I don't know when I'm going to come home or if I'm going to come home. The kids here are saying that most people go to boarding school after. I don't want to go to boarding school. I'm scared of being sent away and I think about it constantly. I want to come home.

I want to see my parents and my friends. There are small periods of time when I don't feel depressed but then I seem to crash down and feel more depressed than ever after. This scares me. I don't know if it's because of sleep deprivation. Because when I crash I feel exhausted and only think about home.... I am hungry all the time. I miss good food.... I want to get treatment at home and regularly see a therapist that can help me figure out what's wrong with me.... I wish I could come home and see my brother. I'm excited about New York. Maybe we can see 'Book of Mormon'...."

His letters would hold our souls hostage. He would hit all the buttons: miss home, miss my brother, you sent me away, I'm hungry, I can't sleep.

We wanted him home. And we didn't want him home.

The rants he thought might persuade us did just the opposite, and alarmed us that nothing had changed. I knew Charles would give us hell for this step, and we did not look forward to that. Complicity was never in his wheelhouse and although he promised to be a therapy poster child at home, I knew that it wouldn't happen. He'd go once or twice and never invest himself in the process. Maybe when he saw others at the school participating, he would do so, too. Herd mentality and peer support can be powerful with teenagers.

He had made progress in wilderness but it wasn't exactly a soul-altering transformation. What he had learned there needed time and space to put into practice without illegal drugs interfering in that process.

Charles' letter, which arrived right before we were to pick him up from wilderness, had romanticized the therapeutic boarding-school experience. He didn't understand that New York was a state and he thought he'd be in New York City; therefore, he wanted us all to attend the play, "The Book of Mormon." His enclosed list included a toaster oven and a mini-refrigerator as well as an exhaustive supply of snacks and groceries. I had no time to reply since we had to pick him up in a day or so, but it foreshadowed what drop-off day might be like, which turned out to be epic Charles-style meltdown.

He was furious when he found out it was not what he expected. My letter had not honey-coated my description and multiple conversations about therapeutic boarding school were had in wilderness therapy groups but my dreamer had conjured up his own fairy tale of what it would be like. He was especially angry that he couldn't have his iPod and earphones, or his mobile phone, although he had been told about the latter. The look on his face as we left bore a striking resemblance to the one on his face when he was kidnapped for wilderness. His eyes screamed deception. We left deflated and in tears, hoping this step would help him find enough stability to come home. *Was this the right move?* Online research had revealed a disturbing past about the school but our consultant had advised us to ignore it as vindictive rhetoric from angry young men and women who struggled before and after they left. Some of what is described probably did happen in the past, but by the time Charles attended it was under new leadership and they had adopted more current therapeutic standards. The degree to which these events of the past did or did not happen does play on my conscience, and I hurt for the children who may have suffered from abuse when they should have gotten help.

Charles was never violent. Thankfully, he never hit anyone or broke anything. Even at home, his most destructive acts were a hole in the wall and a cabinet door that came loose when he kicked it. There was the smashed door at the beach convenience store when he was under the influence but overall, he was not as physically aggressive as other boys were and never threatened me, his father, or hurt others physically.

A therapeutic boarding school was not the place I had dreamed my son would be and it was both difficult for him and for us as a family. We made trips to Hancock for family work and to see him as often as we could, even bringing his dog, Andy, who didn't do the ten-hour trip all that well and limited us in terms of places to stay and eat. Home had not proven the antidote to Charles' mental illness and drug abuse, resources in Virginia had not changed, and the opioid crisis was growing into an epidemic.

There was a mandatory blackout on communication in the first six weeks. At first this rule upset me, but after we experienced a generous dose of *harsh and hateful* from Charles by phone, we understood.

He said, "It is not helping."

"How could we do this?"

"Food is bad."

And so on.

Charles never changed his tune. Every phone call or letter was a dagger to the heart. So many kids seemed to come around but Charles would vehemently stick to tirades on the phone. Eventually he stopped yelling because phone privileges would get yanked, and were his only hope at manipulating his way out, via my guilty conscience.

His music lyrics indicated deep and lasting bonds with the kids at this school and these relationships were important to him. But never once did he reveal that he had invested anything of himself in the experience. As much as he railed to get out of there, he grieved the loss of these friends when he left. He was also very popular there, as he was anywhere he went because Charles was an empathetic listener.

The religious aspect to the school was his main gripe. In his opinion, they were force-feeding Jesus, and Charles was not going to drink that Kool-Aid. While religion can be a helpful strategy for adults in recovery and to some teens, it was out of sync with this new teen population. Even worse, it created an environment of disharmony and resistance. We had been told that the school had a religious aspect but were unaware of how much he'd resist it and how much they pushed it. With so few choices, we had settled on a school that offered the most of what Charles might like and what was convenient for us as a family.

He would occasionally tell a funny story, including one about a teacher who tried to bring up an assignment from the computer to project onto the screen in class. By accident, the teacher posted a bookmarked page with pornography, which sent the class into fits of hysterics. Clearly their teacher had interests besides U.S. history and Jesus. Those stories were rare in our conversations, however.

Soccer season arrived and he worked hard to make the team. Charles was not a great athlete but he loved to play games; he was the perfect recreational-league kid. Surprisingly, he made the school soccer team and he did get to play. He was in great shape and because he was so thin, moved fast and had exceptional endurance. They loved having him on the team even if he wasn't a star player. What I loved is how much hard work he devoted to training and making the team because I had not seen that kind of effort from Charles in years and it deposited a little bit of hope into my needy soul.

Unfortunately, the school would yank the privilege of playing soccer or whatever sport they played if a child stepped out of line in any way. Kids who are struggling need more compassion, not more punishment, but in 2012, this concept was beyond the old guard at the school. Counselors were pushing for more kindness and there would be disagreements between the therapeutic staff and the school staff on how to nurture rather than punish the kids. Yes, they should suffer consequences, but taking away that which brought them an important physical release and some measure of hope seemed unnecessarily cruel in a place as strict and remote as this school was. Charles really needed that outlet and any small infraction would cost them. It had to have driven the coach insane.

I saw many who did go out of their way to provide normal, fun experiences like going to play paintball or a have a picnic. But some of the staff were on power trips, and still other—addicts in recovery—thought a harsher approach would "scare" them out of drug abuse.

Most the staff had the best of intentions and really wanted success for these kids. It was important to them and why they did what they did. It was a time of changing philosophy about the best approach and the counselors were more educated in this regard. The staff wanted to do what had worked in the past but it simply was not an effective strategy for a new generation of kids who had marginal self-worth to begin with.

The staff didn't like that Charles wrote rap music and they thought the context of what he was writing was detrimental so they'd take his journals away from him as if ripping them up and throwing them away was going to remove those thoughts from his brain and the feelings from his soul. They shamed him about his writing and threw religion in his face as his only solution. It took me a while to work through the anger and guilt of his having endured that.

His counselor Rochelle, in particular, did not like or agree with this approach. Telling us she didn't agree did show lack of solidarity on the topic but she wanted us know because, in her opinion, writing was therapeutic, especially for Charles. It is what kept him alive. By taking his journals, the staff created an unhealthy student-versus-staff environment and his friends designed elaborate schemes to get those notebooks back. A friend, Tiffany, and one other young lady hid in an office one day and copied down the words from his notebook on another piece of paper so as not to lose the song, "My Angel." If they had not done this, I would never have seen it.

It wasn't practical to object to everything the school was doing, and figuring what was "Charles exaggeration" and what was really going on wasn't always possible six hundred miles away. There were kids who made remarkable progress in this program; the school was proud of that and dangled those success stories in front of parents starved for results. Who wouldn't want that? What institution wouldn't advertise its successes? On parents' weekend, we connected with others and got the inside story of how the school worked and we were up there frequently for family work over the fourteen months he was there.

Our calls with Charles, the school staff, and counselors were always scheduled. When the school called me unexpectedly one afternoon, said it was an important call, and placed me on hold, my brain went into overdrive projecting catastrophes. By the time Joe, a member of the staff, said "hello," my mind had created a convincing image of Charles in ICU on life support.

"Mrs. Rogers, I need to share something that happened at the school this afternoon."

"Go on."

"Charles walked in on two young men in the dorms today and one of them was in the process of hanging himself."

"What? Is he OK?"

"Charles is fine. Both young men are OK. But what he did was heroic. He called for help and both young men were rescued and taken to the psych hospital for evaluation. I'm going to put Charles on the line."

The scene of him in the ICU vanished. In its place I imagined him walking into the room and seeing what he had, and my body rocked with a violent shiver. My stomach came close to lurching its contents.

"Charles, are you OK? How are you doing?"

Still shaken and in a strained voice, he replied, "I'm OK." His voice trailed off.

"I'm so proud of you, son. What a scene to walk in on. I don't know what to say, I'm so stunned. But both kids are OK?"

"Yes."

"Thanks to you. Can you tell me what happened exactly?"

"I don't know. I walked in and one of them had a belt … the other had …" Then he cried quiet tears because he was not alone.

The urge to embrace my son, thwarted by distance and the gravity of the scene, settled in my shoulders and sent shudders down my back. Those images could never be removed from his consciousness. There was no fixing this for him.

"I'm so sorry you witnessed this. Please do go see Rochelle after this call. Ask to see her, please."

"My friends are OK. I called for help. Screamed for help. Mom, I screamed for help and we got him down in time. They are both OK. Alive."

He was still too shocked to offer more detail but there was a sense of pride in his voice for having acted fast enough to save two lives, and we never got much more information about what happened.

When one of the young men, David, returned to the school, Charles was asked to "shadow" him, a practice where a peer is assigned to be there for another student who was new or struggling. The young man reached out after Charles died and sent this:

> Hi my name is David. Charles and I where at FFS together and in the same house. He always looked after me and had my back. Charles saved me from killing myself one night in the dorm along with another person. After I came back from the hospital he was my shadow and made all the time in the world for me. I just wanted to say I'm so sorry and that he was one of the most caring and supportive people I have ever known. If it weren't for him, I wouldn't be here and me and my family are so grateful. Thank you.

I still did not think of Charles as a suicide risk. In fact, there was a part of me that was convinced it would cure him of any such intention. The school staff had read his music, but no one ever shared with me what they found in those notebooks and up until then, I had barely known of their existence.

Nine months after his start date in June of 2013, Charles earned the privilege of leaving the therapeutic boarding school campus for a forty-eight-hour visit. Eligibility for home visits would come later but only if these initial off-campus visits went well and there was on-campus compliance. We stayed in the nearby Binghamton, New York, area for the visit and picked up our son who was desperate for adventure off campus after nine months of strict rules and confinement. While sitting at a local Greek festival for dinner, Charles asked me for updates on his friends, which prompted me to check my Facebook feed. Cruising the feed and rattling off the latest news, I saw multiple posts about the upcoming graduation, at which my son would not be part. Grief over the loss of life events had kept me from being a regular on social media for the months since Charles had left, and those posts resurrected that sadness, which I masked with fake exuberance. Scrolling through, there was one post by our teenage dog-sitter that jolted me from my pity party and punched me in the face.

One year after wilderness, Cal Reilly, Charles' "woods brother" died by suicide in a nearby park, two days before his 2013 high school graduation. Cal loved wilderness and for the first time in his life, he had found complete acceptance. He wanted to remain in those woods and, of all the kids who'd been in the program, he was the one who set a record for the longest stay.

When I told Charles the news, he shrugged his shoulders and said, "We weren't that close." *You spent ten weeks sleeping in the woods next to this kid under a tarp and you weren't that close?* I was not buying it, but didn't say it. They had, in fact, bonded in those woods and it was tearing him up inside. He disguised his pain with a blank look of indifference, an art he had perfected over the years to hide disappointment, depression, and thoughts of suicide. My shoulders caved and my tears stopped just short of an all-out sob since it was crowded. The pain carved its way into my husband's forehead.

While Charles left wilderness for therapeutic boarding school, Cal had eventually gone straight back home. Before Charles left, he and Cal had planned to meet up on the first break that never happened because Charles had not yet earned a break to come home.

Cal's death shocked the local community where we lived and the teens made a memorial for him in the park in Chesterfield County, Virginia, where he died. As an expression of their grief, they spray-painted messages for him on a bridge in a neighborhood park where he had taken his life. The kids were merely saying their goodbyes and not purposefully defacing property in a destructive sense.

Meanwhile, a handful of adults in the neighborhood were

outraged over the defacing of the concrete around the tunnel and held a hearing. The teens came to apologize, say that it was a symbol of their grief, and agreed upon a date to clean it up. Some of the kids visited the memorial every day that month and they planned a kind of service for cleaning up and repainting: their own way of saying goodbye.

The Hampton Park Homeowner's Association preempted the date agreed upon by hiring painting contractors to do the job professionally prior to the day the teens were planning their clean-up and goodbye ceremony. The association went one step further: It insisted the two recent Cosby High School graduates, both eighteen and friends of Cal, be charged with felony property destruction exactly a month after their friend killed himself in a community tunnel they were accused of defacing.

Charles was outraged by this response to the memorial and wrote many songs to help him deal with his anger and grief. I, too, was at a loss as to why they would do this. The adults apparently thought that washing away the blight of the graffiti would make the entire ugly incident go away. Charles never let on how close he and Cal had become until a lot later after he graduated and came home from boarding school. I had no idea of the extent to which he suffered this loss until I read his rap diaries after his own suicide. He was devastated over Cal Reilly's death, and it is referenced multiple times in the few notebooks we have.

CHAPTER 20

SOMETIMES
IN MY DREAMS
CAL'S SONG[1]

TRIGGER WARNING:
Method mentioned. Emotional content.

Lyrics by Charles Aubrey Rogers, aka Reezin' the Revolutionary

This is real shit,
  not crap rap,
The park I used to trap at
is next to the tunnel
where Cal took his last nap.
Just a coupla weeks away from graduation,
He was supposed to have that gown
and tassled cap hat.

Cosby was where he was supposed to grad at,
But he tied that rope and choked,
No joke,
that ain't somthin' to fuckin' laugh at,

---

1   McAllister "Cal" Reilly was the young man who died by suicide and
was Charles' "woods brother" in wilderness.

DIARY OF A BROKEN MIND

That ain't somethin' to fuckin' laugh at.

I lie in bed
and see you die in my head,
Stay awake and squirm
while my brain shakes with your final words,
"I'll see you back at home Charles in a coupla weeks."
I hate myself. I quake.
I hate this place. I shake.
It's hell.
Stay awake and blame myself
'Cause you were there for me when I wanted to take myself,
And I blame myself,
even though I know,
it's not my fault at all,
But maybe if I was there
I coulda stayed and helped,

You used to tell me to stay myself
cause I ain't like anybody else

Sometimes in my dreams, you speak to me,
You say all is well,
sounds like angels
as they sing to me,
Sometimes in my dreams,
demons scream to me,
And feed to me images
of your final scenery.

It's been over 3 months
since I picked up a pen,
'cause every time I write
I see images of him,
I visualize your end
and I admit I miss my friend
I'll never see again,
I'm just a little empty within,
'Cause I sat and waited
for time we never got to spend

CHAPTER 21

THE RUNAWAY

I think happiness is just a word,
I think this talent is just a curse,
no one pays attention,
they don't listen to the verse.
—*Cold*, by Charles Aubrey Rogers

Charles would earn his first trip home in late summer 2013, about ten months after he'd been enrolled at the Family Foundation School. He reached out to his school friends, made jokes like the old Charles, and our home was once again a buzz of activity, a revolving door of friends, energizing all of us. Drug testing would be done when he returned to school so my husband and I were released from this misery. He claimed to stay clean and by all accounts, it appeared he was.

It was a nice change having my sober younger son at home and life was far less volatile. There was a tension wire suspended inside me that was slack but ready to tighten at the first sign of drug use or trouble. While it had never protected me from shocking events in the past, I remained dedicated to holding onto the tension wire, convinced it would keep me at the ready in the event of cataclysm. Charles met with a promoter, Louis King, about producing a rap album. My husband and I had met previously with Louis to set up the session. He was likable and low key. He was a thirty-five-year old African-American man from a large family to whom he was dedicated, which created an instant easiness and appreciation.

This "present" was Charles' primary obsession on this home visit. He was eager to show the world what he could do; after his dad promised him several hours in that music studio, it was all he could talk about. At first, I was ambivalent about it, self-conscious that we were privileged white parents who were buying their child's way to his dream by placating a spoiled brat with a vision of being the next white rapper. I thought it akin to sleeping with a director to get the part in a movie. Instead of objecting, I stepped back and decided instead to enjoy Charles' joy and enthusiasm, a rare event in the last five years. Watching him get swept up in the passion of pursuing this extended-play album wrapped me in a warm blanket of hope and quieted the mounting fear of losing my son. This session was music therapy and not all that costly compared to his treatment. Besides that, it was an introduction to Louis, who was a good influence and a special part of Charles' life.

When Charles entered the studio, Louis and his partner may not have had any real impression of what he was capable of doing. They were there to do a job. But once Charles laid down the first track and emerged from the soundproof booth for a break, they had become converts. Louis would later share that he had run the initial tracks past a reliable resource for spotting genuine talent, and from there he was invested in Charles' success. He was invited to come to the studio at any time. Louis told me and his dad, "Your son is very talented." For a man who meted out few words, this compliment was savored many times as premonitions about my youngest son's death took possession of my thoughts. I had always been a dedicated disciple of my youngest son's theatrical talent although I had not seen or heard his music, and it was hard for me to make judgment. As middle-aged white parents living in the 'burbs, we were hardly hip-hop experts. I needed validation of my opinion of Charles' creative genius, not something created in my own mind to soothe past failures to help him.

Charles finished that album in a half a day, which seemed to me surprisingly fast. He brought home a CD of the first cut, bolted through the door, and leapt up the stairway taking three steps at a time, his round prize in hand, followed by a posse of neighborhood buddies who had been notified of his arrival prior to this grand entrance. Scottie sat in a chair beside Charles, Daniel and Robert stood behind, Sam was on the sidelines, Randy standing on the stairs and me in the doorway of Charles' room. The man of the hour slid the CD into the iMac that had inhabited our upstairs hallway for the past five years, milking the anticipation by adjusting the volume. His friends leaned toward the speakers like fans following the last seconds of a tied triple-overtime basketball game. Even though he was seated, Charles' posture suggested he was going to spring into action at any moment and his electrified mood was contagious.

The first song, "The American Dream," stunned the tinny computer speakers and the rich sounds created that day in a music studio thawed the anxiety in the room as the inside story about Frank, who appeared to be living the "American Dream," unfolded into the family tragedy we'd seen play out multiple times. The angry-narrator style delivery of his song, based on a composite of true stories, grabbed me, took me prisoner, and altered my perception of Charles' talent as a rap artist. As doubt floated away, the orgy of his words moved all of us to tears. My son had done obsessive and exhaustive preproduction for months and knew what he wanted prior to going to the studio that morning. Friends erupted between songs, fist bumping, cheering, and overjoyed for their buddy destined to be the next Eminem. All of the songs, with the exception of "The American Dream," were personal stories, although this was the first time I had heard any of the words logged into his legendary notebooks, still unaware that any of his songs were autobiographical. I wrapped up the moment and folded it into my mental theater of precious memories. While the album was hardly Grammy-winning, it was an amazing first effort for half a day, and I was proud of my son.

That CD was the grease that eased the transition from home back to school this time. He wanted us to let him stay at home, making a weak argument, but he got back on the plane. I couldn't help but think what future visits would be like minus the inflated excitement of a recording session. Charles cruised along for days on the emotional high but there came a day, like always, when he suffered the hangover, like a deflated balloon. The tedium of a normal day was not enough fuel to energize his existence and it's why he was always seeking sensational experiences such as new drugs to fill that void. It had been the go-to antidote for creating and prolonging excitement but now there was nothing to buffer the after.

While the major theme of this visit had been the treasured hours in the recording studio and subsequent CD prize he took back to share with friends, he didn't let us forget he would be turning eighteen on April 26, 2013. Ever since he'd been forced to go to the therapeutic boarding school he had threatened to leave on this magic birthday when he became an adult. As long as he was underage, we had jurisdiction, but soon that would no longer be the case. Threatening to walk was the only weapon he had and he was an expert at using it to disarm us. While in family counseling in upstate New York, when we thought there was progress, he'd throw that brick into the moment to shatter any feelings of success the session might have held. The decision to send him to therapeutic boarding school had not been Plan A. While his birthday was still several months away, his father and I took the threat seriously and kept in contact with his therapist, Rochelle, who said he'd been saying the same thing to her. She had asked him practical questions—how was he going to live without money, food, and shelter—to which he answered that he had a plan. He wouldn't be the first to leave the school on his eighteenth birthday. Most of them returned after a few days because they had no money and no place to stay.

The Runaway

The idea behind therapeutic boarding school is to allow teens an opportunity to mature and learn to manage their lives without substances. Charles hadn't made much progress by our standards or the school's but he could still serve up a healthy helping of anger and blame.

In those months leading to his birthday, his smoldering rage fueled a flimsy escape plan. With no phone, the holes in this getaway plan were wide enough to drive a double-wide through. In a faulty contact system, a friend was supposed to come and get him and put him up in New York City, where he would be allowed to record his second album free of charge. His defiance blinded what little practical sense he may have had, and on his birthday he did pack some belongings, took the seven-mile trek to town, and hooked up with some young men from Hancock High School. He knew them from having played on their baseball team, and told me he smoked a cigarette and they tried to help him communicate with the ride that had fallen through. We had insisted the school allow a burner phone we had mailed him, with restricted access so he could call only us, his therapist, and one other adult contact at the school. It was for his safety, and not to aid him in getaway efforts.

Emotionally, my flight-or-fight response was on high alert. My Families Anonymous group was completely engaged in the runaway drama and they made me promise to keep them updated. The day he did walk, those were the people who called, texted, emailed me to learn the latest. It was nice to feel the support, which until I joined this group had been rare occurrences.

Charles ended up eating a banana and some junk food the other kids had given him but otherwise he'd gone hungry and slept overnight in a tunnel in the park in Hancock. He didn't sleep well. Neither did my husband and I. He called us several times on the burner phone that night complaining he was cold and wearing all of his socks at once. Charles was never one to suffer alone needlessly. He took people with him on that journey. My husband had to tell him that we were ten hours away and there was nothing we could do about his current circumstances short of calling the police to come to his aid, which was enough to inspire silence on the other end of the line. My husband asked Charles to go to a church and see if there was someone there he could talk to and stay warm.

Rescuing him would violate the boundaries we'd set and it was our hope that his uncomfortable circumstances would inspire him to return to the school on his own. Charles wasn't tough and unlikely to "live off the land" or take to homelessness. This was not a kid accustomed to hardship. Other than wilderness, roughing it had meant going without whipped cream on his iced coffee at Starbucks. Despite the stories of kids being gone for days, weeks, and even making the escape, we knew Charles didn't have the aptitude for outdoor perseverance. Wilderness had helped him understand that nature held all the cards and could be as unforgiving as it was beautiful, but it had not converted him into an Eagle Scout.

He did use that flip phone to call and communicate with his counselor. I was thankful they had a good therapist/patient relationship because that's what ultimately helped him save face and go back to the school. To earn his way back, he had to write a letter of accountability and meet with Mike, one of the heads of school and one of his favorite people. This is the letter of accountability he handwrote:

April 27, 2013

I walked from the school to Hancock, I borrowed a phone to call my ride. He said he would be there in two hours. I checked on Facebook to see if he was still coming and he couldn't so I called my best friend Robert. He seemed willing to give me a ride on May 5 but he wanted me to go back to the school. I didn't want to bank on that. I sat outside the library listening to music and I smoked a cigarette that a kid gave me and one of my friends said he could give me a ride to the Bronx at 10:30 p.m. but I didn't have a phone and couldn't keep in touch with him. I smoked some weed with some kids in Hancock. I couldn't find a way to contact my ride at 10:30 p.m., so I slept in a tunnel in the park. It was cold. There were other drugs that the kids had but I didn't take any. I saw some needles on the side of the road and some heroin and some heroin addicts in town and it freaked me out. I didn't want to become that. I felt like I was going to either be stuck in Hancock or have to do something risky to get out. Either way, it didn't look exactly ideal. My parents really wanted to have me go back to the school, and we had a lot of emotional conversations. I realized if I wanted to have a family and the support of one, I would have to graduate the program. They made that clear. Even though I really didn't want to, it looked like the ends would justify the means if I stayed. I wanted to come back for my parents and dog. I didn't realize the importance my family. I think logically I knew after I talked to Robert that I was coming back when my ride failed but I was too prideful to come back then.

Once he went back, the vise that had gripped my muscles loosened. Letting go and allowing my child to experience consequences was petrifying and not without risk but it was important he understood what being on his own meant.

My Families Anonymous group learned of Charles' return to the school and the reaction set off a flurry of phone calls, text messages, and emails. The warmth of having a support network that held me up when my efforts to do so were fragile gave me permission to laugh at the speed with which our reality show unfolded.

Not long after he transitioned back to the school he still hated, we heard the school had hired a new counselor who introduced a rap club, also known as music therapy. Charles was interested. We were overjoyed.

Charles was never discouraged from crying or expressing pain around me, and I know he appreciated that. However, our culture doesn't encourage emotional expression from males and that couldn't be changed. Rap music therapy would allow him to express that pain, and it was cool to do so. I know other staff members despised his rap songs, were not happy with the new program, and didn't want to encourage Charles to write.

In order to perform at churches, Charles had to "clean up" his lyrics by removing the curse words. He was adamantly opposed to changing any aspect of his music. Anyone who compromised his craft was a fake in his book. His raps were, for the most part, intensely personal and I can understand his wanting to maintain full creative license. But the short of it is, one can't say "fuck" in church. So he did comply although he complained to us about how unfair this was in our weekly phone call. He did not want to indicate that the school was doing anything positive or let on that he was having any fun.

He never did give up advocating that we needed to pick him up and take him home where he would magically change before our eyes and become the child he thought we wanted him to be. I had long ago adjusted any dreams and expectations for my younger son, but fantasies fueled my darker moments to keep my sagging spirits from being washed downstream with my tears. All that hard work and family agony would pay off. I was sure of it. But there were times when I was on the edge of my seat in our family suspense thriller, waiting for the surprise ending to be revealed. When I allowed myself to think of an ending, it always featured Charles and me on stage while he took a bow as the star of a successful recovery story. This was the book I had written in my head, that would one day be published. The fairy tale included my patting the back of another parent with a struggling child and saying it would all get better, pointing to the shining example of my boy, Charles. At the most basic level, my hope was that he would learn to manage his mental illness, acquire healthy coping strategies, and find a medication that worked for his depression. He could become a rap artist, or a monkey trainer in a circus if that was what would make him happy. He was still resistant to any type of antidepressant, so everything tried had to be "off label," making progress difficult.

Not to say that antidepressants work for everyone but he had tried only two, and took no more than a single dose before deeming them ineffective. To him, anything that took thirty days to work was not worth the effort when the drugs he abused instantly put hurt in solitary confinement. The legitimate process was far too laborious and did nothing to quench his insatiable curiosity.

Rap music therapy was the first legal activity that touched the needy place inside Charles that craved something more. His counselor, Rochelle, was charged up about this program and she reported he was making progress for the first time. My mood shifted from yellow caution light to green but as soon as I settled into what progress felt like, we got the startling news that the male counselor who ran the program was accused of having sexual relations with one of the female students at the school and was gone within hours. His expertise in running the program packed up and went with him, and my hope followed. My perspective shifted from contentment to desperation; what was working for my son dangled just out of reach and I tried desperately to bring it back again. An expression of support for the program was folded up in a letter to the head of school but with no one to spearhead it, these efforts took a face plant, bum side up. Even though the ousted counselor was later cleared of the charges, the accusation spread like the plague and parents reacted by changing their child's placement or picking up their kid and taking him home. Some staff had objected to the program the moment it landed on campus, so this was a victory for them. They had advocated going back to the old ways all along.

The head of school was ill-prepared for an incident of this magnitude and it was a major contributing factor in forcing the closing of the school less than a year later. The woman running the school was emotionally undone because it had been started by her father, and it was her baby. There was no disaster plan in place and I know now that therapeutic boarding schools in general had been having a tough go of it starting in 2008 when the mortgage crisis crippled our economy. Few families could afford it given how difficult it was to get a home equity loan, and I think the school was suffering from financial setbacks even when we enrolled him. As expensive as it was to send a teen there, it was costly to support a high school teaching staff and counselor ratio in what was a very remote place to live and work. Reeling from the counselor incident and desperate to keep the school going, I believe the administration started to take more kids from the New York state juvenile justice system.

Prior to this, I would estimate about ten percent of this therapeutic boarding school population consisted of children who had come from the state juvenile justice system and probably had backgrounds of adverse childhood experiences. That balance was sufficient to give those kids a fighting chance. They were often angrier and more unruly, which was understandable given that many of them had no support system and had been victims of abuse and neglect. Most of these kids had no ability to self-regulate their intense emotions. When they were a small percentage of the school population, they had the benefit of herd mentality with kids who were making progress. But with their population increasing to the point where they were becoming the majority, there were a lot of broken windows and clogged toilets that the school was not equipped to handle, from the standpoint of support staff or institutional security. The increase in students from the criminal justice system of the state of New York were enrolled as a last-ditch effort to keep the school running and, in my opinion, was a serious safety risk.

This therapeutic boarding school ultimately turned out to be a poor placement for Charles given the strong Christian/Catholic aspect. A number of the kids did do well there, or well enough given the challenging age group of emotionally immature teenagers who already had substance use disorder or substance abuse issues in addition to mental illness. A staggering number of the kids who went there have died, but the school took in some high-risk kids, and ultimately they had to transition back to states where the opiate crisis was in full swing. Already vulnerable, many of these kids did not survive the epidemic or died by suicide and from addiction-related accidents and overdoses. The school had a checkered past in the early 2000s but had regrouped and made changes by the time we enrolled Charles. Not everyone was on board with that transition, which undermined the success they could have realized with some of these kids.

During the last months he attended this school, Charles was spending far too much time as free kitchen labor. I suspect this was the case because many kids there at the time could not be trusted with a knife and other kitchen implements. He wasn't sent there to be in a 1970s juvenile detention center. I was paying for a therapeutic boarding school and it was far too expensive for us not to get what he needed. The mass exodus of students after the sexual-assault incident also left Charles feeling isolated, and made us uncomfortable and anxious.

While attending a digital marketing conference in Canada, I set up a call with my husband and Charles' counselor. When we asked about his progress, she answered honestly. Charles was not making progress: He was regressing, and fast. It was not an environment that was helping him any longer. She was right and her honesty will always be appreciated. After placing a call to Martha, our educational consultant, she advised we take him out as soon as possible and researched a new placement.

Meanwhile, my husband had searched the Internet for boarding schools and found Wasatch Academy in Mt. Pleasant, Utah. Our educational consultant presented one other therapeutic option but told us Wasatch was a great placement if, in fact, we thought he would benefit from a nontherapeutic environment. She was unsure he was ready for that step and we were skeptical, too. But what choice did we have?

The therapeutic school in New York was angry that we had removed him from enrollment, and did not send his medical records, but Wasatch Academy was successful in securing his high school transcript. I was so wrapped up in getting him to the new school and figuring out from where the money would come that we didn't get a chance to ask again about medical records until well after he died. By then, the records were gone because the school had closed, which had ended their subscription to the electronic medical record system where they were kept. The quick move cheated us out of a transition plan, which became moot when the school was closed less than a year later.

The nontherapeutic boarding school in Utah did provide a lot of support for kids and they valued and nurtured creativity. Many students saw a therapeutic counselor as part of their school day twice a week. Charles would have first period English, counselor appointment, and then history class after that. Counseling was not much of a social stigma, and since it was part of the schedule, no one had to make an appointment and drive anywhere. We wanted Charles to finish his education and I knew that was not going to happen if he returned home.

He was more agreeable to this step but still upset that he couldn't just come home. Once again, he made multiple promises I knew he was incapable of keeping. We still had not found a suitable medication for his depression, which was hard given he was in diagnosis-denial. Due to the stigma, he would admit only to anxiety. Somehow that was a more acceptable mental illness.

As much as I did not want to send him all the way to Utah after not seeing much of him for fourteen months, support services in Virginia were pathetic in 2013. In just nine months he would get his high school diploma and come home.

CHAPTER 22

MY ANGEL

Lyrics by Charles Aubrey Rogers, aka Reezin' the Revolutionary

I floated up to heaven; lifted
   Met a perfect angel and said
"Sorry God, she's coming with this kid,"
Brought her back to earth to live with,
She's my fix,
I'm broke
And she knows how to fix it,

She loves the linguistics that I spit with,
That spot I hit it,
cupid's missiles,
I'm hooked on this princess,
Had 3 wishes
spent 'em all on kisses,
and still I ditch the sickness

What is this?
I feel different love

and its richness got me driftin',
If god won't let me have this angel,
I'll create a private heaven without permission,
As long as by my side is her favorite position,
when the worlds dissin',
I won't listen,
Any place she's not even there,
I don't even care

Without her
there's no point in breathing air,
The entire point of existence,
is completely missing,
If she ain't with it,
if she's distant
I'm looking at life barely living,
With her
every day is Christmas,
Without her I don't wanna live it

She's heaven,
heaven is home,
I wanna stay though,
She holds my heart in her hands
like play dough,
She's my angel,
So it's only appropriate that
she stay on my mind like a halo,

(Refrain)
She's an angel,
I met my maker
and I asked to take her,
She's my favorite,
If I can't have her
I'll make the whole world vanish
like abra cadabra,

I'll make your eyes roll back,
goose bumps, trembles and see black

My Angel

I'll be your triple stack,
I love to see you smile,
and I love to hear you laugh,
Me leaving?
There's no point in fearing that,

Put your ears to my rap and hear clearly
that I love you dearly,
And I'd use my entire hour glass sand
holding your hand,

She's an angel,
and beyond that,
I'd love to say that we're in love
but words can't describe it
I'll try to write it,
But I don't even think God can

Adam and eve had to leave
'cause that garden's for her and me,
She makes me invincible,
bullets bounce right off
like "You ain't hurting me,"
Try to murder me,
and I'll turn death off like it ain't working,
I love to watch your body
while you soak in the bath,

She's so beautiful,
She'd still be a solid ten on the max
if you split that in half,

(Refrain)
She's an angel,
I met my maker
and I asked to take her,
She's my favorite,
If I can't have her
I'll make the whole world vanish
like abra cadabra,

DIARY OF A BROKEN MIND

I miss the sound of your voice
your presence is heaven sent
every thought I have
you're standing next to it.

I'm so in love
and it's evident,
that this everything
I write is evidence,
Nothing can move me
this world can't touch me
She's my angel
and she loves me

Comparison is an aberrant embarrassment,
'Cuz she makes a super models look ugly,
If I could I sing; I would sing to her,
and every time I sleep
I dream of her,
and she's so insecure,
I'm sure for no real reason why,

She's the reason Reezin's even alive,
and when I get this paper rhyming,
I'll decorate my angel with diamonds,
I'm on top of the world
and still climbing,
Ima find where the final height is,

Thinking 'bout Tiffani
while I write this,
said it once I'll say it twice,
That's the girl I wanna die with,

You got it girl,
you know I like it,
Give me everything,
and that body is as beautiful as your mind is,
I locked eyes with the angel of highest niceness,

My Angel

And know exactly
who I wanna spend my life with

(Refrain)
She's an angel,
I met my maker
and I asked to take her,
She's my favorite,
If I can't have her
I'll make the whole world vanish
like abra cadabra,

This is one of the songs that was taken from Charles at the therapeutic boarding school in New York. Tiffani and a friend sneaked into the office of the person who confiscated it, hid under the desk, grabbed the lyrics, and wrote the song down on a piece of paper to save. Otherwise, I would not have it. They were not allowed to have relationships with each other at therapeutic boarding schools and they never even touched each other. He left the school and went to Wasatch Academy, while she was still enrolled at The Family School, and from there she went back home. While he was heartbroken when they broke up, I was glad my son had experienced falling and being in love twice in his life.

Charles' dad took a picture of Charles and me at Wasatch Academy in Utah when we visited in October 2013 for parents' weekend.

CHAPTER 23

UTAH

I'm scared of the future
I can't pass even with a tutor
I guess I'm just a loser
It's a long day looking like the wrong way
Shit is tough, life is rough,
looking in the shadows Ima find the sun
I'm just so sick of the darkness
find a little spark
That's my job as an artist.
—*Silver Lining*, by Charles Aubrey Rogers

According to Charles, school was a waste of time since he was going to be a famous rap star and this gratuitous education was holding him back. He didn't see that his problems with mental illness and drug abuse seriously interfered with that goal. As soon as he got into drugs, there was less music-making and more party drug-hunting. However, he entered this school clean of drug use, and we hoped the remoteness of the school would make it difficult to tap into the drug culture. Given the drug problems in rural areas, I think that was probably false security but I'd have to say that one can't hide a child in a bubble away from drugs and it certainly was not the norm at this school.

This school had a recording studio and an outstanding drama program. Besides that, they had a talented basketball team, which offered a social element that Charles would and did enjoy. What I loved most about Wasatch was that they didn't focus so much on "punishment" but more on helping students find ways to cope. Students suffered the consequences for their actions but it was a more hospitable environment compared to both his therapeutic boarding school and his previous high school in Virginia, and it made a difference.

I will always appreciate their patience and understanding. It was remarkable and unlike anything at other schools. And while it was focused on getting students into college, it was not the intense and insane pressure typical of most high schools and certainly all boarding schools.

There were students from all over the world—Asia, India, France, Spain—and Charles had a roommate from Thailand named Henry who was taking English as a second language. At first, Henry didn't speak much English but throughout the year, this kid and Charles got along very well. The school day started at 9 a.m., and Charles would roll out of bed at the last minute per his alarm clock, Henry, shaking him awake. He'd grab a breakfast bagel and head to the coffee shop for the syrupiest, whipped-cream-topped cup of coffee he could order. Sometimes he'd add a nutritionally vacant doughnut. Weight was never a problem for Charles, and even with all the junk food, he had a ripped six-pack all of his friends envied. I didn't nitpick about his diet. It couldn't be controlled ten feet away much less two thousand miles across the country.

The first semester started out well enough with Charles getting settled in and involved with the drama program. He loved ping-pong, and played a lot with the Asian kids in nonstop tournaments, like he always wanted.

He had a friend named Max, who shared his love of rap music and had had a similar journey of high school, drug abuse, wilderness (in his case wilderness a second time), therapeutic boarding school, and now this school. From the beginning, Charles and Max had a lot in common. The unspoken topic was that they both shared a diagnosis of depression. The music told their story.

The school had parents' weekend in October of 2013, and my husband and I took the trip to see Charles. Randy had not yet seen the school. First on our agenda was to visit his teachers. As always he got glowing reports from English and theater while other classes emphasized that he needed to do more. But he was doing well enough academically for me to be pleased.

The one teacher conference I remember most was the meeting with the theater teacher, Wendy. We walked in, and she stood up and looked straight at us and said, "You know he is a creative genius, don't you?"

So many teachers over the years had focused on his shortcomings—his lack of organization, his habit of not doing homework—and I would get scolded for not having better strategies to get him to get it done. There were days during his school years where I thought I would cave in on myself. Charles seemed less engaged since his years as a preteen; in my mind, since his fifth-grade year, I'd had a premonition that my child was going to die. This one comment lifted my sagging spirits and made me once again appreciate how gifted he was. In the last year, I had heard that only from one other source: his CD producer, Louis, who wholeheartedly believed in him as a rap artist. He had so much to offer yet no one saw past his last test score.

After teacher visits, I met Max's dad, and Maria, the mom of another student, and we talked about our hopes for our boys. There was one issue plaguing my thoughts, and that was Charles' dark mood. When asked about depression, he denied it and insisted he was fine. But lapses in his "face of a clown" façade would appear, and were even captured in photos, and I called his counselor to mention it.

Shortly after that visit, in the middle of October 2013, his album was published on iTunes and his mood rocketed. He had finished it between therapeutic boarding school and starting Wasatch Academy. People from all over the world were downloading and buying his album. He complained that by being stuck at school, he could hardly promote his music properly and once again made an appeal to come home.

Our reply was, "You can come home after you graduate," which by this time was only seven months away with holiday and spring breaks in between. He would come home for that 2013 Christmas holiday, and we would spend it together in North Carolina. He died in 2015, but this was to be the last holiday we'd spend together. The previous year, we had gone to upstate New York and celebrated the weekend before, as he was not allowed to leave the campus of the therapeutic boarding school in 2012. Memories of that 2013 Christmas are very special to me.

There was a difference between this visit and his first one home after therapeutic boarding school a year prior. Charles took more mystery trips out the door that couldn't be rationalized but also couldn't be compartmentalized into a particular category of misbehavior. He edited his explanations, artfully dodging questions with a hint of accusation that I was paranoid. I was always suspicious of drug abuse and he was still angry he couldn't stay at home. He didn't have the time to ramp up his drug use to dangerous levels. Or he did but was better at hiding it. Life with Charles was still a tightrope. All that time away and we had made so little progress in learning to manage his mental illness as he lapsed into the same negative coping strategies he had before. He was still seeing his counselor at Wasatch but continued to refuse medicine to treat his depression and was a regular at the health clinic, as is typical of kids with depression. He had colds, headaches, the flu, and stomach viruses.

Upon his return to school, he was less engaged and his counselor at school thought so, too. After spring break, things digressed further. His girlfriend from therapeutic boarding school broke up with him and that inspired a great deal of drama. The long-distance romance of some two thousand miles apart was destined to fail. They never had the opportunity to touch or see each other. Charles was very upset and used his fist to punch a brick wall. The wall won, so it was back to the clinic for treatment of his busted hand, which turned out to be mostly bruises and scrapes. His counselor, Jim, and I were in touch a lot during this time. At this point, I just wanted to get him through the last few months of school.

And then something pretty wonderful happened. There was a call for students to enter the stand-up monologue contest for the state of Utah. Students would compete in districts and then go to state finals if they qualified. Charles had not signed up, so his theater teacher encouraged him to do so, which he did. Meanwhile, he was cast as the caterpillar in her production of "Alice in Wonderland."

It became a huge hit as it toured venues in the state and everyone at the school was buzzing with anticipation over the production and, specifically, his performance, another of which was scheduled for graduation weekend in spring of 2014.

We were nearing the end, just three weeks until that day. I was salivating for the moment when I would see that play and watch him walk across that stage and get his diploma. I so wanted, craved, needed, and deserved this proud-momma moment. He called us from school excited one day and told us about the weekend in Cedar City, Utah, and having won an award for the state of Utah for stand-up monologue: the only performer in the history of the competition to use his own material.

Charles would never use anyone else's material. In fact, he never knew what he'd say until he went up there. Unknown to me until about two years after his death, I learned that he also won an award for best character actor. A note from his drama teacher after he died:

Dear Anne Moss,

I am devastated by the loss of Charles and I can only imagine how you must be feeling. I wanted to share a couple of stories about him with you. I brought a group of Comedy class students to Cedar City where "Off the Cuff," a professional group of Improvisers, graciously allowed us to perform with them. Charles was amazing and "Off the Cuff" was so impressed with all the boys . . . one said "I thought we would have to carry the evening and help these kids out but NO, not once." As we were leaving Charles said to me . . . "that was the best weekend I ever had." He was so truly in his element and it was one of those moments that make my life worthwhile.

I did a production of "Alice in Wonderland" and cast him as the Caterpillar. At first I was trying to direct him in this way or that then one day it occurred to me to just let him do it his way. It was stunning and everyone in the room knew they were in the presence of genius.

We took this piece to Regional and State Drama Competition and Charles also entered a Humorous Monologue of his own invention. He became an instant sensation at the competition. Girls were following him everywhere and we all felt like we had brought Elvis to a Kindergarten picnic. It was fantastic and we were all thrilled. Though I only knew him briefly while he was at

Wasatch, I feel I got to experience him in all his glory and I will never forget him.

My thoughts are with you,
Wendy

I was upset not to have known about the competition prior because I would have found a way to fly out there and see it. Charles was notoriously horrible about relaying upcoming events to us. He was a person of the moment. Chastising him for not telling me about the competition would have been pointless but the fact is my son's best performance happened without me in the audience and with no future opportunities. It left a nick of regret on my soul.

Not long after that weekend, the dorm manager at the school called me. Charles had had a second infraction for drug/alcohol use on campus. The first one had been a beer with some of the townies a few months prior. On his first infraction, he was tested for alcohol level and it was determined he told the truth of "only one beer." But that was strike one and the students got only two.

This was the second, and it meant expulsion. Although we'll never know the entire sordid story, he sold a substance that was a suspected psychedelic drug of some kind to a girl on campus, but no one knew for sure. When she was caught, she pointed at Charles, which is what she should have done.

The proud-momma moment I had been looking forward to for weeks blew up in my face. Taking small gasps of breath, I fought to maintain composure in the face of yet another crisis with no step-by-step instructions as to how to fix. Who was I kidding? We were in reactionary mode, on standby for our orders. In the last five years, our lives had been punctuated by exclamation points of events that served as battering rams on my mental wellness, leaving me wrung out, hollow, and always on the edge of humiliation and guilt. When would I tip over the edge, throw up my hands, give up, leave for a cave in Peru where my feelings could no longer be dragged over a bed of broken glass? With each calamity, the initial feeling of shock was always the same but with each experience, recovery happened more quickly. Embracing humility and building resilience weren't my goals but these character traits were the result. I learned to pick myself up from the mud, wash off the humiliation, apply a bandage to the hurt, and move forward.

With only three weeks left until graduation, the school made arrangements for him to finish his diploma online. This was unprecedented and gratefulness could hardly describe the elation this news offered. This gift of potential graduation was a tangible reward. Charles had been a very popular and well-liked student, and the play a huge success. They felt let down and at a loss as to why he would cannibalize his own success. My child was suffering, and that translated into increased drug use and what I now suspect was selling on the side to bolster his self-esteem. Charles suffered intense shame for own actions and wrestled with why he had to push the boundaries of tolerance beyond accepted borders.

He had to leave campus within twenty-four hours and they helped us out, but once again, we had to make arrangements quickly. We scheduled him to fly to Georgia to be with his grandparents, Myra and Richard, known to my kids as Meemaw and Grandpa, until he graduated. They made this generous offer, and we accepted. Charles sent a flurry of madman texts, and regressed to incessant calling. He had friends call me on his behalf to beg his way directly back to Virginia. He was furious about this three-week layover before making his grand entrance home. We stuck to the plan and told him he could come home only after he finished his degree online. I did not get angry, scream, yell, or otherwise engage in an emotional firestorm that would have led him to assaulting my senses with a barrage of guilt-speak and illogical reasons why he needed to come straight home.

"You will be in Georgia for all of three weeks to finish that degree. That is the ticket home."

"I am not getting on that plane."

"Let me say this one more time before I hang up, so please listen. We have sent you a ticket and paid for a shuttle that comes at 2 p.m. to pick you up. That plane will go to Georgia and your grandparents will pick you up in Atlanta. You have three weeks to finish your high school degree and then you can come home at the end of May. A high school diploma is your ticket home. If you choose not to get on the plane, just know I'm sending only one ticket, and it's the one you have now that flies to Georgia. If you choose not to use it, enjoy Utah. It is a beautiful state."

Then I told him I loved him and hung up.

My mother asked later that day if he got on the shuttle. I had not checked, texted, or called. That was on him. Coming straight home to face us right away would not have been the best idea had he given it a thought. We needed that three-week buffer to allow our own fury to die down from smoking anger to smoldering cinders. Later that day I got a call from his grandparents that he had arrived in Georgia. I'm not sure why he fought it so. He told his grandmother some of his happiest and most peaceful times ever were visiting them in Georgia, and I believe they were.

He did finish his degree although he was not the most compliant student. Knowing that he wanted to come home so badly was the prize we dangled in front of him in exchange for that diploma. My in-laws were angels so many times in this process and they were instrumental in making sure he got it done. This was no easy task where Charles was concerned as his motivation waned as it does for so many high school seniors. Had he come home, it would never have gotten done and it was important he have that option. Family support really helped.

On Sunday May 11, 2014, I got a Mother's Day text at 9:11 p.m. from Charles:

> "I love you mom.
> I hope you had an excellent Mother's Day
> I know I haven't always been the best son but you've put up with all the pain I've caused and you still love me and I'm working on my final assignment right now.
> After this I'll be finished with high school.
> I'm grateful to have you as my mom."

This was the best Mother's Day gift ever, and I will treasure it always. I immediately took a screen shot and cried.

In May of 2014, Charles came home. He was nineteen and still angry about being put on layaway. I started to search for therapeutic support for him again, which was even harder given that he was now in the gap years of eighteen to twenty-one. He had not softened on the subject of compliance and would go, but it was up to me to make sure he got to therapist appointments. If it had been up to him, he would have skipped his appointment for a better offer, and we would have been left paying the eighty-dollar no-show fee. It never works when parents are more invested in the recovery than the patient. I was, once again, feeling helpless and powerless, and stopped making appointments because there was no point if he wasn't engaged.

CHAPTER 24

I DON'T WANNA
BE A PATIENT

*Lyrics by Charles Aubrey Rogers, aka Reezin' the Revolutionary,
iTunes release*

What's the diagnosis?
    Of the fucking kid that wrote this
No one seems to know it

I'm just broken
They drop me off here and said it's my new home
But I like the old one better
I feel so alone

I wrote you a letter
'Cuz I can't use the phone
And they got folders about me that I don't get to know
In about two weeks me and my parents

DIARY OF A BROKEN MIND

Can call and speak

My mom says, "You should be thanking me,"
I wonder if the world will wait for me
I'm sitting so impatiently
Waiting in line for pills to put me to sleep
Chew 'em up so the sedatives stay stuck in my teeth

Always being watched, I need some fucking room to breathe
"Only a couple more years, Charles and you can leave"
I said I disagree so they tell my parents society has no room
for me
Their lives are so pretty, sometimes I think they are talking
truthfully

Mom thinks I just need someone to talk to
I tried to say, "This is making things worse,"
But they'd rather listen to the man in the doctor costume,
He doesn't care what it cost you
He said, "Your son is sick, when he talks just don't listen,"
I could get raped and beaten, it wouldn't make a difference

(Refrain)
They're at home on vacation
I'm stuck here waitin'
Doctors perfect patient
I hate this
I don't wanna be a patient!
They're at home on vacation
I'm stuck here waitin'
Doctors perfect patient
I hate this
I don't wanna be a patient!
I don't wanna be a patient!
I don't wanna be a patient!

How long has it been?
I miss my home

I Don't Wanna Be a Patient

I miss my friends

Quick, this
Mother fucker needs some counseling
He won't go down
Restrain him and he's still up and bouncing
Family black sheep with a rap sheet

Put me away so they can be happy
Treatment to treatment
Counselor to psychiatrist

Hand me some new meds
And ask if I'd like tryin' it
The amphetamines make me feel uncomfortable
Practically force fed
Creating noise in my head

I'm a fucking walking hospital
I said, "Stop, but they don't listen,"
The docs voice instead, he said,
"It's your choice, it's your boy's meds,"
You take him off, he's as good as dead

Wellbutrin made me feel so putrid
Intuniv made me manic
And it's not even supposed to do shit
They made me take Seroquel when I didn't wanna use it
Lexapro's the next to go
All these meds mixed with the drugs that I'm abusing
"Charles, why don't you just quit using?"

(Refrain)
They're at home on vacation
I'm stuck here waitin'
Doctors perfect patient
I hate this
I don't wanna be a patient!

DIARY OF A BROKEN MIND

They're at home on vacation
I'm stuck here waitin'
Doctors perfect patient
I hate this
I don't wanna be a patient!
I don't wanna be a patient!
I don't wanna be a patient!

I like the pills that put me to sleep
These pills are good to me
Then they check my cheeks
Ask me some questions
And write some shit on sheets
A place for drug addicts, suicidals, and wrists that bleed
Mom still won't listen
Dad doesn't understand
I said, "Take me home,"
They got another plan
I can't sleep in my own bed
But my brother can
I said, "This counselor's a rapist,"
My mom said, "Shit happens, Charles, save it,"

Work on your behavior
Make Jesus Christ your lord and savior
They make me sit in church and hand me the Bible
In wilderness, I couldn't sleep alone cuz I was suicidal
But I don't wanna die Dad,
Can I come back?
"No son, that is where you live at."
Fuck the Allynwood Academy

I don't wanna be a patient!
I don't wanna be a patient!
I don't wanna be a patient!

Fuck the Family Foundation School

I Don't Wanna Be a Patient

(Refrain)
They're at home on vacation
I'm stuck here waitin'
Doctors perfect patient
I hate this
I don't wanna be a patient!
They're at home on vacation
I'm stuck here waitin'
Doctors perfect patient
I hate this
I don't wanna be a patient!
I don't wanna be a patient!
I DON'T WANNA BE A PATIENT!

Max, Charles' friend from Wasatch Academy, believes Charles wrote this after therapeutic boarding school. I think he's right because it reads as if he was reflecting his experience.

This song, currently on iTunes as a single, was supposed to be part of a new album he was working on. He completed this one and we didn't know about it or hear it until after his death. In following up with his record promoter, Louis, he had this one and another half a song that he was writing in Louis' studio just days before his death. Louis also had a lot of photos I had not seen. Charles was truly in his element when he was at this studio and I believe it was one of the few places he found true joy.

Just days before his death, Louis said he came by the studio and sat on a bench most of the day writing. He'd never seen Charles do this. In all the years and all the notebooks he had, I saw him write in them only a few times, which means he probably wrote mostly at night when everyone else was asleep at a time when his brain lit up and his creativity was on. It was a way to combat his insomnia.

The first extended-play release was done quickly, and he wanted more time to create this album. Trouble is, heroin addiction got in the way of his pursuing this as passionately as he had before. Louis told me he never suspected Charles was addicted to heroin and he had seen a lot of people who were. That made me feel better, knowing he had lived with us for at least several months while using and we didn't know, although we knew something was going on.

CHAPTER 25

HOMECOMING

Sometimes I think I won't make it and my dreams a fake,
I'll end up broke, a laughing stock joke beggin' for money to make
that'll spend on coke or cigs leak soaked.
—*Hollow Man*, by Charles Aubrey Rogers

Charles received a rejection letter from Virginia Commonwealth University, the only college to which he had applied. There was little chance of his getting into college since he slept through the SAT, and did not finish. Signing him up for the test again didn't motivate him to show up for the next one and it was a stupid move by me to think it would. He despised standardized testing and despite being wickedly intelligent, it was all we could do to get him to graduate from high school, a painful and expensive ordeal.

If Charles was not invested, there was no way it was going to happen. When Charles was thirteen and Richard, fifteen, I took them to an indoor facility for swim lessons. We live in a river town and Charles had never leaned his strokes, relying instead on a pathetic dog paddle that looked more like he was thrashing about in the water to avoid drowning instead of actually swimming. For these lessons, his brother dove in and got it done but Charles stood on the outside of the pool for two weeks, refusing to put his toe in the water. I had taken them to a heated indoor pool, and he claimed it was too cold.

My husband was disappointed that he didn't get into college since he thought it would be good for him. I was relieved. Charles liked the *idea* of college: the parties, the apartment, the freedom. He had developed few "executive" abilities, and following a schedule, keeping up with a workload, and doing homework were never his strong suits. I was OK with skipping college as an expensive experiment.

Shortly after this disappointment, Charles, at the age of nineteen, got his high school diploma; when it arrived, we celebrated as if he had just won the Nobel Prize. It was an ugly journey, but it was done.

Around May of 2014, he met up with old friends and continued to date someone he had known from high school with whom he ultimately fell in love. When his friends arrived, they had changed so much I didn't recognize some of them at first. Both of my boys were late bloomers, but there was no change in Charles' physical appearance from fifteen to twenty other than his height.

While I was in the living room, his friend William came in to catch up for a minute. William was an intelligent young man who had not been especially advanced when it came to emotional maturity in grade school but that had changed. It was while I was talking with William that I noticed how little progress Charles had made. Mental illness and drug abuse do slow the process but the gap looked more like a canyon and I wondered if my younger son would ever be able to make it on his own. He was always so reliant on others.

Trouble was, he had the charm to get people to do things for him and thus never learned how to do a lot of things for himself. Remember his Thai roommate, Henry, the human alarm clock, who delivered personal wake-up calls? Charles had been bugging his brother to do things for him, too, especially as it related to the computer. Many of the tasks Charles was asking Richard about were ones his brother had previously given him instruction. Finally, Richard had had enough, got angry, and refused to repeat the instructions or do it for him again. There were never two boys more different from each other. Although Richard wasn't always a saint, he was the more grounded of the two.

I remember Charles wanting a sleepover in the backyard at the age of ten. The deal was he could have the sleepover but we were not setting up all the tents. My little boy got on the phone, called his friends, and delegated the task to them. These kids were running around in the backyard building a tent village, and Charles was directing them as if they were his personal orchestra. I laugh at the memory and know that delegating is an important skill but what I didn't know was how often he was depending on others as the glue to keep himself together, not the best overall strategy for navigating life. It nagged at me but there was no way to pin it down and define it as a problem.

Of course, as parents, we thought getting a job would be the magic that would transform Charles into a constructive and contributing member of society, and we pushed him to find one. His lack of motivation that I now know is a trait of depression, had me hyperfocused on finding that "one thing" that would propel him forward.

We discussed jobs and entering community college in the fall. He would start with just a few classes to see how it went and to keep him busy and out of trouble. I was not sure college was his destination and if his goal was to become a rap artist, that was fine, but he needed to support his dream, buy his own gas, and otherwise start the process of being a grown-up.

I insisted he take driver's education all over again, which didn't go over well but he knew that this wasn't a point where I would budge. At sixteen, he had failed his first road-driving test, and I enrolled him in private lessons. A car with Charles in the driver's seat was a deadly weapon, and I had a responsibility not only for his well-being but for the others on the road, too. He had a lot of pride in his intellect, and was humiliated about failing the road test.

Once he had earned his provisional license, he hadn't been driving long before we shipped him off for wilderness and therapeutic boarding school, where he didn't drive at all. Now that he was home, he'd need to take driver's education again to refresh his skills. Freedom from us was the motivation behind his completing it for a second time, although he was no poster child for driver's education this go-round either. No way was I going to sit in that car with him again as a teacher. Memory had not erased the terror of being a passenger with Charles in those earlier learning years when he would stop in merge lanes and drive halfway on the shoulder on highways. My heart was always in my throat, my hands cramped from clenching the handle as I held on for dear life. He took driver's education a total of three times over the years and had a lot of hours behind the wheel that didn't advance his skills as much as I would have liked, but his instructor was good, patient, and thorough, and finally it was good enough.

One day in the summer in 2014, a few months after Charles had returned home, my husband and I were eating dinner out on our deck when Charles and his friends arrived. They sat down with us after we had finished, but Charles was different—weird and overly cheerful—and he nodded off while talking to us, making me feel uneasy.

I looked at my husband. He looked at me. We were sure it was drugs. His friends were trying to usher him away from the table and back inside. They looked and sounded normal. Charles was having none of that. *Was he picking up where he left off?* I gently asked what he had taken and he insisted nothing.

The next day, I pointed out that he was falling asleep in front of us, and again, he said he was tired and denied falling asleep while talking to us.

I did an Internet search for "falling asleep at the table" to see what drug caused the effect, but it turned up nothing at that time. It was opiates—heroin—that caused the "nods." None of the support groups talked about symptoms of particular drugs because those in the group already knew what drug their child was abusing or addicted to. I was having a hard time differentiating which was depression, panic, lack of sleep, or drug use. Teasing all of it apart was a challenge.

On the deck that night, my peaceful illusion that things would be OK crumbled. I was not willing to admit panic and defeat, and I gave myself permission to write off the incident as a one-time event. I had not thought sending him away had fixed all of his problems, and knew from other parents who had gone this route that this was not often the case. But there had been an expectation of progress and there had been so little, if any, despite our many trips to upstate New York for family counseling. Drug tests don't stop people from using and I didn't insist on him taking one the next day, which is a regret. At least we would have known what he'd been taking.

Drug tests with him were always a battle, and the possibility of defeat and potential conflict likely prevented me from going through the process with him that day. Hours of him telling me "I can't pee on demand" and waiting for him to go in there and urinate into a cup were often miserable half-day or all-day events. I couldn't make him pee, or sleep, or stop doing drugs, and some part of me somewhere was throwing up my hands in surrender.

Maintaining sanity as well as the digital marketing company I co-owned took everything I had. I would come back and fight again but there were days when all of it would get the best of me and I needed to hibernate to rekindle that drive. All I could do was keep going to support group.

Late summer rolled around, and it was time to apply for community college. We downloaded the registration and went to orientation, but he could not have been less engaged. I was desperate to get him involved in something and give him a purpose even if it meant carrying him in there and inserting him into a seat. Part of the orientation involved going to the computer lab to learn how to log onto the community college scheduling system. He didn't want to go to orientation, was pissed at me, and ready to go home, but went into the computer lab, where he promptly ignored what was going on and started to text people on his phone.

He needed to be invested in something, and I was losing him. Barely able to hold it together, I hid in the library stacks and let all the frustration and sadness go. Unfortunately, there were no tissues between books, but I didn't want anyone to see me because I was sobbing uncontrollably. I had no idea how I would explain hiding in the library crying, my nose running like a faucet. While he was otherwise occupied, I went to go visit the special needs coordinator, Mark, who was surprisingly good. Just the day before he had asked, "Do you think he is going to make it?" He meant in college, but I remember at the time wondering, "Is my child going to live?"

By November, Charles had dropped out of community college. I knew his drama class, where he was already a big hit, would be disappointed. But something else was pulling him away. Unknown to us, drugs were sucking my child's soul into the depravity of addiction, and there was nothing I could do to stop it despite grabbing for his ankles as he began to disappear down the drain.

Charles was so vulnerable to addiction. Heroin, the deadliest of drug addictions, was becoming a serious epidemic in 2015. I could not find any evidence of drug use. There were never tin foil or needles, just the occasional lighter. All I had were suspicions triggered by odd behavior that fueled gut feelings. He had passed a drug test, and I can honestly say I didn't suspect heroin. Not my child.

That fall of 2014, we had decided to prepare to sell our house the following spring. It was a much-needed distraction. I was still attending my support group although less frequently because readying the house to go on the market took every available hour I had. While putting the finishing touches on the drywall we had installed in the garage to better insulate the room above, I fell off a ladder and shattered my olecranon—the pointy part of the elbow where the funny bone is—into thirteen tiny pieces. I was extremely lucky I didn't die considering all the places I could have smashed my head on the way down. I was mere inches from drill bits, saws, files, and cinder block. Two elbow surgeries and a serious infection landed me in the hospital and tied me to an infusion of antibiotics for eight weeks, which, once discharged, I'd administer at home.

During my stay at the hospital, Charles never visited, which was unlike him. I had become increasingly suspicious of his recent behavior and was on the edge of dread. We had had conversations with him about drug use and our boundaries. Before going to the hospital, I told Randy not to lend Charles his truck because he had totaled his hand-me-down Honda CRV on an icy road in a remote area of the county and I had the feeling he was going places I would not want him to go. I couldn't stop him from using drugs, but I was also not going to make it easier. Besides that, the consequence of totaling a car was not having the luxury of transportation. He asked his dad if he could borrow his truck, our spare vehicle, so he could visit me and then go to a Narcotics Anonymous meeting scheduled at that same hospital, a bogus cover-up to get his dad to agree. He never attended the meeting and the visit never happened but he did drive somewhere that night with the borrowed vehicle.

Sure, I was hurt. But fear was the emotion that took over and fits of panic would hit at random moments. I was frustrated with the elbow injury and the frequent infusions I had to initiate through my PICC line that required me to be awake at odd hours to administer the antibiotics. I had to stay on schedule with my own healthcare to beat the infections and keep up with my business, and I was worried about Charles and what he was doing that we didn't know about. We drug-tested him later and he did not pass so we followed our counselor's advice, which was to tell him he had to leave the house for two weeks. Usually, kids will couch-surf and some will think better of doing illegal drugs. We had to honor our boundaries. My husband and I didn't want to take this step, especially since it would be over the holidays, but we had made clear the consequences of a failed drug test. Illegal drug use was not allowed in our home, a reasonable boundary.

Charles was probably addicted at this point and we didn't know it. He didn't spend Christmas with us in 2014, which will always be a regret. It would have been our last. I couldn't know that, of course. Since we were leaving to spend the holidays with my parents in North Carolina, we did ask him to join us but he was angry we had asked him to leave for those two weeks and said no. After his suicide, I learned that he spent Christmas Day that year with the Morgantis. He was with people who loved him, did not judge him, and I was thankful for that. Mr. Morganti was the dad who, eleven years earlier, had said to his son, Alex, "Tell me the kid in the dragon costume is not the kid we are picking up." Alex said, "I'm afraid so, Dad. That's my friend Charles."

By the time we got home from North Carolina, Charles called and said he was ready to be drug-tested and come home. He passed, so I thought there might still be hope. Could this work? And then a miracle happened: He got a job at Taco Bell, his all-time favorite place to eat. We were all elated. Finally, a good thing had happened.

Randy and I wondered what kind of employee he'd be. He didn't get as many hours as any of us would have liked, and after he got his first paycheck, he asked me the following day for gas money. I told him he'd just gotten paid so he should budget for things like fuel for the car. Curiously, he had a habit of putting one or two dollars' worth of gas in his car instead of filling his tank.

He would often say he could not get to work for lack of gas and those times I offered to drive him. I was not giving him gas money or cash. That was another of our boundaries.

Before getting the job, he had some pet-sitting funds but nothing like the checks that were rolling in then, even with limited hours. Each time he was paid, the funds from those checks were gone right away and we could see no evidence of purchases. He just kept asking for money for this or that and I decided to hide my handbag. I was never sure whether Charles stole from me or his dad. Some of his songs indicate he lifted some bills from our wallets.

In 2015, physicians continued to prescribe opiates by the bucket for patients after surgery. I had ordered a new safe with extra security features because Charles had gotten into my last one. I stored mostly over-the-counter medications there and I took any leftover prescriptions and the dog's medicine, Tramadol, to drug takeback events in the county. The safe would hold prescriptions until I had the opportunity to get rid of them. I shredded paper prescriptions I didn't fill and even during the elbow surgery, I didn't use but one pain pill and got rid of the rest as fast as I could. The surgery has been exceedingly painful but I needed just one pain pill to get through the first night after surgery. After that, I managed on Tylenol and Advil. I didn't want any of that in my house, even locked away.

Charles was having altercations with a woman at work and one day he blew up at her. She was his superior but somehow he held onto the fantasy that they'd keep him on despite the argument. That was not the case. I don't know the whole story, but as Charles was a full-blown heroin addict by now, I'm guessing they were looking for an excuse to fire him. He was not panning out. At the time, my husband and I were devastated. This was in January of 2015.

During this time, the police were stalking young males eighteen- to twenty-five years old in the county, stopping them for anything they could label "probable cause" to fulfill what may have been an arrest quota. I imagine they also suspected Charles' drug use and some dealing to support his habit and were eager to make an arrest. Frequent stops would offer more opportunity to catch him in action. They stopped him so many times for a "rolling stop" that I later installed a DriveCam. We had purchased a used car for him at some point when the chaos had settled and we thought things would be better, which, in hindsight, was premature. I had proof one of his tickets was bogus because the camera showed he stopped for the sign. But before I got the chance to help him fight that ticket, he was stopped again one night after coming home from a friend's house.

He was due home at 11 p.m., and I was worried and angry he had not made curfew. What I didn't know was that he was being stopped on a dark road by a police officer, and handcuffed immediately after being ordered out of the car, as was protocol with males in this age group. Shortly after he got out of his car, his head was slammed onto a police vehicle. While he was being roughed up, he panicked in fear for his life and screamed for help, which angered the rookie cop. Charles had never been beaten up, and he was scared, alone and, vulnerable on the side of the road, handcuffed with no other soul in sight.

The cop, sure my son had drugs in his underwear, dug his hand down Charles' pants without warning, and he freaked out. Charles said the officer shocked him by grabbing his penis. In retrospect, I think the officer did not think a kid as skinny as Charles could be—how should I put this?—as genetically gifted as he appeared. Certainly that bulge had to be a drug stash. It was not. I feel sure this cop had been following my son and knew what I didn't know, that he was addicted to heroin. I'm sure the officer was frustrated that he could not find enough evidence to take him in like a lion with a prize catch. Ultimately, lack of evidence did not stop him from making an arrest.

Once he was grabbed, Charles told me he went into panic mode and started to rant, cry, scream, and pace, his head bleeding and hands still cuffed behind his back, pants unbuttoned and partially unzipped from the surprise search. I used to call this pacing his meltdown mode. They claimed to have tapes of his rant but I never heard them and they were not played in court. He told me he was polite when the officer stopped him but the incident turned dark once he was assaulted; he admitted to Randy and me that he was yelling expletives to anyone who would listen: "He grabbed my fucking dick. He grabbed my fucking dick."

Charles was never violent or physically aggressive but he would yell and cry a lot when he was in emotional distress. The cop finally called for backup once he was aware he had lost control of the situation. Why hadn't he called before he reached into Charles' underwear? When I go for a yearly pelvic exam, a nurse must be in the room with the doctor. If Charles had had drugs next to his package, it wasn't going anywhere while he was handcuffed. There was ample time to check when backup arrived.

They insisted that putting their hands in his underwear was constitutional search, although to this day I seriously doubt it. Others encouraged me to pursue it but a challenge in court would have been an expensive endeavor, and I had my hands full trying to maintain control of what was happening in my family.

Homecoming

It was a botched arrest with pathetic evidence. This officer wanted to save face and ended up leveling multiple overlapping charges, including assault on an officer, which—according to lawyers and a bondsman I would later speak with—was a rookie move. Charles passed the breathalyzer test at the station, but on site he had produced a different result, although not admissible in court, and he admitted to drinking a beer so the possession charge would likely stick. Contents of the stomach are considered possession. The breathalyzer result was .01. That's point zero one, way under the legal limit and even under the .02—point zero two—that constitutes "baby DUI."

To the policemen who had arrived as backup, the arresting officer claimed Charles had taken a swing at him. Later at the station when Charles heard this, he was shocked and pointed out that this would have been impossible while handcuffed. The officer then changed his story, saying Charles threw his shoulder at him in a "football move." Charles was more likely to know how to skip rope double Dutch than he was to know any football moves. He knew he was not a physical force at six-foot-two and one hundred thirty pounds to take on a two-hundred-pound cop with a gun. This officer would tell other officers about the "assault" to rally support for himself against Charles' later complaint for sexual assault.

We got a call from the police station in the morning. I was shocked but relieved that he had been found alive, and the travesty in our criminal justice system began. I was at first angry at him for being arrested. What had he done now? Something in his voice warned me not to be angry. We posted bond, something we would not have done had we had not been suspicious of the arrest circumstances. When his dad picked him up, Charles was in a state, repeating over and over, "This guy grabbed my dick, he grabbed my dick. Why would he do that? He beat me up, Mom. Why did he do that?" Before I went to talk to him after his dad had picked him up and brought him home, I made sure to calm myself. Randy was alarmed and told me I needed to get his side of story on paper. I went for a run first.

As soon as I pulled myself together, entered his room, and saw his

175

face, I lost it. I knew immediately he had been violated. When you've been violated yourself, you recognize the look. He was not faking it. When I was eighteen years old, I was strangled, and barely escaped rape and murder. It was at a Jaycee Haunted House in Fayetteville, North Carolina, where I grew up. I had been coerced into helping a guy wearing a Jaycee volunteer T-shirt to come to the back to join in scaring some of the visitors who would be exiting. My friends all said I'd be good at this and encouraged me to go, not knowing this guy was a predator. He looked legitimate, as he was dressed like all the other members running the event. As I stepped away from the crowd and into the back of the house, the hairs on the back of my neck prickled and he pulled a knife, put the cold blade next to my neck. He forced me into an adjacent backyard, and was sexually assaulting me when I pretended to faint. He became agitated and started to strangle me. I fought back with everything I had and escaped only after kicking him between his legs so hard his sperm screamed for help. I watched him limp away as I struggled to my feet.

I remember running out front screaming, but the police officers who interviewed me dismissed my story as a fight with a boyfriend. Evidence on the scene I had told them about was found the following day; the chief of police visited my house and offered a formal apology for the conduct of the officers that night. I could barely walk from all the bruises from the assault, and red hand marks from the strangling were visible on my neck. I have never forgotten that experience and what it was like to be a victim of sexual assault and mistreated by the law. Charles and I both broke down and cried. I had never told Charles my story before but shared it with him later that day. At this point, I was just listening to him.

I took note of all his bruises and the bumps on his head. He had crusted blood in his hair and strange rows of small bruises up and down his arms. He said he was wearing a thick coat but the policeman had done some kind of torture move up and down his arms that caused excruciating pain. I took photos, and the station sent someone over to take more. I had seen worse altercations from run-ins with the law and I remember thinking how much worse it would have been had he been a nineteen-year-old African-American male. For Charles and us, this was major trauma. The cop had told him after the crotch search, "Nobody will ever believe a drunk teenager over a cop."

Charles was broken. He didn't understand why he would be treated this way by a police officer. I have to believe there were good people on the force then, too, and Charles was the victim of bad luck. I know now that Charles was addicted to an illegal substance and had probably done some dealing on the side, but one can't be arrested without evidence and there is protocol that must be followed from the start. I believe the officer recognized too late that the situation had gotten out hand, delivering a blow to his rookie ego. When he became aware there was not enough evidence to make the charges stick, he made up other transgressions to save face when backup arrived.

At that moment, all I could do was cry and hold Charles while he rocked in my arms and wept. I think this was the lowest I had ever seen him: worse than the break-in at the beach. I was so angry. His life and mine were crumbling.

Charles ended up filing a complaint about the sexual assault and brutality. He was angry, humiliated, and hurt. When he made his original complaint, he wouldn't let the internal affairs officer who came by enter the house because we weren't at home and he didn't trust anyone with a badge. Charles would only make the statement on the front porch in the light of day and he was a nervous mess when I arrived home later that day. We got feedback from this officer that his complaint was credible and worth investigating.

Unfortunately, the complaint inspired a lot of young cops to stalk and make threats off the record to Charles at convenience stores and fast-food joints. I had feared reprisal, and I was right. If I thought he was being stopped frequently before, now it was every time he went anywhere. When I called the local station and complained, they claimed they were not stopping him and later I understood the station was simply acting on the records they had, which didn't indicate any official stops. These were not authorized stops, which is what my son was telling me

They'd run his plates if they happened to see his car, follow him to convenience stores, make a purchase as if they were just dropping in for a snack, and threaten him regarding the complaint he'd filed. In their eyes, they were supporting a fellow officer who had been assaulted. These convenience-store run-ins were off the record, but we had witnesses, who unfortunately were all teenagers and had little credibility when compared to a group of policemen. When we "lost" the plates to Charles' car and had them replaced, miraculously the unauthorized run-ins ceased immediately.

Not long after he filed the complaint, two officers from the division came by to ask questions. They were trying to get Charles to retract his statement. I wish he had. The officers implied he had done so to improve his position in court. If anything, it did exactly the opposite. A vindictive policeman who is trying to protect himself makes a court case far more difficult, especially since he knew all the players better than we did. I recorded the internal affairs visit since they were doing so, too, and I posted it on my blog after his death[1]

In piecing together events, Charles did admit to drinking a beer. He was doing heroin in the wee hours of the night while we slept, so it was unlikely he was high on that substance when he was pulled. I'll never know, however. He knew they had been watching him, and would have been unlikely to take the risk. The majority of the time Charles had heroin delivered, letting the dealer take the risk. He would text the dealer, and the dealer would text him back. He'd walk out of the house and sit in his car by the street until the dealer arrived. I had one DriveCam video from a cold rainy night when he had turned his car on to stay warm. (DriveCam videos come on automatically when the engine is turned on.)

In the video, I hear the sound of icy rain and the windshield wipers squeaking on the windshield. It's very dark but I could make out a sinister, dark shadow of a person in a hoodie passing in front of the car toward the driver's side. I couldn't see much other than black night and swishing wipers but then I heard the window go down,

---

1   Interview with the police and recorded stop as "The Long Arm of the Law Reached Down Charles' Pants" on EmotionallyNaked.com.

there was a shuffling sound, the window went back up, and the dark shadow passed again in front of the car toward the street. Then there was a brief pause, some rustling, and a profound sigh of satisfaction that sounded an awful lot like orgasm. I remember watching it and feeling a cold chill of fear that I was witnessing something significant, but I couldn't interpret the scene or see much more than black on the screen since the cameras were pointed toward the road at night. Other than the one shadow, it was the audio that was revealing. I shared it with my husband who was as perplexed as I was.

Most of the time, he didn't bring heroin into the house but instead snorted it right there in the car in the early morning hours once it was delivered. The DriveCam video was filmed at around 3 a.m. That would explain why the dog was often in distress and would come into our room worked up in the very early mornings. I didn't know Charles was not in the house on those occasions although I have vague memories of the sound of the garage door being opened or closed or movement up and down the stairs and around the house.

In some ways, the police assault incident brought me and Charles closer because I was fighting for him and against what was done to him. Once the internal affairs officer questioned the other officers and were told he was a "junkie" or a "drug addict," any credibility Charles' complaint may have had evaporated. Having substance use disorder demotes a person to society throwaway whose testimony is worthless even in moments of sobriety. As a result, officers who abuse their power get by with it in these situations. But addiction to a substance does not give any officer of the law the right to violate or mistreat another human being. That's not their job.

Since his death, but not because of it, officers in that county now undergo mental health training to encourage tactics other than force for both recognizing those struggling with mental illness and addiction, and dealing with this population more effectively as first responders. The county has also made an effort in terms of recovery resources for substance use disorder, especially in the jails, and officers of the law are always in attendance at my heroin task force meetings. Schools have added suicide awareness programs and in 2018, Virginia was one of the first two states to pass mandatory mental health education in schools.

Ultimately, this assault—compounded by his fear of a trial in a criminal justice system he didn't trust—contributed to Charles' suicide. The people who were supposed to protect and defend had all the power and the system was rigged against him. It was not the main cause or the only one by any stretch. And I did not know how profoundly he was traumatized by the event until after his death when I read his music and Facebook messages.

After this violation, Charles spiraled downward quickly and went into a deep depression. It was like I was seeing water running through a colander. I wanted to plug all the leaks but there were too many and I didn't yet know what I was up against.

Mere days after my son's suicide, after our lawyer showed them the obituary in court, the police who had internally investigated this complaint cleared themselves of any wrongdoing, and sent us a letter stating the matter closed.

CHAPTER 26

JUST TO HURT

TRIGGER WARNING:
Method mentioned

Lyrics by Charles Aubrey Rogers, aka Reezin' the Revolutionary

*B*ack in another institution,
    Guess I'm stupid, feeling useless
even though my music
tight as a noose is
Every day is a nuisance
Bored as fuck I want to do shit
Guess I didn't learn my lesson
Been in treatment
most of my adolescence.
Drug cravings, anxiety and depression
All because of my obsession
I know I'll get by
But all rehab does
is make me wanna get high
I bet God sits in the sky
wishing I'd just die

DIARY OF A BROKEN MIND

They said I got amazing potential
if I'd just try
Since I was 15
I've been fed lies
Said I'd be gone for 2 weeks
I was gone for 3 years.
What the hell, why?
This is my life,
That was my time,
I can never get it back
That wasn't yours to take from me
But this is life
and there ain't no pot of gold after the rainbow
But there's pain through
I promise you there's pain, yo

(Refrain)
Why we put on here on this earth just to hurt,
just to hurt, just to hurt
So much pain in the universe

They said it's gonna get worse
before it gets better
But all I see is hurt
and it's been getting worse forever
It always seems to rain the most
when I'm promised perfect weather
And if you're hurt too,
then we can hurt together

I put these words together,
pain stain in every letter
Cause me and Cal used to hangout,
before he decided to hang down,
Heroin took a home from me
He found a place in the ground
I scream for God to answer
but he ain't make a sound

My demons up against me
and I'm facin' them now

Just to Hurt

I wear the face of a clown
I feel so unloved,
because of the monster
that was created from drugs

(Refrain)
Why we put on here on this earth just to hurt,
just to hurt, just to hurt
So much pain in the universe

I hope this last verse sticks in ya mind momma
I promise Imma fix it this time
I'm putting it behind
cause I can't forgive myself
And you can't give me back time

My emotions drip through these lines
But even in darkness
sunshine sometimes shines through the blinds
You were paying for hope
and I was lookin' for dope
'Cause I just couldn't cope
And I'm just so afraid
that I'll end up alone

I'll always miss my own home
I always seem to fuck things up
I guess rock bottom wasn't deep enough
Even breathing's tough

It's like I'm surrounded by walls
with no escape at all
I'm over 6 feet tall,
But I've never felt so small

(Refrain)
Why we put on here on this earth just to hurt,
just to hurt, just to hurt
So much pain in the universe

Charles with his dad in 2013. Charles was a daddy's boy.

CHAPTER 27

MY SILVER
GOES MISSING

Wish I could go back to the way it was
before I ever had a taste of the stuff
life wasted from drugs
powder replaced faith and got traded from love
hearts now decaying to dust
scratchin' my face as I escape the hate with a buzz
—*Numb me*, by Charles Aubrey Rogers

Two plainclothes Chesterfield County policemen stood on my deck and rang the doorbell, and the skin I jumped out of landed in the next county. Their appearance never ceased to shock me although my ability to recover had improved. Escorting them to my living room was like walking across a rickety bridge over a river gorge. I struggled to maintain balance and composure while my brain chanted, *Stay cool, Anne Moss. Stay cool.* I thought they had come in regard to the complaint Charles had filed but they were not from

Internal Affairs and my mind was whizzing through the catalogue of possible reasons two officers would be here on a weekday afternoon. It was unlikely they were dropping by to get a taste of my famous pound cake.

They didn't make any small talk and right away showed me photos of Charles at a pawn shop and a picture of what he had sold. Once again, I strained to disguise my panic while they paused and studied my reaction. Pawn shops are required to report suspicious activity and the amount of sterling silver he had been selling had come to their attention. It was Gorham by Chantilly, my family's silver pattern and there was but one place he could have gotten it.

What should I do? They didn't say anything about drugs and they measured out their words like rare coins. Maybe they didn't want to bring up what they might be thinking. If this silver was stolen from me, were they looking to press charges or have me press charges? I was unsure and more than a little suspicious of their motives given our most recent encounter with the police. I told them his grandmother had given him that silver. Charles was too young to get it but I said she had insisted so it was his to do with what he wanted. I said I was very disappointed and would be looking into this but couldn't stop him from selling what was rightfully his.

This wasn't entirely true. My mom gave me the silver, not Charles. But I had seen an ugly side of the law and so far they had shown how they could manipulate the system to their favor, which had made us feel under siege. Besides that, I had witnessed some of the judges in action as they leaned over their benches, growling and shaming the accused, many of them kids. I was convinced those judges ate their young. The officers left and never shared their thoughts on why he might have sold the silverware, and I didn't share mine. The room got uneven, and this new crisis slammed its fist into my midsection. My mind was grasping for excuses other than the obvious as to why he might be selling silverware to pawn shops. My brain was thinking "drug use," and then that thought would get pushed away by denial in favor of a more acceptable scenario, each one less plausible than the last.

My approach to the dining room silverware drawer was slow and deliberate. Sliding open the silver box, one solitary spoon sat naked against a backdrop of black, staring back at me. Twelve place settings and the sterling serving pieces were gone. The sterling luncheon knives were left probably because they were rejected for being out of fashion. No one had separate dinner and luncheon knives anymore. All the salad forks, dinner forks, dinner knives, ice tea spoons, dessert spoons, dessert forks, and more than a dozen butter knives were gone. It had to be thousands of dollars' worth of silver pawned, probably for next to nothing. Randy's silver dollars given to him by his grandfather were also gone. It was the only thing Randy still had from his grandfather. I sank to the floor and put my head in my hands as the colors of the room smudged together while my tears fell. My child had been stealing from us.

Where was Charles anyway? His comings and goings had been so mysterious. I had searched his room and the Internet for clues of drug use and those searches had turned up zilch. There had been a number of empty Reddi-Wip cans in cleaning out the house to prepare it for sale. I had also just noticed the day before that cases of hot beer we had bought for a Christmas party no one had shown up for were no longer in our attic. I didn't know until later that it can't be stored this way. Had he drunk it all? Sold it? The pieces of the ugly puzzle were coming together and I wanted to burn it. In cleaning out the house for every substance I could find, I had forgotten about the beer. Charles must have gone to the attic to smoke weed or use drugs so he wouldn't get caught and in so doing had found the stash.

On a phone call to Randy, we decided I would wait for Charles to talk to him. When he came home, I called him to my upstairs office. He had just come back from pet sitting a friend's dogs. No one loved dogs more than Charles. He was immediately on alert something was up.

Very gently, I told him about the officers, the pawnshop photos, and the missing silver. Randy was on speakerphone and asked Charles about what happened. He told us an elaborate story about someone trying to coerce him into selling drugs, a tale that included his having to sell the silver for cash. The story was straight from a movie script and we didn't believe it but also didn't challenge him on it. Instead, we were quiet and listened. I was not angry or yelling. Patience had taken up residence where panic had lived an hour ago.

Looking back, I can at least be proud of how well this conversation and several others we'd had since he'd come back home had been handled: overall, not a lot of yelling or accusations because it was toxic and ineffective.

Charles asked if we believed him. I hesitated and told him it was an elaborate story and I left it at that. I asked him about drug use and he denied it. I was silent and let him tell more tall tales, picturing Pinocchio growing a long nose. We remained quiet and Charles didn't quite know how to react to our silence. We waited. Nervous and fidgeting, he started to fill in all the silence with what I was sure was another fabricated story complete with scoundrels, villains, and drug dealers. No dragons, however.

Then he said, "There's something I need to tell you."

"Yes? Go ahead. I'm listening."

"I was doing OxyContin. But I stopped taking it. Savannah weaned me off."

Then he broke down in tears. His nose ran uncontrollably and he said he needed help: the words we had been dying to hear for five years.

"How can we help, Charles?" I held him in my arms as he shook and my shoulder soaked up his tears.

He was still vague and not telling us everything. But we had arrived at something.

I would find out that a runny nose is a sign of heroin use, particularly if it is snorted. He used every tissue in the box in that sitting. I was trying to figure out how he "was weaned off OxyContin" and he told me his girlfriend had been tapering him off by using hydrocodone. He said he hardly went through withdrawal because he probably wasn't addicted yet but didn't offer from where the hydrocodone may have come. *Don't people get addicted pretty fast on an opiate?* I wasn't sure about any of it.

A few months back, his girlfriend had asked her parents to pay for her to go to a clinic in California where she had gotten clean. I'm sure she wanted him to do the same. She wanted to help him because she loved him. I'm sure neither of her parents were delighted that she was still hanging out with Charles who no doubt was using and a bad influence. I can't say it was the healthiest relationship.

He insisted he was clean but that the urge to use was still there. We kept our mouths shut, trying to pick the truths that were buried somewhere in the fabrications. When someone suffers from substance use disorder and they are using, it's hard to discern between fact and fiction. Manipulation is part of the illness and he wasn't yet ready to make an all-out confession.

Then I asked gently, "How did you justify stealing my silver and pawning it?"

He cried more and then—shoulders drooped as he stared at the top of his dad's desk, catty corner to me from where he was sitting— he described how OxyContin talked to him and why he stole the silver. I titled it, "How heroin talked to Charles," and posted on my blog after his death to help others understand addiction and how it influences the brain. In the office that day, I didn't know heroin had taken my son's brain hostage and he hadn't admitted to being addicted but I would learn later, this is exactly what he was describing. In the script below, I replaced OxyContin with the word heroin since that was the drug to which he was addicted.

How heroin talked to Charles

Charles' Brain: *I'm not going to take any more silver. Not selling any more of it to pawnshops. It makes me feel like shit to steal. I'm never doing another hit of heroin. It doesn't even give me that great a feeling anymore.*

Heroin: *Remember how good I made you feel? I know you can feel that way again.*

Charles' Brain: *No way. I'm not doing it. I don't want to steal. I don't want to be addicted.*

Heroin: *I'm patient. Soon enough you will crave me. You know we can achieve that euphoric high again.*

Charles' Brain: *I won't. I'm not a junkie. I won't take any more. My mom and my dad will find out and be so disappointed in me. I am already such a failure. I'm such a scumbag.*

Heroin: *Just one more hit. And then you'll stop. What can it hurt to take just one more?*

Charles' Brain: *I don't want to. But maybe if the next one is my last.*

Heroin: *They won't miss that silver. Hell, they only use it once a year!*

They love you. They'd want you to have it. It's just stuff.

Charles' Brain: *Yeah. Mom hardly ever opens that drawer. She hasn't missed it at all. She could care less. One last hit and then I'm done for good. This time is the last!*

This was new territory for me. His sleep disorder, the depression he would never admit to, his anxiety, his panic attacks, the drug use that had graduated to opiates. Had we dodged a bullet by catching the drug use in time to prevent addiction? Or were we naïve, so willing to believe our child and hold onto denial?

He had asked for help and we had to figure out what to do next. In the span of fewer than two hours, we learned that my family's silver and Randy's grandfather's coins had all been pawned by our son, there had been serious drug use, and perhaps addiction, or not: All with an elaborate drug dealer coercion story thrown in for added drama.

We were, yet again, in a spot where we didn't have a GPS. My brain was so full of noise and confusion I had a hard time sorting through it all or deciding where to start.

Randy ended up calling his parents and they suggested we send him there for a couple of weeks to get our heads together and figure our next move. We bought him a plane ticket. Little did we, or the grandparents, know what we were getting into.

CHAPTER 28

WHAT THESE DRUGS DO

Lyrics by Charles Aubrey Rogers, aka Reezin' the Revolutionary

I got that shit that'll make you rob, steal or kill,
*   I've seen motherfuckers throw away everything*
for a single pill.
I got that shit that'll make you sell your Xbox,
weed dirty like sex talk,
10 crack commandments;
I wrote the drug dealin' bible.

I'm fiendin', I need it, for survival
Friends stick around like bleach stains
Just call me dude, we don't speak names,
cause when my product leak through each of your veins
you feel the release of pain

DIARY OF A BROKEN MIND

Now pay up 'cause I need the same,

That's what these drugs do
Say that they love you
just so they can fuck you,
But fuck it, you've got fun to have
and a will to lose
and I got pills to move.
I've got drugs to do
so it's nothin' new.
Bricks in check,
let's risk death,
get the cigarette dipped in wet,
I'm not ready for reality yet.

(Refrain)
They'll take everything
That's what these drugs do
Strip your motivation, jail, probation, heavenly elevation
That's what these drugs do

I can see the veins on the side of my pupils
I'm high enough to talk to cupid
He gave me some Jesus powder
and told me how to move it,
your mind is beautiful
and it's cheap to lose it
Plus I drink stupid
and my shrink thinks I'm using.

This hip-hop shit is my theme music
tryin' to reach the scarface dream though it
sip lean, lit weak,
I trip Lucy,
sell amphetamines to buy ketamine,
I've see lives ruined, people die,
but I get high and put it in my music

What These Drugs Do

This drug problem I've fine-tuned it,
I USE it,
Abusive to these hallucinogens,
'shrooms make life cartoons,
Look the moons movin',
My blood itches,
I've scratched my skin to the bone
Fuck stitches, the drugs fuck with us.
Jesus Christmas dust in thick blunts,
hit it once and can't get enough, binges,
woke up already away 3 days in the past,
still baked
If this rush is real, life is fake
Let's see how much pain I can take
before I have to escape

(Refrain)
They'll take everything
That's what these drugs do
Strip your motivation, jail, probation, heavenly elevation
That's what these drugs do

I'm sorry mom and dad,
that little Charlie is a problem bad,
sicker than a vomit bag
Ether-clogged rag,
inhalants make time lag,
Where's my motherfuckin' mind at?
HANDS OFF MY BAG!
Do E pills really kill?
Pink hills, half unconscious,
but I manage to drink still,
My ink sinks into the stationary,
reezin the revolutionary,
Call me a god,
call me legendary,

Me and Mary got married,
space carried loud on the clouds,
I'll come down when I'm buried,
Life is scary,
I know it well

Smoke to heaven,
fall close to hell,
you know the smell?
Chemical dipped hits to your lips,
fuck yea, I sell to kids,
I don't give a shit if little Timmy can afford a brick
Let 'em? cop that shit
Cops can sniff my dick, get a whiff of this,
piff littered with mystic shit,
Lick on this lucy licorice,
liquor slizzerred feelin' like a wizard
when it hits my gizzard and I finish it

Drugs are bad
They fuckin' ruined my life
But I got a couple hits
If you wanna do them tonight

So much of this song illustrates his feelings of unworthiness. How obsessed, yet how much he hated drugs, at the same time. He did sell to support his habit. It's not something we are proud of and the kid remark still eats at me; I was tempted to take it out so readers wouldn't see that side of my boy. They would not have known the difference. I couldn't take out that part because I know good kids who had gotten sucked into selling and didn't even know how they got there.

Drug dealers are notorious for knowing how to groom someone who is young, naïve, vulnerable, and addicted, and suck them further into the culture to a point where they can't find the way out. It is a form of human trafficking. He hadn't gotten that deep into the drug culture, but would he have?

What These Drugs Do

A parent's anger over a child's addiction is often directed at dealers. But as soon as one is arrested, hundreds more are there to take his or her place, and often their own child has sold substances, too. As long as there is demand and money to be made, there will be drug dealers. The fact that the problem has become an epidemic is not because of dealers but because we have a culture that is sick, as well as kids with few coping skills to manage problems so they choose to numb them. Where did they learn this could be a solution?

We parents want to blame. It's the friends, the dealers, the school, etc. The truth is, while some drug addiction comes from being prescribed after surgery, most addictions start with beer in our refrigerators, the cigarettes in our handbags, and leftover medications in our cabinets.

Charles enjoying the hot tub while visiting grandparents, Richard and Myra (Meemaw and Grandpa), in Pine Mountain, Georgia.

CHAPTER 29

REHAB AND RELAPSE

Only 20, I already feel like I wasted my life
You should see the place I reside
I'm vacant inside
And I hate that I only feel like I'm waitin' to die.
—*Mr. Dopeman*, by Charles Aubrey Rogers,

R andy drove Charles to the airport the next day for his flight
to Georgia. He was spitting mad and pushed back hard.
We were perplexed that someone would be mad at the opportunity
to go on vacation after stealing thousands of dollars' worth of his
mother's silver. Charles always loved going to Georgia but he feared
we were shipping him off somewhere against his will and he wasn't
sure he'd land in that state at all. It was a valid concern since we
had orchestrated a kidnapping years earlier. He also had a habit
to support and I'm sure he knew he'd have to score something in
remote and unfamiliar territory to keep withdrawal at bay.

He hit a nerve when he said, "I wanted to at least spend my

birthday with my friends and family and I haven't done that in the last three years." In the face of his anger, we remained unflappable, knowing that an emotional outburst by us would have sent everything off track. We simply explained it would be a while before we figured out what to do next.

Right before Charles boarded the plane he told his dad he was addicted to OxyContin. He told Randy not to tell me, that he'd call and let me know the next day, his twentieth birthday. Later, we learned that was a fib. He was really addicted to heroin. Heroin is a dirty word, dripping with shame and ugliness. Who wants to associate with that?

To illustrate our confusion about what to do, we put Charles on that plane. On the way home, my husband, in his own bewildered state, called and told me what Charles had said. He had been vague about addiction and now he was confessing it outright. So what did it mean that Charles was on a plane headed to Georgia? Would he go through withdrawal? Or had he already been through that? Maybe he's not addicted like he thinks? Were we being manipulated somehow? I tried to compare this to what he had said already and it was all going in circles. I was in alien territory fraught with land mines and no map to point them out.

Randy told me Charles had withdrawn a hundred dollars right after we had given him cash to get food at the airport. Why did he withdraw more money? And why did we give him cash? From what account had he gotten that cash? His account had a zero balance. Then we saw overdraft protection had gone into effect and all the fees associated with it. He could not have taken heroin on the plane. Or we thought he couldn't. I still don't know. And he didn't look high or sick when he got on the flight.

The next day was his birthday, April 26, 2015, and he called me. He sounded defeated but contrite and told me he was addicted to OxyContin. It had been my worst nightmare that this drug would find him. I took a deep breath even though I already knew. I listened as he confessed and thanked him for his honesty, and assured him that while he was down there, we'd figure a plan for the next step to get him help. I was wondering how he missed out on the withdrawal part. But he was not in withdrawal then and I thought maybe it had been long enough for that to happen.

At the same time, I was mourning the loss of not being with my child on his birthday yet again. I had wanted to plan a little surprise with family and friends at the house.

What happened to normal? When exactly did it depart, only to be replaced by chaos and heartache? This disease is insidious and it had my son locked up in its embrace. I knew for Charles, the road to recovery would not be easy. Tough or resilient were not words I'd use to describe my youngest son.

When Charles and his friends were young and playing T-ball, I remember Pete, our neighbor, the team's coach, telling a funny story about the kids trying to come up with a team name. Charles spoke up and said he wanted the team name to be something tough. So Pete asked him what he thought it should be and Charles said he wanted it to be the Bluebirds. Tigers, Titans, or Knights would have been what I would have equated with the word "tough," and Bluebirds would have never made the list.

When I researched the personality of a bluebird, this is what I learned. Bluebirds hold the energy of gentleness. They are not aggressive and will avoid confrontation whenever possible. They are patient and observant birds and choose to spend their time enjoying life. However, if a bluebird is provoked, it will stand its ground and defend itself. The team name ended up being the Bluebirds and the five-year-old T-ball players did cry when they missed the bases, or got hot, tired, or hungry.

The "using Charles" was angrier and more sullen than the thoughtful, sweet boy we had raised but his family and friends were still very important to him, which is why he got on that plane. We thought we had time to think, to discover the next move. That's not how it works, however. We had been thrust in an entirely new universe, one where we knew very little and somehow had to find our way out of the maze. I thought we had time to get educated. But while we were carefully planning the next move, things were unraveling in Georgia.

We got a call from his grandparents later that day. Charles loved to ride a bicycle so he had asked his grandfather if he could borrow his. It seemed like an innocent enough request since that's what he usually did when he went to visit Camp Grandparents in Georgia. They had told him to be back in time for them to take him to dinner for his birthday. He had asked to go to Taco Bell. (No, I'm not kidding. When we'd go to New York City, with the best dining in the world, Charles would ask for Applebee's or McDonald's.)

That part was funny. Comic relief had been rare in this process. But it turned out that he left that day and we suspect now that he went to a neighborhood to score drugs. We were panicked because he didn't answer his mobile phone and we didn't know where he was. Several hours later, he called his grandparents and asked them to come and pick him up. He said he had lost the bike and offered no explanation, but he offered several vague rationalizations.

We were painting our bedroom in preparation for putting our home on the market when the phone rang, and it was from Randy's father, Richard, my oldest son's namesake. It took a few seconds of unreciprocated hellos from us before it registered that this was a butt-dial call, an unintended and unknowingly made call. Randy's dad, unaware we were listening, let loose a stream of expletives and my face registered shock while my husband laughed, realizing I had not known this side of his dad. (Apparently, Grandpa Richard had been a spitfire in his younger years.) Charles' voice was dripping with shame as he apologized and begged forgiveness from his grandfather, who was not in an emotional state to accept apology. Guilt flowed through the phone lines for our having sent him and for hanging on to this call like voyeurs for longer than we should have, so we hung up. At least we knew Charles was safe.

But where had he been? And where was the bike? We'd get that story later. Or would we? It didn't seem like it was the best time to call and talk to him right then. His grandfather was in a mood, Charles was all worked up, and we needed to let emotions cool. I had just had a long conversation with him that morning and we did talk to the grandparents later that day. They had decided not to go out to dinner after all since they were spent and it was late by the time everything settled down. We still didn't get the whole story, and never would.

The next day we got a call from his grandmother. Charles was in the bathroom and wouldn't come out. When he did, he looked dreadful but he claimed he was fine and took the trip with them from Georgia to their condo in Fort Walton Beach, Florida. They picked up Aunt Janice and Charles slept the entire way there. At this point, the grandparents thought he had a stomach virus. Charles had a history of stomachaches and viruses but I wondered if it might be withdrawal. It seemed like days after what presumably was his last usage, entirely too late for that but I was not sure since I'd never been through this. How long is it between last hit and start of withdrawal? And why didn't I call anyone in my support group to ask?

Looking back, my thinking brain was not always attached. Hawaiian Island-sized waves of emotion would send my mind soaring to project terrifying scenarios of my child's future while I tried to coax it back with breathing techniques and practical passages from Families Anonymous meetings. This message, from Helping, from Families Anonymous was one I had pasted onto my phone memos to remind myself how unproductive and futile this kind of thinking can be:

> "… Exhaustion is the result when I use my energy in mulling over the past with regret or in trying to figure ways to escape a future that has yet to arrive. Projecting an image of the future— and anxiously hovering over it for fear that it will or it won't come true—uses all my energy and leaves me unable to live today. Yet living today is the only way to have a life… ."

All the turmoil had me bumping into walls, getting lost while driving to familiar places, and putting strange ingredients in recipes. Meanwhile, there were client meetings and business events and I had to act as if my world was totally together. My job kept me distracted yet it was hard to concentrate on any one task for the length of time it needed to be done well.

Between assignments, I researched to try to educate myself when I saw a website with mortality rates for teens addicted to heroin that included statistics on the starting ages of abuse. The mortality rates, which were as high as eighty percent for opiate abuse that started at age fifteen with contributing risk factors such as depression, threw a truckload of water onto my waning pilot light of hope. I waffled between wanting to be more educated but not wanting to know more because fear was taking my brain prisoner.

The guilt of having sent my son to see his grandparents while we did our research sat right next to fear. What have we done? We sent him to Georgia to be with grandparents and now they have to deal with this? What the hell were we thinking?

Before I got into a boxing ring to beat myself up, I lapsed into pep-talk mode with my alter ego, my habit since I was fifteen. Interior conversations have always kept me from being consumed by fear or self-deprecation. The deal is I can fight back and forth with myself but in the end my conscience and alter ego must come to an agreement and end in solidarity on positive note.

> *My conscience: Why the hell did you send him down there when you knew he might be addicted?*
>
> *Alter ego: I didn't know.*
>
> *My conscience: You didn't know? You've been going to Families Anonymous for four and a half years! What are you, a moron?*
>
> *Alter ego: But he never had a "drug of choice." And FA is about finding your own life in the chaos. Setting your boundaries. All of this is new.*
>
> *My conscience: And now your in-laws have to deal with all this shit! You think they are equipped for all this?*
>
> *Alter ego: Who is? And he was not entirely honest. I'm guilty of being naïve. I've not had time to get educated on this. We didn't know he might be addicted to an opiate until three days ago.*
>
> *My conscience: You're emotionally spent, too. You needed a break to think.*
>
> *Alter ego: I did. They did ask him to come. It was a mistake to send him. I know that now.*
>
> *My conscience: But it was not on purpose was it?*
>
> *Alter ego: No. And I can't go there and punish myself right now. What good does that do? It won't help me, or the grandparents, and least of all it won't help Charles. And that's the goal, right? To get him help?*
>
> *My conscience: Yes that's the goal. As long as he is alive, there*

202

is hope. And I'm going to keep that pilot light of hope burning no matter what it takes.

Alter ego: That's my girl. You can tell them you are sorry. But you have to focus on your son and the next steps. You can do this. Take a deep breath; we're in for another ride on the emotional roller coaster.

It was the next day when Myra, my mother-in-law, said Charles looked gravely ill. So they took him to an urgent care center. The nurse came out to talk and Grandpa Richard asked what was going on. They refused to tell him. He erupted in a you-have-to-be-kidding-me rant and demanded to know what was up with his grandson. There was no way he was going to walk out of there without information no matter how many HIPAA laws they were hiding behind.

"Mr. Rogers, we believe your grandson is going through withdrawal. We are not equipped to deal with that here. We'll give you the names of places to go."

So they went to the ER. In the waiting room, Charles laid his head on his grandmother's shoulder. When she told me this story, I remembered the most recent Thanksgiving when he had done the same. I was still doing my round of antibiotics for the deadly infections from my elbow surgery. The boys had followed me into the sunroom at my cousin's house while I infused big balls of antibiotics through my PICC line.

I remember thinking that my presence was needed in the kitchen to help my cousin clean up after the holiday meal. But I couldn't leave that rare moment. Charles fell asleep on my shoulder and Richard was engaged in deep conversation with me. Neither of them was on the phone texting or watching videos so I was riveted to the spot and in the moment. I felt warmth and love from my boys who had both grown up. So, yeah, I knew how Charles could lay his head on a shoulder and transport someone back to a time of innocence and love. I couldn't help but cry. My baby.

Charles had just turned twenty and he was an adult so there were many things we did not know. He was ashamed, and told the nurse he didn't want us or his grandparents to know he was addicted to heroin.

From there, his grandparents checked him into detox. It was for four days so it was our turn to find where he went after this. He couldn't just come home because he was not ready. We were not ready. I was on the phone two days straight figuring out insurance, next steps, and approvals. My husband and I finally had a plan not at all like the one we had made just a few days ago. How many times had this happened? Too many. But before it was drug abuse and now it was more. We had been unable to prevent this but we had delayed it. Would this help? I told myself it would. Why not? I needed to believe.

It was my job to tell him the next step would be rehab after detox. I worried that no matter what I said, it would not penetrate, like the time he had the impression therapeutic boarding school was like a college dorm despite my telling him differently. How were we going to avoid his having an epic meltdown? Was that possible?

After detox, my father-in-law drove Charles to Georgia from Florida, my husband picked Charles up in Georgia to go to the southwestern part of Virginia to a rehab facility there. I got feedback on the facility from my support group. Mixed reviews, but they assured me, like anything, it depended on where they were in their own minds with respect to using and recovery. A place is only as good as the person's mind-set going into it, and this was a challenging age that few facilities wanted to take on, in part due to the high relapse rates of this population. Those statistics don't look good on the back of a sales brochure.

I called Charles and outlined the next steps but it did not penetrate. I figured I'd text him as Randy approached so he was more prepared but it didn't prepare him at all and he had another Charles-style meltdown. Others had told me over the years that their child had tantrums, too, but when and if they were ever to witness one of Charles', they would quickly declare him the champion. Charles invested every ounce of his blockbuster passion in whatever emotion he was feeling at the moment. It had been an challenging couple of weeks and I longed to curl up in a cave until all of this settled but my husband was in the middle of it and had been driving many hours over two days. Stress had stretched our patience past the edges of ourselves but it was important that I not check out for a break right then.

Charles continued to make the plea that he had complete control, was going to stay clean, and showed no willingness to go into rehab. He was going to find a job, go to Narcotics Anonymous meetings, lead meetings, become the pillar of the recovery community, go to Africa to help the starving, and become a famous rap artist whose accomplishments would eclipse celebrated rapper Eminem.

My husband was doing this alone. Over the years we had had to tag team. But I made an error this time and should have been there with him. Charles' emotional storms could escalate so fast, we would get swept away in anger that would touch down like a tornado. It usually took hours for him to shrink from Incredible Hulk back to Bruce Banner. If and when he was cornered, his weapon was relentless badgering, and he was a pro.

Once it got started, he'd find any vulnerability he knew we had and repeat it over and over like an auctioneer on speed. If we were not in the room, he'd call or text incessantly with long diatribes of the unfairness of whatever boundary we'd set. He would make us feel as if whatever step we were trying to take was lunacy and would end up a failure. As much as I loved Charles, these emotional tsunamis were unbearable. Randy was trapped in a small space, a vehicle, with all that emotion directed at him with no escape.

I thought again about single parents. How hard it must be for a co-parenting couple or one where one person is responsible. Charles refused to go in. For more than seven hours he stayed in the truck and would not get out. My husband's voice, usually robust and lively, was almost inaudible over the phone.

If Charles was this adamant, the chances of this working were not great. I talked myself out of my defeatist attitude, reminding myself that it would help nothing. This was all we had. We didn't have an alternate plan and even now I'm not sure what Plan B would have been. Coming back to our house where we are ill equipped to handle something like this was not an option. Besides, we were about to put our house on the market. If we needed additional cash to help him, we'd have it. I was starting to feel as if I were in a race to get the house sold before it was too late.

Charles' age group was a population few facilities wanted, and this one had a bed and accepted our insurance. Besides that, he was in the same state as we were, which was rare. We worked out a plan that Randy would have to leave and let Charles decide whether he wanted to roam free in Southwest Virginia or go in and have a warm bed, food, and a tapering off of medication. The issue was how to get him out of the truck. We decided if it came to that, Randy would take Charles to the police station and ask them to remove him from the vehicle. Charles was unlikely to put up a fight. He was not physical even in meltdown mode. We hoped it would not come to that. I had to be there for my husband even if it was on the phone.

Their grand entrance had attracted a great deal of attention by now and a young man walked out of the facility and walked up to talk to Randy. He told my husband that Charles would soon start to feel the effects of withdrawal, that four days of medication just got someone out of the worst of it, but that they would continue the detox process when he was checked in. There was still a journey of pain to come. But once he was feeling bad again, we had a better chance of getting him in there.

We didn't know any of that.

The medication that had kept Charles feeling spunky in the truck started to wear off and as it happened, the edges of his anger lost its fangs. He simply didn't have the strength to go on once he was feeling sick again. The young man got into the vehicle with Charles and talked to him. He told Charles that soon he would start to hurt; inside there was relief, support, and a lot of others suffering as he was. Charles started to soften.

Ultimately, he did walk in with this young man to whom we were most grateful. My husband said it was the worst day of his life. At that point anyway.

When Charles called home that week, he screamed and shouted how much he hated it and how angry he was with us for putting him there. He wanted to come home and he kept asking, why couldn't he do that? No logical argument was sufficient. Withdrawal makes people very angry; it made Charles angry, for sure. I started to dread his calls, yet waited for them at the same time. Not one of them was pleasant until near the end of his stay. On one call, he was so chipper and upbeat that I almost didn't recognize who it was on the phone and stared at caller ID to make sure it was not an imposter. One decent call was all it took for a flicker of hope to come to full flame.

He wrote this to me in the final week in rehab, an 8 a.m. test on May 2, 2015:

I know you don't trust me a lot but I've actually turned over a new leaf for myself

I'm going to earn your trust back

I felt terrible these past couple days (I feel much better now) and it made me think

It made me hate myself

For the things I've done. I want to move forward I'm not sure exactly how but I know I'm not going to go back to taking OxyContin

It was an artificial happiness

I liked it because I didn't have to work for gratification and I didn't see the things it was making me do and how wrong they were until it was too late. I cried a lot in before the hospital and in the hospital

Withdrawal made me feel so alone

I was left with nothing but the guilt of my actions

I want to go over to a 3rd world country where they really need help

Like in Sudan where the civil war is

Or relief from the earthquake Nepal

I think I will feel better with myself by helping people that TRULY need my help

They have trips to go to places like that and I think after I help you get the house ready to be sold and earn you and dad's trust back

And show you I can be good

And I need to go to meetings

I could go over there and actually help

I've been watching a lot of movies

Where they help people in reform camps in Sudan something like that would make me feel good

I love you

He reached out to other kids at rehab, shared his rap lyrics, and encouraged them to get out from under the covers and go to meetings. Charles was a great cheerleader. Everyone loved how his writing expressed their feelings, too. In one of the groups, a young lady asked to borrow his notebook as people often did. She ended up checking out of the facility and, as the story goes, she lay the notebook on her bed and asked her roommate to make sure Charles got it back. But that never happened.

Multiple calls later to the facility turned up nothing. I tried reaching the young lady who had borrowed the notebook—Charles had messaged her on Facebook—and she said she didn't know where it was and told me she had put it on the bed. He wanted that notebook back. I wanted him to get it back and after he died I was possessed with tracking it down.

He'd had that particular notebook throughout his therapeutic boarding school stay, detox, and rehab, and it was filled from front to back. But Charles never saw it again. And neither did we. I mourn the loss of that one in particular, and I hope it's helping someone. I can't bear the thought of it having been thrown away.

CHAPTER 30

HELL ON EARTH

TRIGGER WARNING:
Self harm and suicide method mentioned

Lyrics by Charles Aubrey Rogers, aka Reezin' the Revolutionary, YouTube

We were created equal
*   There should never be kings amongst people*
Where's the balance between good and evil
Why were we created from our roots to be deceitful?

Bred to be lethal, death is the end
I guarantee there ain't a sequel
Theories of a fantastic instance
To keep us separated from fear of nonexistence

Holocaust, genocide, puppet to a government
Livin' lies,
this is 1984 re-visualized
A 17-year-old with a rope around his neck
Because he's just so sick of livin' life

DIARY OF A BROKEN MIND

Girl's wrist slit with a knife
Mid-40s a man digs a ditch for his wife
That he killed by surprise

One act of emotion
can send it all in a backward motion
As black as the back of the ocean
As natural as change
Is natural erosion, chemical corrosion
Missiles explodin',
take a chance and roll the dice
Let's take a look at life through this criminal's eyes

What if Titanic missed the ice?
What if Osama did it twice?
Took the buildings plus a bigger price
And God just missed it
Like, he loves us
But doesn't care for our position,
He loves us
But he'll send us to hell for one wrong decision
I guess the love is somethin' that I'm missin'

Led by crooked cops
and twisted politicians
Misery or happiness,
choose your nutrition
If there's a God where is he?
I tried to pray but the line was busy
Welcome to America the free land
Free for Wall Street
and the suits on C-SPAN
Free for the rich man

Religion starts wars,
but so does ignorance
Greed and the God with the world is belligerent
Change is comin',
Ain't shit different
Recession, depression,

Hell on Earth

this human disease infection
No hope for a cure,
fuck a research session
Come on teacher,
teach your lesson

These are my words,
Mark this
Live with meaning before death forever
Eternal darkness,
peace at last,
no more hardships
Hard to comprehend in the human mind
Impossible to envision leaving yourself behind

Nothin' is for sure,
I can't prove it
But you've only got one,
why waste it before you lose it?
I'm searchin' for beauty in the dark
and music is my spark
In the shadows I can almost see it,
feel it
I'm close,
but I feel alone and scared
I turn on the light
and nothing's ever there
This world is desolate and cold

"Go to school, Charles,"
Do what you're told
and hope that your cycle
Of reality never gets old,
'cuz one day everything
You know and love will collapse and fold

World War Three is already here,
neo-Nazis, KKK
And government-bred fear
Lock yourself in your house

with your bread and your beer
And pray to your gods
that the world doesn't end this year

I scream into the clouds
but nobody hears
A little boy shot for rockin' the wrong colors
Raised to think that thugs were his brothers
Daddy's dead, who's gonna tuck you under the covers?
Dark and alone, hell is in the place and it's home

Quick, Franny, run,
Poppa screamed when he saw the gun
Watched as they shot his son,
he lost it after that
'Cuz that was all he had
No more little boy callin' him Dad
And his wife died four years back
Who dreamed of becoming a dancer
Came so close
but lost her life to terminal cancer

You'll make it,
you can push through
But he never got to hear her answer
She made him promise to look after their son
And make sure he hangs out with the right kids
He said, "Of course,"
but forgot to comprehend
How fucked up life is,
now he watches his son
Lowered into the ground next to where his wife is
He had everything he'd ever wanted
and didn't neglect it
Remember, life can crush your perfect world in under a second

So if you got somethin' good
You better respect it,
hold your world and protect it
The only thing guaranteed in life is death

Hell on Earth

And everything looks sweeter
When you haven't any life left

This is hell on earth,
we dwell in a curse
Mutter words,
please never get worse
Pray havin' the curse,
Can't fathom unbirth
Fear of havin' the berm
and leavin' this earth
Drownin' in fear,
if hell's a place
Then we're already here

Who busted the locks off Pandora's box?
Famine, disease, war and violence
Women as slaves,
masking their face in foreign countries
While the world sits in silence
Crack, drugs, pimps and dope,
but through all the terror
I can catch beauty and a glimpse of hope.

I saw this song before he died when he was at Wasatch, the nontherapeutic boarding school in Utah from which he had graduated.

These parts in particular were chilling and I didn't know what to make of it:

A 17-year-old with a rope around his neck
Because he's just so sick of livin' life

and:

So if you got somethin' good
You better respect it,

hold your world and protect it
The only thing guaranteed in life is death
And everything looks sweeter
When you haven't any life left

I was stunned at the content that scared me, and awed by his talent. Those conflicting emotions would hit at the same time and I would freeze. I tried to have a discussion with him about this song, too, but was dismissed.

The volume on conversation about suicide was not turned up high in 2015, at least not on my radio. It's so painful to know he had displayed classic textbook signs of suicide and I was unaware. The crying at the beginning of this song on YouTube indicated depression. So when I saw it, I ached that I could not hold my child and make the bad go away. The monster under the bed was now living in his head.

About three days after he died, I was sitting at my dining room table with friend Karen and we watched this video on YouTube. It was like I was seeing it for the first time.

These passages jumped in my face and told me how stupid I was to miss such obvious clues.

All from the lens of "after."

CHAPTER 31

SATURDAY CHARLES

This world is crushing me but I lift the weight,
Look at a star with a different face you'll see tomorrow
The world will be a better place.
—*Silver Lining,* by Charles Aubrey Rogers, on SoundCloud

Insurance released him from rehab after three weeks so we didn't get the benefit of even the meager extra week. Cured, time to go home. I was sorry because it was in the last week he had started to like it, get into it, and share his rap lyrics with the other patients. The recovery process had just taken hold when he was tossed back into a chaotic world he wasn't prepared for yet.

According to the rehab center, he was a model patient other than his phone calls to me, and he got an award from the center as well as a sendoff party. Only Charles would have become so popular so fast. Only Charles could touch so many so quickly. I knew he needed more time there: at least that extra week, but ideally three months.

While he was in detox and rehab, I had not told many people what was going on. No one was asking anyway. Few had asked about

Charles for years. When I talked about him, people would change the subject and ask about Richard.

On a walk we took together around the neighborhood one day, I told my friend Karen I was not sure he would make it. She listened without judgement. Charles was so fragile and opiates such an evil epidemic. It was bigger than him and the rest of us. Meanwhile, getting a home on the market was a life event with additional stress. This would free up some funds as we were out of money. Most of the expensive things we did were not covered by insurance and were paid for out of pocket or by a home equity loan. I had become a pro at selling items online to support our depleted checking and savings accounts. Would the house sell in time to help Charles? He had that ridiculous court case coming up. After the long arm of the law reached into my son's pants and I found out about the police stalking incidents, I wanted out of that county.

We made it clear to Charles that we loved him no matter what, and supported recovery and good health. After rehab, we decided to pay for a room for Charles in a recovery house. I couldn't take more sketchy strangers in the house and drugs delivered to my driveway in the wee hours of the morning. His cooking at 2 a.m. with the stove burners left on, and alarms from a smoke-filled kitchen were putting our lives at jeopardy. Allowing him behind the wheel of a car was putting our neighbors at risk.

No longer could I tolerate being tired from the dog reacting to the stranger with Charles outside, strange noises in and around the house, doors left open, strange spills, vomit on the floor, mystery holes in the wall, and surprise visits from police. At a point, our own lives needed separation from chaos.

This opiate addiction was beyond us and peer support is known to be more effective. We had already made the decision of no Suboxone because the recovery houses wouldn't take residents who were on it. We wanted him to do the Vivitrol implant. We knew it took away cravings but so far he was refusing to do it. Getting Charles to agree to anything that might involve needles was always a no. Final no. He never used a needle for heroin and I heard from others he didn't even like watching others shoot up.

We went back and forth on Suboxone. Randy called someone to get his opinion and I did the same. There were no really good studies on Medication-Assisted Treatment (MAT) in 2015 that I could find. By 2018, studies revealed that MAT patients have higher survival rates. A leading detox expert I interviewed in 2018, Dr. Peter Coleman, had said in his experience, his younger patients benefitted from longer-term use of Suboxone. Dr. Coleman would do the Suboxone, sometimes for years for some of his teen and young adult patients, to keep them alive until they had the opportunity to develop the emotional maturity to work a recovery program. Then he'd follow up with a kinder detox off Suboxone, do the Vivitrol implant once they had been referred to a recovery program. In his experience, the Vivitrol implant wouldn't work if you weren't committed to recovery. And people of that age rarely are.

One of those arguments is probably likely to remain controversial, and we were trying to make this decision with little experience, time, and limited outside counsel. The rehab center was not making any specific recommendations. I don't think it was for any other reason than the epidemic was stretching existing resources to the breaking point. In short, no one had time because so many patients were flooding into the communities.

Randy insisted on picking him up from rehab in the southwestern part of the state. He had intended to take him straight to the recovery house as advised but came by the house first because he had forgotten the checkbook he needed to put a down payment for rent. He called me at a stop on the road, elated over how good Charles looked compared to the last time. Both were in such good spirits, it was infectious.

He and Charles came in the door and my boy looked fantastic. He was happy and lively. The dog was going crazy, he was so happy to see Charles, and Charles was equally as thrilled to see Andy. I am sorry there is no photo of him that day, but I was drunk with love and relief: too in the moment to snap a picture. But I have that image burned on my retina and remember the untucked buffalo plaid shirt he was wearing.

He was beaming and telling jokes again. How subtle and slow the changes had been while he had become addicted. God, how I'd missed this version of him. How he made me laugh that day was a throwback to earlier days when he'd have us all doubled over, grabbing at the arms of furniture to remain propped up for fear of falling over laughing. No one could think on the spot the way he could and tell jokes that were perfect for the audience in front of him. His gift was timing. And it was a gift. Slowly my son had been taken over by heroin, and now my child was back. My underlying feeling of panic evaporated, and we were still blissfully unaware he was using heroin. We still thought it was pills, and no one had told us any differently.

Later, I would refer to him on this day as "Saturday Charles." I can see him now, sitting in the chair across from the sofa, telling me about all his future plans. Then he told me about the increase in hepatitis and AIDS cases that had sprung from the heroin epidemic and about some of the people at the facility in Galax. He told me how many loved his music and had promised to download his album. He shared so many stories with us that day, and I know that Charles had made a lasting impression. He was unforgettable, and I have run into people who had met him during his stay there who make the effort to mention it.

Randy and I couldn't help but feel good: his hug such welcome relief from the toxic stress that had defined our lives. There had been so little joy in the last several months and years that we were starved for it. Adamant, Charles told me he was going to leave opiates behind forever.

I didn't think it was going to be that easy for him. That I did know. I didn't dwell on it, for the sake of enjoying the moment. Some hope had been restored and I wanted to freeze him and this moment right where it was so I could tuck it away and savor it.

Randy told Charles it was time to go and he said he needed to get some shirts upstairs. As he packed the extra clothing items, Randy and I reveled in the lullaby of that happy moment.

Before they left to get checked into his new temporary residence, Charles said he wanted us all to go to lunch the next day and we made plans to do just that. Charles loved his family so much.

Randy and Charles arrived at the recovery house and listened to all the rules, and then he and Randy went to the grocery store to stock up on food. Randy then told Charles we would be by the next day to pick him up for lunch, and left.

He looked so good, sounded so good. I slept well that night for the first time in months. Mindfulness CDs littered my bedside-table drawer but I didn't need them then. I was so excited to see my son the next day I could hardly wait.

CHAPTER 32

FORGIVE ME MOMMA

Lyrics by Charles Aubrey Rogers, aka Reezin' the Revolutionary,
YouTube, Anne Moss Rogers reciting lyrics

I *just want to apologize for all my lies*
and all the times you stayed up at night traumatized
from when I said I wanna die,
When we argued, screamed and cried

I used to wonder if it was possible
for a soul to bleed inside
I was trapped in the dark,
But I see the light
Your love would never budge,
even when I would scream and cuss,
puke and get drunk.

I wasn't raised that way,
I know it cut like razor blades.
But you never ever fade away,

DIARY OF A BROKEN MIND

But Ima graduate,
I'm get this paper made,[1]
every dreamer needs a believer
and I'm paving the way

(Refrain)
Forgive me momma,
I tried the fast life and got addicted momma
Forgive me momma
I wish I was different momma
Forgive me momma

My actions were ugly,
teenage druggie,
looking for anything to numb me,
pathetic, scummy.
But you still love me.
I would cry when I wanna die
and you would hug me.

I was so angry when you sent me away,
in my own personal hell to stay.
I hated every day,
put me off on layaway
cause you were terrified by the way I lived my life.
I was still your little kid inside,
the same little boy who said Momma, "I lost my tooth,"
was the same kid saying I need bail from you,
I failed you.
It hurts but that the truth
I got worth to proof,
I know you love me
and I love you too.
You're my mom,
the only one I'll ever have,
I'm sorry I was bad,
all the tears I could sit in a bath,

---

1   Charles' reference to "getting the paper made" indicates he wrote this
while in Georgia with his grandparents when he was finishing up his high school
diploma online. I believe he wrote this on Mother's Day.

Forgive Me Momma

I'm sorry Mom,
I'm sorry Dad.

(Refrain)
Forgive me momma,
I tried the fast life and got addicted momma
Forgive me momma
I wish I was different momma
Forgive me momma

Apologize for the dirty words of my songs,
you didn't raise me wrong.
But anger blinds and burns strong.
I remember when you told me Cal tied that rope,
tears flushed your face
and sobs choked in your throat.
I sat in silence,
refused to show any expression of pain,
my brain played the same sad note
but I kept it bottled up
and never spoke except the raps I wrote.
It hurt and no one was supposed to know,
when everything leaves,
all you have is hope.
All you have is family.
I took that for granted and I can't stand it.

(Refrain)
Forgive me momma,
I tried the fast life and got addicted momma
Forgive me momma
I wish I was different momma
Forgive me momma[2]

---

2   This one is on YouTube but I'm actually the one reading it. It was close to the first anniversary of his death, and I wanted to share it. Of course, it's my favorite..

It's hard to fathom how my cute, bubbly fun little child turned into a
teen who suffered so much emotional pain.

CHAPTER 33

RELAPSE

Friends stick around like bleach stains
Just call me dude, we don't speak names,
*   cause when my product leak through each of your veins you feel the*
release of pain,
*   Now pay up 'cause I need the same."*
—*What these drugs do,* by Charles Aubrey Rogers

We called on our way to pick Charles up for lunch and he said he was taking a walk. It was a beautiful day so I didn't blame him. He loved being outside. We arrived at the sober house, eager to see the bubbly, fun "Saturday Charles" again. It had been intoxicating the previous day.

The house was neat and quite nice. The house manager didn't know where Charles was, and we took a tour.

Charles had texted that he went to the river and got lost. He had zero sense of direction and, like me, couldn't find his way out of a box with breadcrumbs and a ladder. He should have been back, though.

We were texting and calling, but he wasn't answering. I noticed the house manager, Lee, was equally as confused, and I thought he was thinking something and I am not sure I wanted to know.

Where was he? Finally, he called.

Awesome. He is fine.

He told his dad he was at a McDonald's on Commerce Street. The house manager's eyebrows shot up. I read his reaction and tried to calm myself. I think, again, "It's fine. He's fine." But I wondered what he was reacting to, and I buried those sparks of concern because I was still high on the love from the day before, not willing to be pushed back into angst.

My husband and I went to pick him up for lunch. At McDonald's, before we go to lunch? We got there and my husband insisted he should go in but couldn't find him. We finally got a text saying he was in the bathroom because his stomach hurt. "Post-withdrawal symptoms," he told his dad through the bathroom door.

In the car we waited. And waited. And waited. With each moment, the anxiety intensified. After about thirty minutes, he came out not looking at all like "Saturday Charles." In fact, he looked as if he'd slept in the trunk of the car the night before. He got into the back seat and again said he was suffering post-withdrawal. Randy and I were both alarmed and confused.

On the way to the restaurant, which was not far, Charles kept falling asleep, and alarms in my head were triggered. What is this? He kept blaming everything on post-withdrawal and I didn't know if it was true or not. I hadn't researched this part.

I tried to look up information on my phone but grew frustrated and abandoned the idea. I'd seen him doze off like this on my deck that day about a year before, and one time when we went to dinner. "The nods," but I didn't have that phrase.

We arrived at Crossroads Restaurant in the Forest Hill area and parked the car. Charles still felt nauseated, and I let him lean on me on the way in. I wasn't sure what to think but it didn't matter, I wanted him to lean on me. We ordered and got our food.

Charles kept saying what a great cheese sandwich it was. He repeated himself a lot. Something was wrong. We were seated outside when he turned his head and threw up on the ground. Then he said, "Sorry," turned back around and continued to eat as if nothing had happened. Randy and I stopped eating and stared at each other. *What should we do? Is this really "post-withdrawal?"*

The waitress came out and didn't look happy. The diners nearby were not so happy either. I was sure they were not, but there was a bigger issue for me, except that I was not sure what it was. He was not right but we didn't know what was wrong. Post-withdrawal? Drugs? But he had no money. So it couldn't be that, right?

We dropped him off back at the recovery house. I hugged him and he told me he loved me. He hugged his dad and said the same. It was our last hug and, as always, the feeling of that embrace offered temporary reprieve for whatever was ailing me. Randy and I talked on the way home about what was up with him and then we got a call from the house manager. "Did you guys notice anything weird about Charles?" We had to say yes.

My organs tied themselves up like a washcloth being twisted and wrung out. The house manager said he was going to drug test him. Charles could never pee on demand. When he got anxious, he couldn't go, or wouldn't go. I'm not sure which. They were pumping fluids into him, and no pee.

We waited for hours, went to bed, and woke up the next morning to the house manager call, saying, "It's dirty," meaning he tested positive for Benzodiazepines (Xanax) and opiates (heroin or Oxycodone) plus other drugs and addictive substances that dealers of street drugs put in the mix. Still we are unaware he had been addicted to heroin and not just the little white pills.

It had been less than twenty-four hours, and he had relapsed. Randy immediately had a eureka moment, and blamed himself.

He had brought Charles home from rehab to the house for the checkbook, even though he had been advised to take him straight to the recovery house. He figured Charles must've had money stashed in his room. That was how he was able to buy drugs. It must have been why they recommended he go straight to the recovery house from rehab. Charles had walked the four miles downtown to score drugs. Randy was beating himself up and I tried to talk him out of it. I would never have seen "Saturday Charles" had he not stopped by. If he was determined, he would have figured out how to score drugs, and obviously he did.

The recovery house policy was to take him somewhere but he couldn't stay there. It was a sober house, after all. He was cleared at the hospital and they took him to the psychiatric hospital. They turned him down because he was a drug addict. The response they had was, "We don't take those patients anymore."

So where do you take a child with mental illness and addiction for acute care? Since he was now over eighteen, they took him to The Healing Place in Richmond, a place where people with nothing left go for recovery and, surprisingly, it's one of the most successful programs in the country. Not a country club and at the time, only a few whose lives were at risk from withdrawal qualified for medical detox. The others had to gut it out because funding would only go so far. With just one hit, I thought withdrawal wouldn't be that bad. We let them handle it because we had no idea what to do. Lee, the recovery house manager, called or sent texts with updates frequently. This was our first rodeo with the disease of addiction. Later I would learn it was not unusual for kids this age who were addicted to opiates to be in and out of rehab seven or eight times before finding recovery for any length of time.

He was checked in and about to go back when someone he knew walked out of the bathroom. Charles and this friend, Mac, talked. The house manager had to leave us because he had to be at work. He had gone above and beyond as it was, and we were grateful.

Later, The Healing Place called Lee and told him that Charles had walked out with his friend. Lee couldn't believe the odds of him seeing someone he knew, the only person he actually saw, as a matter of fact. He wondered if it was a coincidence and later I found out that it was.

Relapse

We were stunned, frightened, and our crushed souls ached for those fleeting but previous "Saturday Charles" hours. To date, no one had taken more time to explain what was going on than Lee had. He was straightforward and honest, and we were thankful for the information he provided.

We didn't know where Charles was. But when he texted us earlier he was mad. "The test is wrong," he said, and they were sabotaging his effort to be clean. This was not true, of course. Manipulation is such a frustrating part of the disease and I had gotten past feeling betrayed and violated by the lies. Getting emotionally worked up about being lied to was akin to getting mad at a diabetic for having low blood sugar.

We were outside when the house manager called and told us we needed to know something. He told us it was not OxyContin Charles was addicted to, but heroin. And because they mix Xanax with it, he was addicted to that, too.

He had no needle marks because he snorted it. I had no idea you could snort it. I kept thinking there was some way to stop him from getting to heroin and it turned out that's what he'd been using for eleven months. Or was it longer than that?

The addiction was so new and recent. I had been reading like crazy but there was so much to learn. I failed in self-care at this time, and didn't go to my support group where I could have gotten answers to at least some of these questions. Why did I abandon the one thing that had been working for me at the time when I needed it most? I didn't know "the nods" and the vomiting were signs. This was like fighting an invisible monster and I had crawled back into isolation, especially as I was focused on getting the house on the market.

All these years of struggle with sleep disorder, ADHD, depression, and drug abuse, and now a full-blown heroin addiction. Charles told us at some point, way in the past, that smoking pot "wasn't like he was doing heroin." And here we were.

Now I didn't know where he was, or who he was with. Randy said he thought he was down at VCU with his old buddies. I let him hold on to that fantasy. I knew that's not where he was and my heart sank. I was a wreck. Premonitions were assaulting me, and I was not feeling confident he would live through this, which left me feeling desperate, immobile, and incapable of making logical and informed decisions.

I begged in silence to whoever might be listening to spare my child. *Please spare my child.*

CHAPTER 34

HOLLOW MAN

Lyrics by Charles Aubrey Rogers, aka Reezin' the Revolutionary

*S*o many things I've seen
   but empty at only 18
and I wake up midscream
only to discover I wasn't even asleep

I'm just a fuckin' freak,
I'm just a fuckin' creep
Waiting for the day to end
so I can try and fall asleep
Failure gets to me
and hurts deep
Sobriety doesn't work for me,
it hurts to breathe,
escape packin' perks in my cheeks,
I'm awkward
nervously,
not my heart

DIARY OF A BROKEN MIND

I wear my fucking shirt on my sleeve,
keep it all hidden purposely
cause talking shit out
don't work for me

(Refrain)
I'm a hollow man
Shell of a person
Drown sorry with the alcohol I swallow
Damn
It's hard to feel when you're hollow man
I'm hope it's better tomorrow
Damn

I want a life without pain,
I want to like every day
My own place to stay
where I can escape the rain

Sometimes I think I won't make it
and my dreams a fake,
I'll end up broke,
a laughing stock joke beggin' for money to make
that'll spend on coke or cigs leak soaked
so I can hide my misery in an overcoat
till I finally go and croak

But no, this ain't no suicide note
It's a reminder that this is do or die yo
Cause I know I'm dope,
put my soul in every rap I ever wrote

Music fills my empty,
makes my hollow float
To the tops where I gotta go,
I won't choke,
But it's so painful
I gotta smoke
but even after I swallow
the high goes

Hollow Man

and the hollow flows
and swallows whole

(Refrain)
I'm a hollow man
Shell of a person
Drown sorry with the alcohol I swallow
Damn
It's hard to feel when you're hollow man
I'm hope it's better tomorrow
Damn

Friends left,
some I'll never see again
I wrote so cold that it freeze my pen,
No one listens to real rap,
they want mainstream trap crap
It ain't easy pleasin' them

But I bet when I'm deceased,
at peace when my final season ends,
they'll listen then and say
ain't another rapper dope as reezin is or was,
cause I'll be done with the dust
unable to feel the love

Right now I'm just lost in the drugs
and I don't follow God
cause who could allow the holocaust
and all this blood,
you call that love?
I call it neglect,
my father taught me respect,
then how come I still feel hollow as death
When I got a family
and I'm obviously blessed
I'm still poppin' X
to arrest the stress
Fuck who got now,
I found solace in my promise

DIARY OF A BROKEN MIND

that I'll follow up next

So be happy,
fuck wallowin' depressed
Cause life without purpose
is just a useless tomorrow till death

CHAPTER 35

SHARING THE NEWS WITH RICHARD

My brain is on fast forward and rewind at the exact same time.
—*Wilderness Suicide Lyrics*, by Charles Aubrey Roger

The night Charles died, we called our loved ones to share the tragic news. Both sets of parents said they would be at our house the next afternoon (June 6, 2015). Fortunately, the house we had just sold four days prior to Charles' death would be our home for another four weeks.

The last person we called the night we found out (June 5, 2015) was Richard, who was twenty-two at the time and living in Winston Salem, North Carolina. He had just graduated from the University of North Carolina School of the Arts with a degree in filmmaking. We knew he stayed up later than both sets of parents whom we had started to call at 9:30 p.m.

Prior to that, dialing a phone was a challenge for which we weren't capable. We found out at about 7:30 p.m., and I had to tell his girlfriend first, a heartbreaking, gut-wrenching call as yet another person experienced the stab of loss and guilt that follows a suicide. It took me a while to recover. She had broken up with him, but I know it didn't mean she did not love him still. We have never blamed her at all. In fact, I'm thankful he had had the opportunity to fall in love in his short life. Twice. She had her own recovery to think about, not getting sucked back in to the depravity.

We called Richard at about 11:30 p.m. and I told him his brother had died by suicide. His first reaction was, "Oh, no."

Without missing a beat, Richard said, "You guys are great parents. I love you both. You did everything you could and I tried, too. Charles and I were raised in the same house by the same parents and I don't see anything you did wrong. You helped him as much as he could be helped. You couldn't know he'd kill himself."

I know he said more but that's the part I'll always remember. I was amazed by the wisdom that came tumbling out of the mouth of my twenty-two-year-old son at a time when we needed it most. He was so calm and collected, as if something had taken over him. For the second time that day, I was shocked, but this time it was good shock, and I was stunned into silence.

The worst part about the suicide of my child was that I felt as if I had failed at the one thing most important in the world to me: seeing my child successfully ushered into adulthood. I had hoped wilderness, therapeutic boarding school, and rehab would help Charles build a toolbox to manage his depression, and successfully bridge the gap from adolescence to thriving adulthood. That's not what happened. And what had happened was far worse than any tragedy I could have dreamed up.

Charles did not do this because he didn't love us but simply because his brain betrayed him and made him think no one would care if he died. To his sick brain, he thought death was his only option from the physical pain of withdrawal, the emotional pain of his depression, and addiction.

The rap diaries offered me the insight I needed to understand. So I was not left without answers. His soul is there on those pages and I feel it when I read his words, listen to his raps, or watch his videos. That's a precious gift. He was a precious gift.

And on the worst day of my life, someone told me I was a good parent and it happened to be the other most important person in the world to us: one who had grown up in our household.

I did torture myself still. But I would also replay what Richard said in my head when I hurt the most, and it did help me pull it together and face the day. Sometimes it was the only thing I could grab on to. After Charles' death, I called Richard, often in racking sobs when I was at my lowest. I didn't hide my ugly, naked pain. He never once tried to talk me out of my tears, scold me for my grief, or try to escape. He was unusually patient and comfortable with it.

I always took a couple of minutes or so and we would both talk about Charles and then I wanted him to tell me all about what he was doing. And that's what he did: told me about his short film and his latest work project. I just listened and let his conversation and his passion for film sweep me away to somewhere else. A lot of adults I ran into after it happened didn't give me that minute to talk about Charles but talked all around the subject. I know it's out of fear of saying the wrong thing. It's also so close. No one wants to imagine this kind of loss, which left me feeling isolated and ostracized. Some people even tried to talk me out of my grief because they were uncomfortable with it.

But not Richard. How did he know to let me have that time?

The death of his brother fast-forwarded his maturity. Because I had focused so much on my youngest, saving his life, I left my eldest to fend for himself, he who was in college most of that time, and that delivered another stab of parental guilt. In retrospect, I could see that something remarkable had happened. Richard had grown up. The kid who was once less mature for his grade level had leapfrogged ahead of most of his peers.

He has struggled with anger and frustration and the "How could you do this to us?" more than I have, which is understandable and natural. Richard had grand plans to move to Los Angeles right after graduating from college to live his dream as a filmmaker but was left so stunned by his brother's suicide he was unable to make that move for another two years. He shared with me later that this was his brother's gift. By staying in Winston-Salem for those years, he was able to gain more experience in film editing at a local firm, and build lasting relationships that later gave him a stream of income that would sustain him when he did move to Los Angeles. He shared with me that when strangers would ask, "Do you have any brothers and sisters?" he answered, "No." They then asked, "So you are an only child?" And he said, "No," again. He told me he is OK with talking to friends about it but it's too heavy a conversation to go into with someone you've just met. I had to chuckle at how confused someone must be when he hears those responses. Richard must come across as mysterious. My eldest is the family introvert and when he tells me these stories, I think how hard it must be that his only sibling killed himself.

While I don't feel Richard has fully grasped "addiction is a disease" or even Charles' clinical depression, he's making an effort to understand, and it's a learning process. I can't usher him through that journey. I have to allow him to move through it at his pace with no lectures, just listening and asking questions.

When life started to get really chaotic and Charles was calling Richard and having long conversations about party drugs and rap music—two subjects the older brother was not into—he had to create a boundary. Conversations had become a one-way street. He wasn't asking about what Richard was doing and as a result, they grew apart. Like us, Richard didn't understand his brother's disease or his obsession, and was frustrated. He tried to help, to steer the conversation and his brother's interests in other directions. I remember doing the same when I went to college, my own brother having struggled with drugs and alcohol as a teenager and young adult. At some point I had to make a life for myself that was separate from the bedlam that was then my family. When one child goes off the rails, the family dynamic shifts. I, too, had to minimize my exposure and become more independent as a result of what was happening in our family, so it was easy for me to recognize that Richard had to do the same.

Richard had just graduated from college and was excited to start his new life and pursue his passion as a filmmaker. He had just achieved his greatest accomplishment since learning how to walk, and this was followed two weeks later by the worst thing to ever happen to our family. It did indeed force him to stop and regroup, as it did all of us. Until he read the first draft of this book, he had forgotten how close he and Charles had been growing up. He hadn't understood what we had gone through as parents, and our frustration with the lack of help from a broken mental health system. Seeing the whole story laid out helped him understand.

Richard (white shirt), Randy to his right, and both sides of our family at his college graduation from the UNC School of the Arts.

CHAPTER 36

BALLAD OF AN ADDICT'S SORROW

Lyrics by Charles Aubrey Rogers, aka Reezin' the Revolutionary

I put my whole life to a waste
  from this high that I chase
    My mother hates the sight of my face
Say my name and you'll choke on the taste

My girl say she love me
but act like she don't give a fuck if she dumped me
My soul is so ugly,
I ain't nothing but a junkie
Or a least that's what my father said

All I know is that God is dead
I fell to rock bottom
and landed on top of my head
Sick of cops and the fed
Oxycontin is like oxygen,

DIARY OF A BROKEN MIND

I snort train rocks till the pain stops
And my nostril is dripping with red
I tried stopping
And did the opposite instead
Being harassed by officers
the second I pop out my bed
Was gonna finish college
But I dropped out instead

CHAPTER 37

GRIEF WRITES ME
A LETTER

I know you love me and I love you too.
You're my mom, the only one I'll ever have,
I'm sorry I was bad, all the tears I could sit in a bath,
I'm sorry Mom, I'm sorry Dad.
—*Forgive me momma,* by Charles Aubrey Rogers

Dear Anne Moss,

I came on strong at the beginning and want you to know, I didn't mean to hurt you. You stumbled numb through those first days and months because I had to protect you. One can take only so much pain and agony at once. I watched you in your agonized moments knowing that these would be building blocks to emotional healing. You suffered under my weight and tried unsuccessfully to lift it yourself when you tired of it. But I have a mind of my own, and just when you thought you couldn't take another minute, I would drift away.

At first, you thought moving forward or "getting better" meant getting past me. But then you learned it was about incorporating me into your life in a way we could live together. I will never go away because I represent the love you have for your child. I am the reminder he lived, and loved you. I hope you understand I'm not the nasty, bad thing people make me out to be. I'm not something people should avoid or be ashamed of either. I'm not a "weakness." Quite frankly, I don't know where that comes from.

You feared this journey because it was so foreign to you. For some reason, people think that's what they are supposed to do. The fear of not knowing what lies ahead or how to manage life going forward is part of the reason people try to avoid me.

How do you keep a job? How do you stay married? How do you do normal life? How do you make it through birthdays or the holidays? How can you survive the pain? How do you answer the question, "How many children do you have?" You just do because you have no other choice.

As you travel the path to healing, I will inspire you to do things you would never have done, meet people you would have never have met and help you become someone you never knew you could become. You'll be stronger for having had me in your life because I make life matter more, and this agonizing experience can transform you from an ordinary human being into an extraordinary one. That's your son's gift to you in death.

I am sorry loss has to hurt so much but the path to joy is often through intense pain. Remember, I didn't take Charles away. I'm the one who reminds you he lived.

I'm part of life. But most of all, I am love.

Yours Truly and Always in your Heart,
GRIEF

CHAPTER 38

THE DAY AFTER

I'm low, so low, in a boat to hell in myself as it rows. I'm low, as low as it goes.
—*So Low*, by Charles Aubrey Rogers, SoundCloud

The day after Charles' suicide, I opened my eyes. The unforgiving agony of loss ground itself in my face, and the weight of it pinned me to the mattress. Nature's anesthesia—numbness—had not kicked in to offer protection. I was left naked and vulnerable to the full-body assault of grief in the sunrise that yanked me out of fitful sleep and showed me the day would happen, no matter what. There was no fast-forward button. The rest of the world would go on despite my tragedy. How could it do that? Neighbors were probably drinking coffee or sleeping in, not yet aware our hearts were under siege and the kid who had orchestrated a hundred games in our cul-de-sac was dead.

I was the mother of a child who killed himself. That truth was woven with razor wire and had written itself into my autobiography overnight.

My husband and I held each other, sobbing, and the persistent "coulda, woulda, shouda" ritual began to run on autopilot, as it would for most of the first year after he died. *How would we tell people our child is dead? How does anyone in this state of mind plan a funeral?* The thought of getting dressed in itself was overwhelming; how would all the rest happen? And we had sold the house: We had to pack it up and move, too. On the days when my premonitions wouldn't stop—the day the morbid list was written—I had prayed for Charles not to die before we moved and got settled. I had once prayed that my child would stop abusing drugs. On this morning, I prayed for endurance. *Give me the strength to see myself through this nightmare.*

I will survive this. I will. Believing it is the first step.

There is no easy way out of a loss of this magnitude. There is no avoiding it or skipping around it, and I had to feel the pain in order to have the incentive to pull myself through it. In short, I couldn't heal if I couldn't feel; numbing myself would only prolong the agony.

In my lifetime, I had suffered a broken neck, and survived attempted rape and murder, a near strike by lightning, a benign brainstem tumor, two craniotomies, and radiation treatment. I had flatlined on the table during a diagnostic procedure, and contracted two deadly infections following elbow surgery. The most devastating of all, though, was losing my son to suicide. Asking myself, "Why me?" only fosters bitterness.

Did those earlier incidents help build my resilience? They had to have. So went the process of pushing myself forward at a time when the desire to curl up and fade away pulled at me at every step.

I had not yet called Martha, my best friend since first grade, to deliver the news, as it had been too late the previous night. She worked with autistic kids, something that took considerable physical strength with the more disabled students; by Friday she was usually wiped out. At 5 a.m., it was too early still. My mind started to churn and a spark of inspiration told me to check Charles' phone records. Grief turned into determination as the desire to fill in the blanks of my son's final story propelled me forward. Perhaps the last phone number he had called would provide answers.

The morning after the most devastating news of our lives, we had an appointment to look at houses. Others might think this was crazy but being in motion was crucial to my being up at all. Out-of-town family would not be arriving until the afternoon and the fear of us being alone in that house with recurrent tidal waves of hurt was paralyzing. The house tour would be a distraction from unrelenting pain before my family and friends could fill the house and support me because life right then was too heavy. I also needed to know where I was going to land. A child's death by suicide combined with nowhere to live was too much uncertainty. Lee Anne, my real estate agent and first cousin from my mother's side, wouldn't be coming to get us for another three hours.

A wave of panic seized my lungs and turned my mouth to sandpaper as I held my phone to call the last number Charles had called, listed on the Verizon website. That fear was followed by grief that took me to the floor for the fifth time that morning.

How could Charles do this? Didn't he say he hated suicide? And how the hell did the kid—one who once had to ask friends to put together a tent—figure out how to fashion an instrument of death in the state of mind he was in? Who found him? Where had he been living exactly? Would I ever get answers? Where is his phone?

I thought about the child who would cuddle up to me with warmth and love. I took a deep breath, and thought for a second about what I was going to ask this person when they answered. If they answered. *Oh, please answer.*

A young man did answer the phone and I explained that Charles had killed himself and I saw that his number was the last one he had called. There was no blame meted out; all I wanted were some answers. His suspicions softened, and he began to talk. He met Charles twice and knew him as "Reezin." The last time he'd seen him was when he was helping someone move a sofa, and Charles had been there. In a last-ditch effort to score drugs, my son had reached out to him. But this person wasn't selling anymore; He had gotten out of jail a few months back; he had a family and it was time to focus on them. How could I argue with that? Good for him to turn things around. I found out, though, that Charles had probably been going through withdrawal and was out of money. He told me he sounded awful and was hard to understand. Later a friend of his would tell me he looked awful, too. This was news we didn't have before, and I thanked him for his time.

A text ping from Wendy Holt, a neighbor across the street for the past nineteen years, sliced through the silence in my kitchen. Our kids had grown up together, and for a split second an image of all of them outside in the driveway eating popsicles came to mind as I longed for the days when life had all been about the ice cream man and worrying about the summer heat.

> Wendy: "Hearing rumors this morning. Is everything OK with y'all?"
> Me: "No."
> Wendy: "Charles?"
> Me: "Yes. He died."
> Wendy: "Are u home?"
> Me: "Yes."
> Wendy: "I'm coming over."

Wendy arrived with her husband, Trey, and the son closest to Charles' age, Tucker. They, too, were in disbelief and for a while all of us sat there crying, attempting to talk. It was so final, so raw, so unreal. Eventually, the Holts made their way home and Wendy said she'd be in touch to help. I envied the fact she could walk across the street back to her life when I was dragging an anchor of devastation. She'd be there for me, though. Putting together anything to eat took single-minded concentration that was beyond my ability, so access to someone with a working brain would be essential to planning a funeral service.

The word suicide burned a new hole in my heart. Why didn't I see it coming? During all the counseling, intense outpatient and support groups, suicide was never mentioned. Later I would learn that depression and substance use disorder increases the odds six times that a person will die by suicide. Not one of the mental health professionals mentioned it to us as a possibility. In fact, little was said about suicide at all, anywhere, at any time.

I agonized over that last text conversation with Charles for the second time that morning. Meanwhile, my friend Martha woke up on June 6 and said she had an instant feeling of alarm: "I have to call Anne Moss."

When she called, I told her that Charles was dead. Without hesitation, she said she'd be at my house by afternoon. We cried together on the phone. She was grieving, too.

How do you share the news your child is dead? It's not like it's a life event you plan for, like paying for college. After digging through photos in my dining room drawer and finding the one that felt right, I made my way upstairs, and scanned that photo of Charles to post on Facebook. Calling everyone wasn't an option and word had begun to filter through the neighborhood. The picture would scan only in black and white; my mind was so mushy that I realized it would have to do. I added the message: "So very, very painful. No parent should ever have to endure it. I love you, Charles. I can't believe I'll never see my baby alive again. RIP."

I walked through the house in a trance, confused as to where to go or what to do. Grief stalked me. *How did I end up in this macabre club?* It would take me to the edges of myself, chew me up, and spit me out. Pounding the floor with fists, my wails and screams were absorbed by the walls and carpet, and the love for my youngest child had nowhere to land. My husband would find me, and hug me as we wept together. Again I told myself, "It is not as bad as it was last night when we got the news. It will never be that bad again. You are going to survive this. You are. This is one day. You will make it to the next day. And then the next day after that."

That number the officer had handed me: Where was that? This could offer some answers. Hunting it down, I shared with my husband that it was time to call but it was a disappointment. No real news existed other than an explanation of paperwork that would have to happen regarding the body. Would there be a toxicology report and medical examiners report? Always the more practical one in emotional situations, my husband took the phone and got the details about his last belongings and how to get them. No way that was happening without reinforcements so it would have to wait until after our house tour when my family was here.

Real estate agent Lee Anne came over to pick us up. She was flustered, her eyes swollen, and she talked about Charles. I was relieved to have something to do and someone in the house other than just the two of us. We could hold it together for the first house appointment since we would be meeting with the contractor who was renovating the home. The other homes would be empty.

During that first tour, all was well until we walked into one of the spare bedrooms and the contractor asked, "Do you have any children?" Stunned by what is usually a normal question, there was a pregnant pause until I shattered the silence with this response: "I raised two boys. One is a filmmaker living his dream. And my youngest, Charles, died by suicide. Yesterday." Jaws dropped, feet froze in place, no one exhaled. The contractor looked as if he'd been struck by lightning and I quickly assured him it was not an offensive question but a normal one. Surprisingly frank and together, it felt good to be relieved of the awful secret. But there was shame, too, for having blurted it out.

I am sure he was amazed we were there at all.

I am amazed we were there at all.

Denying Charles' death would be catering to the stigma that his was a less than noble death. There was no hiding how he lived or died. It's a conversation killer only if I allow it be. I wanted people to start to talk about this because there had been silence for too long and was having consequences in our culture.

Distraction as a means of escape no longer worked on subsequent home tours. My child was dead, my world had collapsed, and I wanted to go home. My decision on where we'd live next was made, and my husband agreed. Lee Anne said she'd take care of the contract. She was a godsend in this process when we had to remember to breathe.

Back at home, family and friends surrounded me with love and the Southern tradition of dropping by, bringing barbecue, booze, and boxes of tissues. When laughter erupted over a particularly funny story about Charles, the immediate guilt of enjoying the moment froze my vocal cords. To give myself permission to let go, I reminded myself how much my younger son loved to make me laugh.

People were talking openly about his addiction and depression because that's how we wanted it. When drug addiction first hit my family, I literally folded up inside myself, cut myself off from a social life, and lay in bed at night embracing my agony in isolation. For a while, all the ugliness of our suffering stayed within our home.

The day after, my business partner, Howard, struggled with how to share our family's tragedy with clients, while at the same time managing the business and his own grief. I wrote this message for our blog so it could be shared by newsletter:

Celebration of the Life of Charles Aubrey Rogers

Anne Moss Rogers' son, Charles, 20, died by suicide, June 5, 2015.

Charles was a creative genius who was articulate, intelligent, funny, and loved to rap. He was currently in the process of producing a new album when he died by suicide.

While he lit up every room he ever entered, he struggled with anxiety and depression, addiction, ADHD, and a sleep disorder. A deep, soulful, and sensitive young man, Charles loved and treasured family and loved dogs, funky socks, drama, and writing. But most of all, he loved people—his friends, his family. He was one of a kind, a true nonconformist. Charles Rogers was Peter Pan. He was just never meant to grow up.

My business partner and I had worked out many just-in-case disaster plans, including what would happen if one of us died. But the death of one of our children was not one of the scenarios. His wife, Kelly, had just asked about Charles a couple of weeks ago. She was one of few who continued to ask.

The house would be full for the next week with friends; my niece, Aurora, and her mother, Kristy; my brother, Gene; Charles' godfather and his wife; Haigh cousins; Hearring cousins; my Families Anonymous support group; and our neighbors. Randy recounted what he knew over and over to Charles' friends. He needed to talk, too, and Charles' friends surrounded him, completely engaged. One of my son's oldest friends, Jacob, arrived late, collapsed in our driveway crying, and we sat together on the warm asphalt grieving together. Very few of his friends knew about the heroin and they suffered guilt, too. Charles' relentless pursuit of drugs scared them as it had us and they had distanced themselves. He was reckless and spent too much time throwing up only to go out and do the same. They wanted time with Charles, not this frightening new version of him.

Charles didn't tell any of us he had ever suffered thoughts of suicide and watching my child self-destruct for the last five years was my introduction to powerlessness and humility. Charles was stubborn about accepting any kind of help or intervention. That's what depression does when fueled by social stigma. Denial is part of its charm, judgment so crucial to its success, and shame is where it thrives. It silences people. To Charles, using a drug to numb those initial dark feelings and avoid killing himself was a perfectly logical way to manage thoughts of suicide.

What will I do when I'm all alone and not surrounded by all these people? That thought would leak in, then be pushed away so it wouldn't ruin the love and support that was necessary for my surviving the day. It was beautiful weather, perfect for early June in Virginia. The dining room, living room, den, and kitchen were full, and people spilled out onto the deck and into the yard.

We had to plan a funeral, do paperwork for the body, and make choices no parent should ever have to make, particularly in this state of mind. My list. I went back to it again.

1. Call family
2. Call Martha
3. Call MaryJo about helping me get the church

Oh my God, I picked out a church? I couldn't even remember doing that. This list was my defense against premonitions that Charles would die. It had given me peace and now it was offering me guidance at a time when my brain was in a fog.

We had once regularly gone to a local church but stopped going when Charles' sleep disorder worsened. He was too young to be left alone but waking him to drag him to church during the precious sleeping hours he needed was nothing short of cruel. Richard was not going if Charles wasn't and it just was not worth the hassle and arguments. That's not what church was about. We stopped going, and had not gotten back into the habit. Charles and Richard had been baptized in an Episcopal church and if we were planning a memorial service, it needed to be at a large space because people

The Day After

would be coming from all over the country. The memorial service was also time-sensitive because family was already here from various states. We made an appointment for later in the week and took three friends with us since my husband and I were suffering from grief dementia.

My husband left the house with his father to retrieve Charles' backpack, and when they arrived home, my husband's eyes were rimmed in red. "Charles has every family photo in that backpack," Randy said, and caved into his hurt again. Clutching that backpack and embracing a moment of welcome isolation, I sat alone in the dining room with my son's belongings, rocking back and forth trying to catch the faint scent of my boy that one day would become stale and nonexistent. His computer was not there but the pink pawnshop receipts were. That would be a trip for the next day as I was sure there would be information on the pawned computer.

The inventory list in the backpack gave me pause. The handwritten list of contents didn't look very official. I would have expected a typed inventory of some kind but this one looked more like a grocery list scratched onto a scrap piece of paper:

Red Cosmetic bag: Reezin the Revolutionary business cards
Toilet articles
1 stick empty box
Headphones
iPod
Smoking thing
Watch
Family letters
2 medicines—hydroxyzine and clonidine
Shoestrings
Phone
Clothes
Flipped over was a description of a dinner someone had delivered that said,
"Ham—Brown Sugar & BBQ Sauce Glaze
Broccoli w/ olive oil, salt, and pepper
Corn & Tomato Salad

None of the containers need to be returned. Enjoy, Rhonda.

This confused me. Then it started to register. In taking inventory of the backpack, someone had grabbed the first leftover scrap of paper he or she could find and listed the contents of the backpack—the last possessions of my dead child—on the back of a note with a takeout order on it.

I continued to examine what was inside and pulled out the plastic Ziploc bag meant to protect the package of letters from me that he had saved. While he was away at wilderness and therapeutic boarding school, I wrote him every single week. I wanted him to know he was loved. By the time he was at Wasatch Academy, he had his phone so this was not necessary. When fitting all of one's belongings into one backpack, choices must be made about what is most important. In looking at the inventory, I saw what was important to Charles: It was family. It stirred regret and a depth of sorrow only parents who've lost a child can know.

The list didn't include the family photos as part of the contents. Charles apparently unblocked me as a friend after he walked out of detox because he wanted the family photos. He must have gotten someone to print the pictures because he had every one I ever posted on Facebook.

This time I huddled up to the grief and wept as I curled up on the floor with his last remaining possessions, ones he had last touched just forty-eight hours ago. Other than his ashes, which we could not bring ourselves to pick up for three years, this was as close as I would ever be to my son after death. There were six of his notebooks. Where were all the rest? Not quite ready to read all of them, I read one and made a date with myself to sit down and truly slide between the covers of those notebooks and feel what he'd written. They did have answers.

In the coming years, the lyrics painted a portrait of my son and answered the "why" behind his last act on earth. Around 11 a.m. every day that week, neighbors and friends came by to pay their respects, leaving around 5 p.m. How they knew to do that was driven by Southern tradition, and those not from the South simply followed the lead of others who were. There was never an official message sent out but word filtered throughout the community that we needed our neighbors, friends, and family.

Various family members from out of town were farmed out to available rooms at neighbors' homes. After they left, my family and childhood friend Martha watched old YouTube videos from Charles' Timeboy1408 years. Richard showed us his short film, "Cottonmouth," for the first time. Surrounded by family, the grief was more tolerable and evenly distributed. It allowed me the opportunity to absorb the love in the room and fueled my strength to move forward.

Charles' phone had so far revealed nothing. Already the password screen on his phone was telling us we could try again next week. With each attempt, it would push the "try again" date that much further out. First it was by minutes, then hours, days, and weeks. The next try would push it to months later. The code to get in died with my son and that thin screen between me and my boy's last words and pictures might has well have been a high-security twenty-inch-thick steel vault door. The irony of holding those locked secrets in my hand fed the helplessness of being on a journey for which there was no compass.

The next day, my mom, Martha, and I packed into the car with the pawnshop receipts. Martha drove, which was far safer than having me behind the wheel. The phrase, "Mom, I have nothing," replayed in my head as I recounted the conversation with his dad the Monday prior to his death when he told us he'd pawned his last possessions. He had pawned his computer and his beloved bike, which he never rode with a helmet. Funny, how I worried about a head injury when what I needed to worry about was the enemy living inside his head.

From Stuart Court Apartments on Monument Avenue where he'd been staying, it was a twenty-minute walk for him to the Golden Goat Pawn Shop. On the way there, he had ridden his bike one last time. It would be years before I pieced all of this together.

There we stood, three women in a pawnshop. We could not have stood out more if we'd been wearing green fluorescent pantsuits. The man at the counter looked at us, then at me, and then down at the pink slip I held in my hand. It would be the last time he made direct eye contact. He knew what had happened and took the pink slip for the computer. We couldn't have been the first misfits to collect a loved one's last possessions after a drug-related death. When he came back with the computer, I handed him a credit card and he told us they didn't take plastic. Cash only, of course. We left and went to an ATM to withdraw the cash—well, my mom withdrew the money since our bank account was still suffering—and returned to the shop. It felt grimy to be there, and it reeked of desperation. The bike would not fit into the car with the three of us in it and Randy would come by later to get it. Every time I see the Golden Goat through the car window, my heart seizes, because in my mind, it goes with the phrase, "Mom, I have nothing."

I had the computer and there would be answers and passwords. His phone code was not in it but email and social media logins were. Charles never wrote on the computer and there wasn't much on it. Even a lot of the history was cleared, a habit he had started in ninth grade.

As coincidence would have it, the community room for after the service had just been completed. I felt the comfort of my friends and something else: gratitude. My heart swelled with love for all of the people who helped me at a time when putting one foot in front of the other was all we could manage. I was surviving. Randy was surviving. This would be a beautiful service where we would remember my youngest: his gifts and his struggles.

We asked the minister to be frank about what had happened. There would be a lot of young people in attendance, and a sugar-coated, fairy-tale sermon wasn't what was needed to help us heal. Charles was an incredible, vibrant, empathetic, and soulful human being, but he suffered two diseases that drained his hope and left him feeling he had no other option. In the years after his death, I would learn more about suicidal thinking, and I have boiled it down to this definition: It's a brain attack that causes an irrational episode of emotional pain so great, that people who suffer from these thoughts think death is the only option. They feel worthless, that their loved ones would be better off without them.

That moment comes on with extreme intensity and can last anywhere from a few minutes to several hours. Twenty minutes is about the average length of time when sufferers are in the most danger of following through. Most who suffer these thoughts have a mental illness. But not all who suffer mental illness have thoughts of suicide. There is never just one reason someone suicides, and often there are several factors including health history, family history, and environment. When they are younger, they don't yet have the coping skills to manage thoughts so dark and intense. Those who are older have simply been worn out by fighting the dark demons. From my point of view, those who suffer recurring thoughts of suicide are courageous and strong.

For after the service, we wanted people to tell stories about Charles; this was scheduled for the community room. Who would be the catalyst to get people started? His theater friend, Kevin, would be perfect, and he was delighted to be asked. The young people entertained us with funny stories about Charles that my soul craved. My neighbor Wendy thought to videotape some of these stories. Kids came from all over the U.S. and there were not enough places to sit in the church so the crowd spilled out onto the sidewalk. Many of his friends from the therapeutic boarding school in upstate New York and Wasatch Academy in Utah attended.

At the very back of the church were three young people, one of whom was in a wheelchair. These kids had polished up as best they could and had come to Charles' service. They were probably new friends he'd met when he was out on his own those last two weeks. Maybe he had lived with them. These kids were also suffering from addiction and had not yet found recovery. They had come from an apartment down the street, where Charles had died, but I didn't know it at the time.

How brave of them to come pay their respects. They were stricken with grief and tears, and my husband made his way back there to thank them for coming. Seeing them there—victims of our culture, society's outcasts—they looked vulnerable and ostracized. We could read the shame on their faces, and saw their grief, which squeezed my heart. These kids had moms and dads, too. How many friends had these kids lost? They had to be frightened. In trying to make my way back there, I was sidetracked by the guests and all the love.

Mac, the young man who found Charles, also came with his family, and it was the first time I learned he had discovered the body. He had gone to the same therapeutic boarding school in upstate New York and had walked out with Charles from detox in Richmond just two weeks prior. Hearing him tell the story of finding my son filled in some big blanks. Pale and sweating, he was grieving, in shock, and still using, which would account for his trembling posture. But good God, he dressed in a suit and made the effort to join his family to pay his respects, and speak to me, which is courage that will never be forgotten or dismissed.

Friends got the food together, and helped with the funeral planning, as well as packing and cleaning of our house for our move. I limped through life, barely making a contribution, but a fire was building. My family had suffered a triple stigma: substance use disorder, mental illness, and suicide. No one was talking about suicide and someone needed to do so. Talking about suicide doesn't give someone the idea but does the opposite: creating an environment where someone is more willing to reach out. Did I have the courage to take this taboo subject public?

CHAPTER 39

PAIN TURNS
INTO PURPOSE

"Even in darkness, sunshine sometimes shines through the blinds."
—*Just to Hurt,* by Charles Aubrey Rogers

I began to write about Charles' mental illness, starting with Facebook, and had the itch to do a follow up to a popular article of mine that had been published in 2014 by the *Richmond Times-Dispatch*. There were still a lot of rumors flying around about what had happened to my son despite our openness on the subject. People needed to know who he was and what had happened, and how families suffer with these diseases without emotional support. It is a story that is both beautiful and ugly.

These were uncomfortable topics. I was uncomfortable about going public with them. Grief-stricken and terrified, the voices that tried to hold me back were drowned out by the ones inside pushing me forward to share. The thought of speaking out inspired fear equal to that of walking a tightrope over a moat of hungry alligators.

Had my child been diagnosed with cancer, there would have been a lot of support. This would be my coming-out party on the subjects of addiction and suicide. It could be met with fanfare or disdain, anger, resentment, and even rejection. The *Times-Dispatch* agreed to let me write a follow-up to that 2014 article and I set my sights on it. It gave me a purpose. They say two of the most stressful events in life are loss of a loved one and moving. And we were going through both at the same time.

The renovations on the house we were moving into were not yet completed, and we had to be out of the home we had sold, leaving a gap of several weeks in between. Friends offered their residences but the dog was an issue. So I booked multiple Airbnb places during that time. Being nomads as grieving parents was so ridiculous I can hardly fathom how we got through it, but we did. Our rental choices were more limited because we had a dog—thankfully, a well-behaved dog—and each place that we rented required the extra effort of appeal for animal approval. It was Charles' dog and boarding him for ten weeks was not an option. My husband could not be separated from him, and Andy provided us with much needed love and support. The dog was grieving, too. We moved out of our old home in July and into our new home in September.

I worked on this newspaper article during this time and on into the fall of 2015. In November, my husband learned that he had to go to England for business. My brother-in-law and his wife lived in England at the time so I asked Richard if he was free to join us, and we booked the trip. With little notice, my brother-in-law and his wife graciously said we could stay in their spare rooms.

The highlight of the trip for Richard and me was the Harry Potter tour. Two buses and a train ride to the outskirts of London took us to the famed studio where actors and actresses spent years together making the movie series based on the popular books. They opened up the grand double doors to start the tour and the huge group— babbling multiple languages—surged forward, prepared to be awed. The first step involved being seated in a dark theater, watching a short film, and going over housekeeping rules. Charles would have loved this tour. At the moment when that thought hit, grief ambushed me, and tears followed as I struggled to suppress the shaking that often went with them. Surely it was dark enough in the theater for my moment of ugly-momma grief to be incognito.

While fumbling awkwardly for a seat in the theater, a concerned Warner Bros. staff member approached and asked, "Are you OK?" Momentarily stunned, I blurted out in a whisper that I had lost my son to suicide in June and expressed how much he would have loved the tour. Her response was thoughtful and empathetic; later, she found me and handed me a note that said, "The ones we love never truly leave us." She also said she had recently suffered an untimely loss of a cousin in her own family.

As hard as this journey has been, and it has been brutal, there have been moments of unsurpassed kindness that have renewed my faith in humanity. It's been in this journey of grief where I have met and come to know the most magnificent individuals.

I put aside my article that week in England with Richard. I managed to enjoy London and the company of my eldest who was not afraid of his mother's tears. Once back home, the article took priority. Writing it was like throwing myself onto the street to be run over multiple times. However, there was a release of pain that kept me on task. I was driven by purpose. There would be days when only two sentences would get written before my insides would crumble and the weight of loss would push me into darkness; my ability to string a coherent sentence together was lost. My first versions were disorganized, ugly, and angry. It allowed me to express emotions, make discoveries about this new journey, and reflect on my child. I kept at it, knowing it would come to me. And that's half the battle.

By early December 2015, it was finished. My friend, Karen B., reviewed it before it sailed via email to the editor of the paper. Sending it provided intense pride and relief. It would be February of 2016 before it would actually publish.

Writing helped me find emotional healing. Running certainly had. My legs felt like one-hundred-fifty-pound weights, and frozen eyelashes and tears stung my face throughout the winter, but pounding the pavement was part of my journey and physical release. About one mile into a three-mile trek one day, the cobwebs that clouded my thinking cleared, and inspiration hit. *I need to start a blog.* Facebook had been my venue for posting and venting, and everyone was encouraging me to write a book. After taking almost five months to write a twelve-hundred-word article, there was no way I could tackle an endeavor that big yet. The ideas for how it would be structured, however, were already being assembled.

As a preteen, I had kept a diary, but other people, including my brother, would break into it and broadcast its tender, private contents. Humiliated by my own words, I abandoned journal writing for decades and opted for "alter-ego" conversations that helped me work through my feelings to make decisions. This time my diary would be public to begin with, putting to rest any fear of diary break-ins. Of course, writing a live journal, with all my hurt and fears out there naked to the public, was petrifying, triggering multiple episodes of self-doubt. But while running one morning, the title popped into my head like a text message: "Emotionally Naked." Sprinting home as fast as my leaden legs would carry me, I dashed inside to look up the domain name only to learn that EmotionallyNaked.com was reserved but not being used. After placing it on a watch list, it was released by its owner two years later and I snagged it. Waiting to start this new endeavor was not an option, however, because I was a woman possessed. But who would want to be exposed to my ugly, naked grief?

No one had been interested in conversation about Charles for years. No one wanted to talk about substance use disorder, mental illness, suicide, or even grief. Why would they want to do so now? These voices of doubt were drowned out by my passion and the need to put the thoughts in my head on paper, so to speak. My husband and I were part of a grief group—Full Circle Suicide Loss Support Group—but I needed more. Becky, our counselor, encouraged me to write, and blessed the project. Facebook friends were cheerleaders, too. Immediate family may not have been comfortable with it initially, but there was a force outside my control pulling me in that direction. Charles was chanting in my ear to go for it, and it was energizing to release those emotions.

I went back to the old domain name I had owned since 1999: annemoss.com. I installed a simple, standard black-and-white theme and called it Emotionally Naked. It had to have a "naked" design, too. No bells and whistles. No sliding pictures. Emotionally Naked does not translate to "fancy." I was hyperfocused to get it up and going.

In a self-imposed break from my obsessive task, I was on an errand when one of the editors from the local newspaper called to say my article had been published online. It was February 5, 2016, a Friday. While pulling into the closest parking lot, beads of sweat formed as my face heated up. My heart raced as the editor explained it would run in print the following Sunday. I squeaked out a thank you. There was a jolt of excitement and then one of intense fear. This is it. There might be negative or cruel comments and some would not like what I was doing. Our culture was in a place of change but the stigma was still strong and debilitating.

Alter ego: *What the hell do you think you are doing publishing this story?*

Me: *I've been writing this for months, where did you think it would go, the shopper's weekly?*

Alter ego: *You are airing an ugly family story, making Charles the poster child of heroin addiction and suicide. Is that how you want him remembered?*

Me: *Right now no one seems to remember him because no one is talking about him at all. I wrote this to honor my son's struggles and how he died. I'm not ashamed.*

Alter ego: *You could lose clients over this. It makes you look like the biggest loser.*

Me: *I suspect others are dealing with this behind closed doors. If I lose a client who dumps me because I lost a child to suicide, maybe that person is not the kind of client I want.*

Alter ego: *True. I hadn't considered that. What about your mom?*

Me: *She's just worried this might be a vulnerable time for me. She knows I always color outside the lines.*

Alter ego: *So what's really bothering you?*

Me: *That no one will read it. Or care. That it will be dismissed and then I will be, too. My friends will not want to be with me anymore because this ugly is contagious.*

Alter ego: *Is that reason enough not to share it on social media? You do all that work and then stop short of sharing it? That doesn't sound like you.*

Me: *Yeah, you're right.*

Alter ego: *So here's the deal. You take a few minutes, drive home, share it first with family, business partner, and employees, then Facebook. After that, shut down the electronics and take a walk.*

Me: *Deal.*

Ultimately, the terrified child in me got only momentary consideration. It was time to shore it up and, like it or not, this was my coming-out party. The title was, "Honoring my son who died by suicide is not the end of my story." Initially the editor had used "committed suicide," words I had banished from my vocabulary because that phrase insinuates a crime and suicide is an act of deep despair and an alarming public health issue.

My husband got to see it first. Then I sent a link to my mother and another to my business partner. I explained that it would be shared on Facebook and that others would read it and know our family secrets. I was sure no one but friends would read it anyway.

My business partner and employees were supportive as was my husband. Mom was wary I'd catch flak at a vulnerable time but she was supportive as were my dad, my mother-in-law, and father-in-law. My knees were shaking when it was shared on Facebook and I walked away from social media to walk next to the James River with my husband and our dog. *Would I be fanning flames of hate and anger?*

Meanwhile, the article began to go viral, with shares and comments; By Sunday, it was off the charts. Other people were reading their own family stories in mine. There were so many mothers, fathers, sisters, brothers, friends who were suffering the scourge of addiction and the lack of resources for mental illness and substance use disorder. So many parents who had lost ones the same way we had: suicide. Still others had lost one to overdose.

Out of the thousands of comments, there was just one harsh one: "You kidnapped your son out of bed? No wonder he killed himself!" I replied, "Everyone is entitled to their opinion." I pitied him. Other readers mobilized like hungry piranha, blasting the guy who had posted under a fictitious profile. Ultimately, he deleted his own comment.

The original article has since been moved online at least twice, and all the original comments and the ones that followed are now lost. I regret not capturing a screenshot of all those stories.

Empowered and euphoric from all the support I had craved for so long, it occurred to me that I might experience an emotional crash after all this attention. And it would happen. Although it trended for weeks, I was glad I had prepared myself for it. I decided to think of the overwhelming response and support as kindling for my purpose and my passion.

No longer were we fighting for Charles' life. I had already gotten the call no parent ever wants to get. It was time to lead a movement for change. How would that happen and take shape? There was no set path but many others, fueled by the pain of their own losses, were starting to fight the same fight. Looking for solidarity and partnership in this effort would help propel the message forward.

The opiate epidemic was starting to take an astounding number of lives in 2015. No other epidemic in history was getting as little attention or funding as this did. By 2017, more awareness and efforts in this direction were occurring. Society had simply considered those who suffered drug addiction to be "throwaways" or morally corrupt. Studies that proved otherwise were not mainstream, and it would be a long time before people would start to understand addiction as a disease. The resurgence of a drug that had become a mere blip on the radar after the seventies was making a huge comeback. Greed and opportunity had revived it. Those little white pills invented and heavily marketed by pharmaceutical companies served as breadcrumbs to the drug and far deadlier formulations.

After decades of "the war on drugs," which had failed miserably, we were still knocking our heads on the same wall, expecting less miserable results. In the U.S., spending on incarcerating those with drug or alcohol dependence or addiction skyrocketed into the billions from the 1980s on. In 1980, nearly a half million people were incarcerated due to drug-related charges; by 2006, it had increased almost five times. In the 2016 election campaigns, there was still substantial rhetoric by politicians who thought we still needed to be "tough on crime." Arresting our way out of this had not proven a valid strategy. Yet politicians found it far easier to put people on layaway and label them as bad guys than it was to tackle the issue.

But it was starting to cost us economically and in terms of lives lost.

Add to that a huge culture shift: Families were no longer growing up together in the same town, and technology and digital screens were seducing our kids. Our culture was becoming less connected, creating the perfect storm for this drug epidemic to flourish. Those who were predisposed or suffered from depression were the most susceptible. To those kids who suffered from depression, how could something that makes you feel so good be wrong?

In the seventies when I was growing up, medicine cabinets were not full of juicy leftover prescription drugs that had become the norm by 1999. Doctors, strapped for time by new guidelines for patient visits, were not discussing pain expectations but instead writing prescriptions. Pharmaceutical companies were marketing their drugs aggressively as magic pills that would make pain vanish, not fully disclosing their addictive potential.

It was nine months after Charles' suicide when I was asked to speak and tell my story. Most guidelines would say this was too soon, and it probably is for most people. I had been a public speaker for years, having given hundreds of presentations on social media, digital marketing, content marketing, search engine optimization and women supporting women in business. Public speaking was a lead-generating tool for my digital marketing business. The first talk was for a small, intimate crowd, perfect for beginning this discussion. When I took the stage for the first time, Charles was with me. The stage was where he found peace and happiness and where there was love, support, and understanding for me.

Facing the first-year anniversary of Charles' death, not knowing what to expect, I wrote about how we reacted to the news of Charles' suicide and titled it, "The Final 48 Hours." Pouring my pain into that post took me back to sitting in the back seat of that police car. When it was time to hit the publish button, my hand hovered over it, shaking. I had shared every post on Facebook until then but this one sat in limbo, published—but not shared—until my subscribers made that move for me. *There was insurmountable guilt for having advertised such naked grief. Why would I do this to people? Will my friends ever want to be around me again?* For two days, it remained a mystery to me as to why tens of thousands were reading and sharing this story from my three-month-old blog.

My message inbox pinged, and it was a note from a young lady, Lauren, from Virginia Beach. She said two days prior, she had thought about taking her life and went on to say that reading a post from a mother who had felt such devastating pain as result of losing a child to suicide had changed her perspective. She reached out to her mother and father and told them what she had been wanting to say for four years: She suffered from depression and suicidal thoughts. Now empowered to seek help and looking for validation, she stated she was going to keep trying to find the right medication and support. My article had helped her find her voice, and I could not help but feel a part of that story. She transformed her life and graduated from college with her family's love and support.

This was a turning point for me. The power of telling my story to educate others overwhelmed the fear of telling it. A blog really could save lives. I was finding purpose, or rather it was finding me, and the side effects of this new passion meant there was considerably less interest in my digital marketing firm. I kept expecting that passion to return but it didn't, and morale at my firm was dwindling and my business partner was doing the lion's share of the work. My productivity was pathetic; it was unfair to everyone involved and I had to recognize this and make a change. But we had people depending on these jobs, so it could not be a rash decision.

In pondering the notion of selling my partnership, I picked up the phone, prepared to call business partner Howard to discuss it. Coincidentally, he called me at the exact time my phone was in my hand and introduced the same topic, as if a teleprompter with my wishes pasted on it was in front of him. He approached the topic tactfully although this was not the first conversation we had had about what my future with the firm might be. Before that, I had been lost in the fog of grief and gripped with uncertainty.

A decision was made: By January 2017, nine months later, we had merged with another firm and my partnership had been bought out. It was an amicable transaction and all parties were gracious and thoughtful.

There has never been a moment of regret. After being offered the position as president of Beacon Tree Foundation, a youth mental health nonprofit on which I had served since 2010, I accepted. I left a successful and profitable business to work for free at first.

I'm thankful I had the opportunity to pursue my passion. My husband had a new job, which helped, and there were checks coming in from the sale of the business to supplement until I found a new way to make a living. Not everyone has that opportunity and that choice. Again, this was something to be grateful for, especially to my husband who supported this choice without a moment's hesitation. There are times I'll read a post to him and he'll ask, "Are you going to publish that?" This is usually the question that inspires me to hit that send button.

Before the conversation on suicide becomes mainstream, it will be uncomfortable. There is no right group or right time of day. Not many do a search for "suicide speaker" and even fewer want to book me as a motivational speaker for fear that it will bring audience morale low.

Who would have thought I would want to talk to parents of those suffering, reach out to students, talk to those in crisis, speak to audiences about my story, and write about the most taboo of subjects every day of my life? Ten years ago, I would not have believed it if someone had told me this was my purpose. When it finally found me, it had the highest price tag ever: the suicide of my son. For a long time, my mind held me responsible for Charles' suicide until, one day, I was finally ready to forgive myself.

Instead of feeling guilty for owning it, there is another way to see this. I owed it to Charles and his memory to be my best self. And he gets the credit for inspiring me to do so. He once asked, "Mom, are you pursuing your passion?" To which I pondered and he responded, "If you are taking that long to answer, maybe you aren't.

"You should always follow your heart," said the child with world's biggest heart.

CHAPTER 40

BALANCE

Lyrics by Charles Aubrey Rogers, aka Reezin' the Revolutionary

*M*y style of art is unusually beautiful
Like a man accepting a death unsuitable
Dying alone in the desert without a funeral
A bittersweet feeling you can't get from pharmaceuticals
Nothing's quite as beautiful as a tone that's musical

This is death to autotune
This is death to the cubicle
This is 5 minutes of world peace
This is a taste of the good life
An escape from the hood life

This a scapegoat from the pain
A place away from the rain
Something real you couldn't fathom to feign

It's your very first kiss
It's happiness, sadness, anger, and bliss

DIARY OF A BROKEN MIND

It's something beautiful, that's what music is

This is your last 3 seconds after your birth
This is music, the only thing that ever gave me worth
This is death to the government and freedom to the people
This is lock on Pandora's box and proof we were created equal

This is good and bad, happy and sad
This is the dark side, this is murder, this is hate,
this is war and this is rape.
This is the end of the beginning
This is death and this is fate
This is lack and this is gain
This is health and this is pain

This is my sanctuary
This is my home
The only place I don't feel alone
It's a story of hope
An addict putting down the pipe,
a child beating cancer,
broken wings finding flight
A man praying for an answer

I found my place amongst these beats
And my passion with these stanzas
Now they're tellin' me they know what my issue is
at the same time they askin'
What's my problem is,
like why do I do these things
and drink till I'm wobblin'
Then they act like they know me
Just 'cause they got a damn degree or PhD

I just wanna be free from the wrath of society
And if you open your damn eyes you should see
that these pills and this therapy and these drills ain't for me,
I tried your plans doc,
I used it
The only thing that works for me is music

CHAPTER 41

FORGIVING MYSELF

TRIGGER WARNING:
Method mentioned briefly

… if you make it through today, you can make it through the next.
—*Find Beauty,* by Charles Aubrey Rogers

The fantasy of Charles becoming the poster boy of rehabilitation had been one I had entertained throughout our worst family crises. Surely all the hard work, heartache, tears, and money spent would pay off. Truth is, Charles was not a trophy that could be polished and put into a glass case to demonstrate superior parenting skills.

I know now he suffered from thoughts of suicide for a long time, and conversations and reactions that puzzled me before became clear after his death. Why couldn't I have had that clarity when he was alive? The answer is, because it's the gift of "after." My life and even the one that came before, is something seen through a lens that was off limits until a tragedy of this magnitude happened.

There are no do-overs. And in the coming days and weeks after it happened, it was all about adjusting to that reality. My grief was about learning to live without the child I still loved, and accepting that parenting is not about perfection but recognizing what I did right.

We have sketchy information on the last two weeks of Charles' life. Some of the gaps have been filled in but there is a process in accepting that questions remain. We know he had been found in the early hours of June 5, 2015, by Mac and a group of other friends. After Mac discovered the body, he freaked out, as anyone would have done, and frantically called his parents, who came immediately.

After rehab, we had to make a decision as to whether to let Charles come home. We could let him do drugs in his room and put us all at risk, and drag us into the mayhem. Or we could let him be uncomfortable and force his hand to ask for help. So far nothing we had done had pushed him off the path of self-destruction. I couldn't fix this for him. He needed to invest himself and I was hoping to see that. Was this the right thing to do? I still don't know.

That last text haunted me for more than a year. It was time to let it go. Time to forgive myself.

The last text stalked me because I was laser-focused on the isolated conversation of June 4, 2015, the day before he died. Why didn't I react like a normal mother to an obvious cry for help? But one day, several months after his suicide, I looked at the texts that came before it, to see it all in context. There were streams of rants, denial, and manipulation, the hallmark of substance use disorder and mental illness. The ones that came before reminded me of how conversations often went, and how confusing it could be to discern fact from fiction.

When he was using, he was lying most of the time. This was my mind-set when he reached out in his last desperate phone call. It was important for me to understand that, in my own insane state of mind, I could hardly hold myself accountable for knowing what was truth and what was manipulation. He had to own his own recovery. While we could provide support, this was something he had to do for himself.

The conversation picked up before his very last text to me. It started in late May when he is checked into the recovery house, right after it had been discovered that his pee test registered "dirty": This meant positive for drug use, specifically opiates, benzodiazepines, and other substances he did not know about because he was on street drugs, which can be a mystery mix of addictive and deadly substances. He was making a case for his innocence and telling us why he left detox. Several times, he referred to Methadone, but Charles was detoxed with Suboxone.

This time when looking back at the text, I read the last words of June 4, 2015, in a broader context that included all the manipulative rants that came before.

> May 24, 2015, 10:00 p.m.
> Charles: I'm not lying I physically cannot make myself urinate.
> I know I'm clean.
> Me: OK. You need to deal with this. I can't help.

> May 24, 10:00 p.m.
> Me: You need to eat ice chips. You are dehydrated. If you don't keep some liquid down you will end up in the ER.
> CALL ME.

> May 25, 2015, 2:17 a.m.
> Charles: I was throwing up.
> Sorry.
> I have to pee now but I gotta wait till morning.

> May 25, 8:13 a.m.
> Charles: He's sending me away cause of my detox.

> Me: No. He's sending you away because you took opiates and benzodiazepines. Detox is long gone by now.

> Charles: No it's not.
> I was on methadone for 21 days and I've only been off for 5 and I was still withdrawing and I tested negative for morphine and I tested negative for oxy.
> Methadone stays in your system for weeks.
> Look it up.

May 25, 11:34 a.m.

Charles: I need my sleep medication they're not going to give it to me.

I stay up for 3 days and start hallucinating.

It's very important mom.

June 2, 2015 – (After he has left recovery house and walked out of detox with a friend)

Charles: That was the main reason I left that place is cuz he said he was going to tell you I used heroin.

HEROIN SHOWS UP ON A FUCKING DRUG TEST AS MORPHONE! HE EVEN TOLD Me: "NO YOU DIDN'T TEST POSITIVE FOR MORPHINE."

And I said, Well then look it up!"

Fucking look and find anywhere and that will show you heroin doesn't come up as morphine and he refused to do it.

Charles: I was on fucking methadone detox for 21 days. METHADONE IS AN OPIATE. METHADONE CAN ALSO STAY IN YOUR SYSTEM FOR WEEKS.

It gets in your damn bones and I'd only been off for a couple of days and David was still withdrawing on day 58.

But I'm done explaining this shit.

I know what I did if you don't wanna believe the truth.

Even though the drug tests proves that wrong, go ahead and be ignorant and yell at me for shit.

Me: Love you, Charles. Always will.

June 4, 2015 (the texts after his last phone call)

Charles: "Mom, I'll go to fucking rehab, just listen to me."

"Mom, I'm trying to tell you something and ask for help but you won't fucking answer."

"Mom PLEASE ANSWER ME."

Me: "I am. I have a job and there are things I have to do. I want you to get help when you are ready. Are you ready? Really?"

"We sold the house and there are just calls we have to take."

The last piece of the text conversation is the hardest thing I have ever made public in my life, and it's the second time I have done so in this book. Every time I read it, my heart sinks into an ocean of regret. The dismissive tone makes me wonder who that woman was, when in fact, I'm just at a loss as to what to say and it followed two hours of phone conversation that was hard to understand due to his symptoms of withdrawal. I was overwhelmed and decision-impaired. There was a moment of me sitting on the bed after talking to him that last time, thinking, "Will this haunt me the rest of my life?" Since his death, when other parents who have been in the same situation have called me, they are just as emotionally spent and confused at this point as I was.

To move forward, I had to forgive myself, to remember that message in context of all the crazy manipulation and mayhem of addiction, given the knowledge available at the time. It's hard to go from maintaining boundaries to rescue mode in an instant. The line between enabling destructive behaviors versus empowering recovery is razor thin, and always shifting, and laced with myths we've adopted as truths because we don't know any better. Walking that tightrope is difficult even in the most emotionally stable of circumstances.

What would have been the outcome had I done something different? Would I have been the one to find him dead? Would he have shown up if I had driven to meet him? Would he have told me where he was? Would he have willingly gone back to detox and rehab? Would my son be alive today?

The reality is that living with a user who wreaks havoc creates impossible living conditions. It is heartbreaking to have to walk the love-and-let-go approach as a parent and it's risky. We knew that. I was losing him and helpless to do anything to prevent his self-destructive path. Sometimes it takes self-evaluation by the person who is addicted. Sometimes it means pain and consequences from actions to find the incentive to change. Reality takes a user to dark places, such as homelessness, jail, or worse. But it also has provided the moment of truth and turnaround for many. Loving and letting go was a gut-wrenching decision that sent me into emotional turmoil.

I must remember that he adamantly denied suffering from depression and was rarely compliant to any kind of treatment that required personal investment. At that age, he wanted an instant cure:

"Instant" like he felt when he first started using drugs to numb his pain. I did not know he was in a deep depressive state, that he was in withdrawal, and had no clue he was suicidal. Charles thought of himself as trash, as if he no longer mattered.

In my darkest hours of grief, that's what hurts the most: I missed the clues that he was in a place so dark he didn't want to live. There was despair in his voice during his last phone call, and I didn't go with my gut. Subconsciously, I contributed to his feelings of worthlessness, but for me to have taken the leap to think suicide a possibility was unrealistic.

He had no idea what an antisocial drug heroin was and how it isolated him from his loved ones and friends. For the first time, Charles experienced rejection, and he was not in a state of mind to see his way back. I know now that he should have gotten a call or text from me every day those last two weeks just to say "love you," and let him know he mattered no matter what he was using.

But at some point, I had to stop torturing myself for hesitating to choosing the correct option in an instant. Because I had no idea that my hesitation would cost me the life of my child, that he would hang himself that night or early the next day.

Surely there was time to call, to ask advice and weigh the options. That was not the case.

He had relapsed within hours of rehab. And so had we.

Charles simply never had many inner resources when it came to helping himself. That's the part I knew in my heart and agonized over his whole life. The reality is that in that moment of intense emotional pain, a loved one acted on irrational thoughts that I can't alter.

To change my mind-set, it's important for me to focus on being grateful. Randy came home from his trip the day we got the news, and I didn't have to hear it alone. Our marriage survived a child's suicide—not always the case—and my son, Richard, is thriving. Family members on both sides as well as friends have been there for us. And my blog, Emotionally Naked, and the community we've created have provided more than was expected. We've developed a community of caring and no judgement. Together our voices have reached others and saved lives.

Forgiving Myself

Torturing myself for mistakes that are all too human will not bring Charles back or enrich my life. There are regrets that will always needle me, but I have forgiven myself because I know my son would have wanted me to.

My husband and I celebrate Charles' memory with his friends from high school in 2018.

CHAPTER 42

FIND BEAUTY

By Charles Aubrey Rogers, aka Reezin' the Revolutionary

*T*he sun is shining,
   all I need is you and me and rhyming,
but you're not here
so there's only me and music,
but I can still appreciate life's beauty,
because there's so many unfortunates

Sadness is something I haven't truly earned,
self-pity is undeserved
because there's too much tragedy on this earth,
for my self-centered toss and turns
and inside burns

It used to be 'woe is me,'
my days rained black
but I can even find beauty

DIARY OF A BROKEN MIND

in where the rain is at,

I was suicidal,
but I came back,
and I love life
but still put pain in my rap,
'cause it's real,
I want my angel back,
but Ima get some stacks,
my dream won't crash,
and soon enough
she'll be in my lap.

It's all okay in the end,
I've got family and friends,
Ima rap till I get a milly and the Benz,
that shit is easy to find beauty in.

Ima win a Grammy,
then do it again,
even when my ink shoots sadness,
there is still beauty
drooping out of my pen.
I spit hallucinogens so dope,
clean addicts hear and fear
they'll started using again.

(Refrain)
Even when you're feeling sad truly,
you can look and find beauty,
I put in my music,
so, when you feel your mind's useless,
look deep and find beauty.

Stand face-to-face with sorrow
and I can still wear a smile
with enough to go around and borrow,
because if today sucks,

Find Beauty

it'll be better tomorrow.

Life is tough, suck it up,
people are corrupt and fucked up,
tough luck, get over it

I got motivation I can move boulders with,
when you get older, kids,
you'll be glad someone told you this,
this world is harsh
and you don't want to feel
how cold it gets.

It's too quick
I wish I could get a hold of it,
but that's life,
we all fold into an end,
we all meet death,
so count everything good you have

What makes you blessed?
What relieves your stress?
because if you make it through today,
you can make it through the next.
You can progress.

I never thought I could do it,
until I found my soul in this music
and found beauty now every day I use it.
Some people say if you're sad you choose it,
I don't believe that crap,
but you can try to lose the blues
instead of excepting that you're drowning in it
with concrete shoes.
Kick them off
and swim up dude,
Life's got too much to do
to give up so soon.

DIARY OF A BROKEN MIND

(Refrain)
Even when you're feeling sad truly,
you can look and find beauty,
I put in my music,
so, when you feel your mind's useless,
look deep and find beauty.

School sucks,
but I'll graduate eventually,
maybe, unless they pay me
and I can leave
and be perfectly free,
we'll see

But in the meantime,
I won't quit,
this is my world,
I own this,
my tone is,
SO SERIOUS;
so passionate, so real;
I spit shit you have to feel,
you can find the crack of light
like a toy in your happy meal.

I'm not always acting right,
help you just a little bit,
my rapping might.
Never give up,
you have to fight,
so, when you look back at life,
you don't say, "I wish I actually tried,"
on your final last night.

You don't want a conscious
that Bites with regrets
as you sit in fear of what's next,

Find Beauty

it's just Death,
but what's Death?
It is something more
or something less?
I'm not sure
but you can't escape
and you can't run,
so, you better find beauty
before that end comes.

ACKNOWLEDGMENTS

This is my first book and was both a labor of love and therapy for my grieving soul. Writing it was agony at times but growth and self-discovery was more than worth the tears invested. I began writing it in my head the day after my son killed himself because the story stalked me and wouldn't let go. Prior to typing the first word, my tribe at Emotionally Naked (EmotionallyNaked.com) encouraged me to a write a book; it was one thousand blog posts and two and a half years after my son's death before I typed the first words in January of 2018.

I owe by biggest thank you for my writing friend and beta reader, Susan Casey, a fellow author whom I met by phone before starting this memoir who said, "I was meant to help you with this book." For a grieving mother and publishing virgin taking on a project of this magnitude, those were the sweet words I desperately needed to hear. I had no idea where to start, and she advised me to get that first draft down on paper first and edit later, which I promptly did. Her encouragement and gentle, but straightforward, advice is why this got done and got done well.

I want to thank publisher Ray McAllister, who believed this story needed to be told and offered patient, steadfast guidance, and to Lori Ross for making the connection. I must add Karen Owen for her expert editing touch and suggestions, and my proofreader, Kelly Browning.

Thank you to my family, including my in-laws, Myra and Richard Rogers, and my parents, Anne and Bobby Nimocks, who weathered the tough years of Charles' drug abuse, addiction, and diagnoses of depression and addiction, and read the early drafts of the manuscript and offered feedback.

To my son, Richard, a talented writer and film editor, who was there for comfort when I thought I would not survive another day with the suffocating pain of losing a child to suicide. He dove into one of my early drafts of this book and declared it a blockbuster, worthy of a later film. (I have to love that enthusiasm and support.)

Not all marriages survive the death of a child and I'm thankful my husband, Randy, and I had each other, and didn't resort to blame but instead supported one another. He has backed me financially through the writing of this book after the sale of my business, and supported my passion for dragging taboo topics into the spotlight through speaking and writing. He was one-hundred percent behind this project even though reading it in manuscript form took him several months.

My love to my niece Aurora who drove with her mother, Kristy, to Charles' funeral, adored her cousin, still grieves the loss, and started a mental wellness club at her high school. She has wholeheartedly supported my effort to write this book.

Huge thanks to childhood friend Martha, who was at my house as fast as she could make it the day after Charles died, and helped me pack up his room because our house had sold before he died. She never stopped supporting my advocacy, and had the intuition to call whenever this project was overwhelming me. To my book club and the ancillary members, who held up the world when it was too heavy and encouraged me to keep writing my way through grief.

To Robert, Sam, Jacob, Daniel, Alex, Scottie, William, Joslin, Courtney, and the rest of the crew for being there on Charles' birthdays and death anniversaries, and telling me who was whom in some of the photos. A special shout-out goes out to Rowan for keeping in touch along the way and to Max for helping me

Acknowledgments

figure out the syntax and words of Charles' rap songs. To Louis King, who believed in Charles' talent: He opened up his studio and his heart, and helped me fill in some blanks regarding Charles' movements prior to his death.

And finally I am extending a special thanks to agents Wendy L and Anna L, for opening my proposal and reading it. Although they didn't represent it for publishing, their guidance and feedback helped me to make more informed decisions.

—Anne Moss Rogers

TIMELINE

September 2010 – Charles goes to Cosby High School. From small private to public school, only a public school would accommodate his DSPS sleep schedule.

August 2011 – Richard leaves for college at the University of North Carolina School of the Arts in Winston Salem to pursue a degree in filmmaking.

April 2012 – Charles is kidnapped out of his bed and taken to wilderness program in Clayton, Georgia.

June 14, 2012 – Charles gets out of wilderness in June and goes to Family School therapeutic boarding school. There 14 months.

July 2013 – We take Charles out of therapeutic boarding school, Family Foundation School, because the ship is sinking after the sexual misconduct and trial. We never receive his therapeutic records from his stay there.

July 2013 – Charles does his *American Dream* EP (Extended Play) album for iTunes release.

August 2013 – Charles starts Wasatch Academy in Utah.

October 2013 – Fall Family Weekend, Wasatch (early October). Later that month, album, **American Dream**, is published on iTunes. (It's now a free download on SoundCloud.)

May 2014 – Charles is expelled from Wasatch for drug infraction, his second, and goes to Georgia to visit grandparents and finish online.

This is when I get the Mother's Day text.

June 2014 – Charles comes back to Midlothian, Virginia, after graduating.

September 2014 – Charles starts John Tyler community college. In November 2014, he drops out. I break my elbow in November 2014, and am hospitalized right before Thanksgiving for infection.

December 2014 – Charles has to leave for 2 weeks as he is using, and breaking one of our rules. He couch-surfs for two weeks and refuses to go with us to North Carolina for Christmas. He spends it with the Morganti family.

January 2015 – Charles gets his first job at Taco Bell.

February 2015 – Charles arrested by a rookie cop who sticks his hands down Charles' pants; a severe spiral downward.

March 2015 – The case is continued when cops don't show up. We're told this is called "judge shopping": They don't like the fact that we got the "good judge," and continuance increases their chances they'll get one sympathetic to them.

April 2015 – Police visit and tell us he's been selling our silver to pawn shops. Charles confesses to being addicted to opiates on April 24. He says he is off them and goes to Georgia to see grandparents. Charles spends his twentieth birthday in Georgia.

April and May 2015 – Richard graduates from college. Charles is in detox, then rehab, on Richard's graduation weekend, then goes to a recovery house.

May 2015 – Charles relapses the day after he's in recovery house. He goes back to detox and walks out with a friend. For two weeks, we don't know where he is.

June 4, 2015 – Charles calls me for the last time.

June 5, 2015 – We get a visit from the Richmond police telling us that our son has killed himself. My life is forever changed.

RESOURCES

EMOTIONALLYNAKED.COM
Find support groups, book, and podcast recommendations at
EmotionallyNaked.com under Resources:
- Resources > Grief
- Resources > Addiction
- Resources > Mental Illness
- Resources > Suicide

Free eBooks for download on the Resources page.

SUICIDE HOTLINES
If you are experiencing thoughts of suicide, please reach out.
- United States 1-800-273-8255
- United States Text hotline- Text "help" to 741-741
- For other countries, search "Wikipedia List of suicide
  crisis lines" or "suicide crisis lines."

ABOUT THE AUTHORS

ANNE MOSS ROGERS is a writer, owner of the blog, Emotionally Naked, and a professional public speaker who captures hearts and fills them with hope. Since 2010, she has been a board member at Beacon Tree Foundation and advocates for youth mental health. Her career started in advertising as a copywriter and she co-owned a digital marketing firm from 2010-2017, selling her partnership after Charles' suicide. Originally from Fayetteville, North Carolina, and now residing in Richmond, Virginia, she is graduate of UNC-Chapel Hill with a BA in journalism. Married to her husband, Randy Rogers, since 1986, they raised two sons: the late Charles Aubrey Rogers, and Richard Rogers, currently living his dream as a filmmaker in Los Angeles.

CHARLES ROGERS was born April 26, 1995, and died by suicide as a result of depression and addiction on June 5, 2015. He attended Woolridge Elementary School, Millwood School, Cosby High School, the Family Foundation School (a therapeutic boarding school), and graduated from high school in 2014 from Wasatch Academy in Utah. Deep, soulful, passionate, and empathetic, Charles loved and treasured family and friends. He was a true artist, an off-the-cuff comedian who loved to entertain and act. He loved dogs, funky socks, drama, writing, performing rap, and making people laugh. But most of all, he loved and cared about people. As many artists do, Charles lived life on his own terms and was a true nonconformist. Charles Rogers was Peter Pan: He was just never meant to grow up.

For more, visit EmotionallyNaked.com.com and AnneMossRogers.com.